Modernity as Experience and Interpretation

To Ariadne Lou

Modernity as Experience and Interpretation

A New Sociology of Modernity

Peter Wagner

Polity

The right of Peter Wagner to be identified as Author of this Work has been asserted in accordance with the UK Copyright, Designs and Patents Act 1988.

First published in 2008 by Polity Press

Polity Press
65 Bridge Street
Cambridge CB2 1UR, UK

Polity Press
350 Main Street
Malden, MA 02148, USA

ISBN-13: 978-07456-4218-5
ISBN-13: 978-07456-4219-2 (pb)

A catalogue record for this book is available from the British Library.

Typeset in 10.5 on 12 pt Times
by SNP Best-set Typesetter Ltd, Hong Kong
Printed and bound in Great Britain by MPG Books Ltd, Bodmin, Cornwall

The publisher has used its best endeavours to ensure that the URLs for external websites referred to in this book are correct and active at the time of going to press. However, the publisher has no responsibility for the websites and can make no guarantee that a site will remain live or that the content is or will remain appropriate.

Every effort has been made to trace all copyright holders, but if any have been inadvertently overlooked the publishers will be pleased to include any necessary credits in any subsequent reprint or edition.

For further information on Polity, visit our website: www.polity.co.uk

Contents

vi *Contents*

Preface

In the afternoon of 25 August 2007 the skies darkened over Arcadia. Fires were destroying vast areas of the Peloponnese and had created smoke clouds that turned the sunlight orange and gave the apocalyptic impression of a very early dusk. More than sixty people died in the fires. A state of emergency and a day of national mourning were declared in the country.

The summer of 2007 had been characterized by extraordinarily high temperatures in the south of Europe, going often far beyond forty degrees centigrade. This phenomenon was generally attributed to global warming, the persistent rise of temperature due to irresponsible human activity on the earth. But it was also clear that fire was unlikely to break out accidentally in so many places at the same time. It was widely assumed, and could sometimes be documented, that the fires were deliberately started, most likely for reasons of individual profit-seeking, to turn protected reserves into buildable land, but other more politically targeted strategies are not ruled out.

The darkening of the skies over Arcadia offers a sign of our contemporary modernity swinging out of its always precarious balance. The inability to halt the process of global warming that will make ever larger parts of the earth uninhabitable shows that the notion of a common world, which needs common measures to be preserved, has been radically weakened or has even withered away. If the pursuit of individual gain was the driving force of the arsonists, as the most probable explanation suggests, then so little sense for the common exists that a small individual advantage is seen to justify destruction of a highly valuable, almost irreplaceable common good. If fires were set for strategic political advantage – a rather less likely reason – then 'the public thing' itself barely figures on the mind of those who committed these deeds, be they Greek or international actors.

All of those accounts capture aspects of our modernity, and none of them is specific to this example and to this region of the world. To be modern means to see oneself as autonomous; it means to reject any source external to oneself as a guide to one's action. Whoever sets incendiary devices, be it by igniting them in a forest of the Peloponnese or be it by refusing a signature to the Kyoto agreement, is likely to justify their action only by reference to their own will, by no source outside of themselves. Such a modern self-understanding found its first strong expression in the ancient Greek city republics, most importantly Athens, not far from Arcadia, and also burning these days. These republics were strongly committed to collective self-determination, to a radical concept of autonomy, in which there was no brake to the will of the collectivity – and sometimes this meant the ruin of the city.

In ancient Greece, two elements existed that are rather absent today and that mark a significant difference between this early manifestation of modernity and our own. Even though the ancient Greeks did not accept any ruler over them, first, they knew about the precarious nature of their modernity and they had a term for its most important peril: hubris. When human strivings hubristically overreached the capacity to master the consequences of one's action, then life in common was at risk. And even though, second, the ancient Greeks recognized the dangers created by over-ambitious individuals and had a means to counteract those, namely ostracism, expulsion from the polity, they did not see these dangers as the most significant ones because ruthless and instrumental individualism, which is so frequent in our world, was absent in theirs. Greek modernity knew and cherished the expression of personal freedom but it was based on the idea of collective autonomy, and individual ambition was unlikely to upset this way of ruling the common life.

Our current modernity is clearly different. Individual liberty and instrumental action are not only driving forces that are recognizable in all walks of life, the fires in Arcadia being only one dramatic example among many others. They are even hailed as the epitome of modernity in sophisticated accounts of social and political theory. The aims of this book, which I was about to finish on 25 August 2007 in an Arcadian village, are, first, to understand this aspect of our contemporary modernity and, second, to suggest that modernity, even today, can be otherwise.

Maybe one is always rewriting the same book, but the situation changes and thus the words. My first writing about interpretations of modernity, without using exactly those terms, was a comparative political sociology of the European social sciences (published as *Sozialwissenschaften und Staat* in 1990). This was during the second half of the 1980s and there was a sense that modernity was undergoing radical changes, but the existing words for them were highly inappropriate. My second attempt (*A Sociology of Modernity*, 1994) tried to approach the question of our contemporary modern condition through a historical sociology of transformations of European modernity over the past two centuries, an analysis of 'successive modernities' as Johann Arnason would later call it. This was after 1989 and the fall of existing socialism; and it was also after I had first left the European continent and had gained direct experience of North American modernity. The words given to this analysis mostly stemmed from some kind of thick historical description and stayed close to the experiences of continental Western Europe. To fully spell out their meanings, my third attempt tried to take some distance from this 'case' and widen the conceptual horizon (*Theorizing Modernity*, 2001). This move suggested to me even more strongly that modernity could be, indeed had to be, analysed in terms of plurality and of possibility. As necessary as this step may have been in times of supposed *pensée unique*, of neo-liberal hegemony, as I still think, it may have conveyed too little a sense of the limits to possibility in history and invited too general and too abstract an idea of the contingency of modernity. The current work tries to remedy this imbalance by reintroducing the specificity of the experiences of modernity and to relate existing interpretations of modernity to those experiences.

As it happened, much of the research for this book was pursued at the European University Institute in Fiesole. EUI is in many respects a most privileged place for a researcher in the social sciences. If there is any place where the 'new sociology' I am proposing, a truly interdisciplinary endeavour in terms of current disciplines, should flourish, then this should be there where the transcending of national intellectual horizons is more easily possible than elsewhere. In particular, in my opinion, EUI should be the place where constructive work at a reassessment of European modernity with a view to the contemporary global context could take place. However close or not EUI may have come to live up to its promise, I am glad to have had the opportunity to work there for eight years and to develop much of what follows in this book. In particular, I had the good luck to work with the historian Bo Stråth for much of the time on an interdisciplinary research programme analysing European modernity. I am very grateful to him for his intellectual and institutional companionship. The outcomes of our common work, we hope, will also be available in book form very soon. Most importantly, I take this opportunity to thank the doctoral researchers of EUI with whom many of the following ideas were shared and developed in numerous seminars, workshops and conferences.

From 2003 to 2006, my research also benefited from generous support by the Volkswagen Foundation programme, 'Key themes in the humanities', for the working group on 'Modernity and contingency', which I co-directed. This group possibly did not realize all of its immense potential, but it enabled me to reflect anew on my ideas about significant experiences and their interpretation in European history in the framework of workshops on the period around 1800, the First World War and '1968'. Traces of these discussions will be found throughout this volume.

This book is being finished just after I have started teaching and researching at the University of Trento. I would like to thank my colleagues there for granting me an extended summer period to conclude the writing. I look forward to discussing the outcome with them.

Nathalie Karagiannis's presence in the following text is stronger than any word in this preface can express.

Melana, August 2007

1

Ways of Understanding Modernity

> CLOV: Finished, it's finished, nearly finished, it must be nearly
> finished [...]
> HAMM: And the horizon? Nothing on the horizon?
> CLOV: What in God's name could there be on the horizon?
> [...]
> HAMM: The end is in the beginning and yet you go on.
>
> Samuel Beckett, *Endgame* [1957], 1958, pp. 6, 21 and 41

Modernity as experience and interpretation: the agenda

We are all modern today. The idea that modernity could come to an end, strongly proposed for several years from the 1970s onwards and, as one may think, anticipated by Clov in Samuel Beckett's *Endgame* of 1957, has not been found convincing. Rather, we may have witnessed a grand revival of modernity during the 1980s and 1990s, covering now the entire globe and gradually reaching towards each and every individual, as the theorems of globalization and individualization suggest.

But modernity today is not what it used to be. Modernity was associated with the open horizon of the future, with unending progress towards a better human condition brought about by a radically novel and unique institutional arrangement. This expectation arose in the decades around 1800, as revealed by the analysis of conceptual change in political language, pioneered by the late Reinhart Koselleck from the 1960s onwards and in different ways by Michel Foucault and Quentin Skinner. And it found one significant expression in the evolutionist strands of the social sciences, first during the nineteenth century and then in the sociological theories of modernization during the 1950s and 1960s. But there is nothing on the horizon of the future today, and even the question of what there should be remains unanswered.

Thus, maybe we are modern in different ways today – in a different way than we used to be until the 1960s, and also in a variety of different ways at the same time. This is a theme that has been addressed in recent years in an increasingly persistent manner under headings such as 'multiple modernities', 'successive modernities' or 'alternative modernities'. My own *Sociology of Modernity* (1994) tried to give an account of the transformations of West European modernity over the past two centuries and make some comparative glimpses on the different modernities of the USA and of Soviet socialism. The argument remains plausible, I would maintain. But it has made inroads in neither scholarly nor public debates. Recent sociological analysis of modernity by and large only accepts that the moderns needed to make some adjustments in the light of the problems they themselves had produced. Modernity thus became reflexive, rethinking its own achievements and failures (Anthony Giddens, Ulrich Beck); or flexible networks are said to have replaced, or at least complemented, the iron cages of modern life (Manuel Castells, Luc Boltanski and Eve Chiapello). Public debate, in turn, sees modernist globalization taking its course, resisted only by marginal movements in its centres and by fundamentalists at its peripheries.

To say that we have remained modern, but are so in a different way today, is, however, not satisfactory.[1] It begs the question about that which is variable in modernity and how change in modernity occurs. The aim of this book is to provide an answer to this question. Its basic assumptions can be spelt out in a rather straightforward manner:

Modernity is a way in which human beings conceive of their lives. As such, it needs to address the questions of how to govern life in common; how to satisfy human needs; and how to establish valid knowledge.

Modernity's specificity is the commitment to autonomy: to giving oneself one's own law. Thus, the modern answers to those questions cannot be derived from any external source of authority. By implication, any answer proposed is open to critique and contestation.

There is no single uniquely modern answer to those questions: much of the philosophy of modernity, from Immanuel Kant to Jürgen

Habermas, tried to find such a unique answer. Much of the sociology of modernity, from Emile Durkheim to Talcott Parsons to recent neo-modernization theories, claimed to have identified the one institutional structure of society that is specifically modern. However, the very transformations that modernity keeps undergoing suggest that there is a variety of modern answers to those questions.

The difference between varieties of modernity is a difference in the answers given to those questions: such difference is often certainly related to the cultural background against which modern answers are developed – the 'cultural programmes', as Shmuel Eisenstadt puts it. To assume, however, that contemporary, say, Japanese modernity is determined by the long-term cultural legacy of Japanese society underestimates the dynamism of modernity that has often been observed. The commitment to autonomy renders the acceptance of any prior answers difficult and contestable. Rejecting any cultural determinism of 'multiple modernities', however, does not suggest, in turn, that answers to the questions are under constant revision. Modernity is not a permanent revolution either. Rather, the answers that any given collectivity of human beings – for the sake of brevity, any given society – elaborates to these questions can be traced back to significant moments of their common history.

The experience of significant historical moments constitutes the background against which specific answers to those questions are elaborated: this proposition takes up the common view that modernity emerged historically as a profound rupture with the past, as a rupture with 'tradition' as the common sociological parlance has it. From a modernist perspective, the significant historical moments that put modernity firmly into place were a particular sequence of great revolutions: the scientific revolution, the industrial revolution, and the democratic revolution. After those revolutions, this view holds, the adequate answers to the three fundamental questions were found once and for all. From then on, modern society is said to have unfolded rather smoothly and progressively, and all remaining difference between societies is seen as due to either 'backwardness' or relatively insignificant cultural difference. The significance of these moments in the history of European modernity will not be doubted here – against objections from some forms of post-colonial studies, which tend to see Eurocentrism wherever European history is studied, and of more recent historiography, in which the idea of major social transformations dissolves into myriads of small occurrences that do not add up to anything significant.[2]

4   Ways of Understanding Modernity

The interpretation given collectively to the experiences of those signifi-cant moments is that which gives shape to a specific variety of modernity: experiences, namely, do not 'speak' on their own – they need to be interpreted and given meaning in human interaction. While the approach I propose here agrees with established wisdom about modernity in regarding those revolutionary transformations as highly significant moments in European – and to some extent North American – history, it takes issue with the view that such a rupture occurred once and for all, and that the evolutionary programme of modernity just unfolds from that moment onwards. In contrast, I suggest that the experience of those moments differed considerably between societies and that the interpretations given to them were contested from the beginning and continued being revised in light of further experiences with their consequences. As Hamm in *Endgame* has it, there is some end in the beginning. But how to go on is not endlessly determined by the beginning.

The objective of this book is to spell out the above programme. In this light, the remainder of this chapter will do the following. First, it will review the variety of existing approaches to the study of moder-nity in some more detail. The aim here is to demonstrate that an analysis of modernity in terms of experience and interpretation does exist already but that it has not been elaborated in any systematic way. Second, to provide the underpinnings of a more systematic elab-oration, it will discuss the status of the three questions raised above for a historico-sociological analysis of social configurations. For these purposes, the questions are rephrased as *problématiques* to which any society needs to give an answer. The question about the rules for life in common constitutes the *political problématique* (to be analysed in Part I of this volume); the one about the satisfaction of needs, the *economic problématique* (Part II); and the one about valid know-ledge, the *epistemic problématique* (Part III). The book will proceed by demonstrating how different answers were given 'within moder-nity' to these *problématiques*.

The meaning of 'within modernity' requires a clarification to avoid misunderstandings. It here refers to the predominant presence of the idea of autonomy in the social configurations that are analysed. Wherever human beings hold an understanding of themselves as autonomous beings, there is 'modernity' – the ancient Greek democ-racies, for example, were highly modern in many respects. The analy-sis of modernity as the experience with, and interpretation of, human beings giving themselves their own laws entails a broadening of the concept of modernity and allows a widening of the spatio-temporal perspective for the socio-historical investigation of modern practices.

At the same time, though, the term 'modernity' cannot escape reference to the all-too-widely accepted idea that modern societies are those that have evolved in Western Europe and North America during the past two centuries. Working by means of conceptual retrieval and aiming at a review of historical experiences, much of my own analysis draws on such existing scholarship and will often refer to Western Europe and North America for examples and illustrations. However, my analysis in terms of *problématiques* takes distance from any conceptualization that presupposes a tight link between the concept of modernity and recent Western history. This double orientation may appear as ridden with contradictions, most clearly of a strong tension between a very broad and general concept, on the one hand, and the need to be specific, on the other, as experiences and their interpretations are, first of all, local and particular. While I acknowledge this tension, I rather see it as both inescapable and capable of fruitfully widening the scope of the analysis.

To underline the specificity of experiences and their interpretations, the general analysis of the three *problématiques* in terms of modernity will be followed (in Part IV) by reflections on the specificity of European modernity – as an example of modern experiences and their interpretations, not as the origin of modernity or its model. The choice of Europe as a 'case' is doubly motivated. First, the author of this book is European, and the book is, therefore, also a reflection on his own experience with the recent transformations of European modernity. Second, European modernity – as any other – is today more than ever set in the context of a global socio-political constellation. One of the tasks of Part IV is to see in what way the European interpretations of modernity can contribute to addressing the novel problems emerging in this constellation, which is more suitably described as one of dispute over ways of world-making than as one of one-dimensional and inescapable tendencies of globalization (see Karagiannis and Wagner 2007).

Modernity: beyond institutional analysis

As briefly introduced above, the social sciences of the early post-Second World War decades worked with the assumption that contemporary Western societies, called 'modern societies', had emerged from earlier social configurations by way of a profound rupture. This rupture, although it could stretch over long periods and occur in different societies at different points in time, regularly brought about a new set of *institutions*, most importantly a market-based industrial economy, a democratic polity, based on an idea of national belonging plus rational administration, and autonomous knowledge-producing institutions developing empirical-analytical sciences. Modernity, thus, was located in space, that is, in 'the West', meaning Western Europe and North America, but it tended to get diffused from there and gain global significance. Once such 'modern society' was established, namely, in this view, a superior form of social organization was reached that contained all it needed to adapt successfully to changing circumstances. There would, thus, be no further major social transformation. Once it had emerged, modernity stepped out of cultural context and historical time, so to say.

During the 1980s, it was exactly this key conviction of the modern social sciences that was challenged by the idea of 'post-modernity', often understood as the assertion that Western societies had transformed into an entirely new form of social configuration, based on novel forms of social bond. As such, the assertion was most prominently made in Jean-François Lyotard's 'report on knowledge' of 1979, titled *The Postmodern Condition*, but as a hypothesis of an ongoing major social transformation it has guided much sociological research since. At roughly the same time, the spatial connotation of the term was also challenged. The rise of Japan, and other East Asian economies somewhat later, to compete with Western economies in global markets suggested that non-Western forms of modernity could exist. The Iranian Revolution, in turn, inaugurated the idea that modernity could be successfully challenged in societies that had appeared to have safely embarked on the long process of 'modernization'.

This is the context in which the term 'modernity' came into use in sociology. The idea that modernity was neither established in its final form once and for all nor immune to radical reinterpretations outside of its space of origins was now more readily accepted. Nevertheless, conceptual change in much of sociology remained rather limited. The term 'modernity' tended to replace the earlier concept of 'modern society', but it often simply continued to refer to the history of Western societies since the industrial and market revolutions, and since the democratic revolutions and the building of 'modern', rational-bureaucratic nation-states. In the work of Anthony Giddens, to cite one major example, modernity kept being addressed from the angle of 'institutional analysis', and these institutions are those that arose in the West over the past two centuries. All that happens today is that they undergo an internal transformation towards what Giddens calls 'institutional reflexivity' (Giddens 1990, 1994). This is not a major step beyond Max Weber's assertion 'that in Western civilization, and in Western civilization only, cultural phenomena have appeared which [...] lie in a line of development having *universal* significance and value' (Weber 1976 [1904–5/20], p. 13). The reader may note that I omitted Weber's insert 'as we like to think'; I will come back to this.

With 'modernity', thus, sociology proposes a key concept for understanding socio-historical development but oddly makes this concept refer to only a single and unique experience. 'Modernity' is one large-scale occurrence, the origins of which can be traced in space and time but which tends to transcend historical time and cover all socio-cultural space. This view has been radically challenged by work in philosophy, anthropology and post-colonial studies over the past three decades. From the angle of philosophy, with support from the historiography of concepts, the question of concept-formation in the social sciences came under scrutiny. Questioning the facile presupposition that phenomena in the world can always be constructed as empirical 'cases' that are to be subsumed under 'concepts', attention was redirected to the actual 'work' of the concepts, to that which concepts are employed to perform, in social-scientific inquiry. Concepts are proposed not least with the purpose of relating experiences to each other that are otherwise simply separate and different. Particular emphasis was given to the suppression of time in such conceptual labour by virtue of postulating the timeless validity of concepts. From the angle of anthropology and post-colonial studies, related issues were raised with specific regard to the, so to say, conceptual relation between 'modern' and 'traditional' societies, between colonizers and colonized. While maintaining the suppression of historical temporality, so the critical argument goes, time was here re-instituted into concepts in the mode of a 'denial of coevalness' (Johannes Fabian). And even where a greater sensitivity existed, the degree to which a mere application of concepts that were generated in and for a specific context, most often a European one, to other socio-historical situations could be problematic was often underestimated (Derrida 1978; Lyotard 1979; Koselleck 1979; Fabian 1983; Asad 1995).

Until now, however, it is quite open how such critiques of the conventional social and historical sciences relate to the task of analysing entire social configurations over large stretches of time. Much of the critical work operated in the mode of denunciation and thus tended to discard rather than aim to rethink key concepts of the social sciences. Many of those established concepts, however, do address actual *problématiques* of human social life, even if they may do so in an overspecific or unreflective way. Thus, work at conceptual *criticism* would also always need to be work at conceptual *retrieval*, i.e., an attempt to understand both the limits and the potential of those concepts. This book should be seen as a contribution towards a rethinking of the concept 'modernity' in the light of such conceptual retrieval.

As we have seen, the sociology of modernity operates mostly by means of a distinction between historical eras, by some assumption of a rupture, a major social transformation. Such distinction demands specification as to how these eras differ, i.e., a conceptualization of what is modern. In other words, the term 'modernity' inevitably carries a double connotation; it is always both philosophical and empirical, or both substantive and temporal, or both conceptual and historical (Yack 1997; Wagner 2001a). The conceptual imagery of a 'modern society' as developed in mainstream sociology, characterized by a market-based economy and a nation-based democratic polity, aims to reconcile the historical view of modernity, as the history of Europe, and later the West, with a conceptual view of modernity, namely a social configuration composed of sets of functionally differentiated institutions. It provides what I will present here as the first of a variety of possible ways of conceptualizing modernity, namely *modernity as an era and as a set of institutions*.

At a closer look, this imagery sits in an uneasy relation to any array of dates in European history against which one may want to test it. Were one to insist that a full set of functionally differentiated institutions needs to exist before a society can be called modern, socio-political modernity would be limited to a relatively small part of the globe during only a part of the twentieth century. This tension between conceptuality and historicity was resolved by introducing an evolutionary logic in societal development. Based on the assumption of a societally effective voluntarism of human action, realms of social life were considered to have gradually separated from one another according to social functions. Religion, politics, the economy, the arts all emerged as separate spheres in a series of historical breaks – known, as mentioned before, as the scientific, industrial, and democratic revolutions – that follows a logic of differentiation (Parsons 1964; Alexander 1978). A sequence of otherwise contingent ruptures can thus be read as a history of progress, and the era of modernity emerges through an unfolding from very incomplete beginnings. In this view, indeed, modern society came to full fruition only in the USA of the post-Second World War era, but 'modernization' processes were moving towards that *telos* for a long time, and have continued to do so in other parts of the world.

In conceptual terms, this perspective on modern social life aimed at combining an emphasis on free human action with the achievement of greater mastery over the natural and social world. The differentiation of functions and their separate institutionalization was seen as both enhancing human freedom and as increasing the range of human action. Thus, it provided a sociologized version of the Enlightenment combination of freedom and reason, or of autonomy and mastery, or of subjectivity and rationality (e.g., Touraine 1992).

In direct contrast to this affirmative, even self-congratulatory conceptualization of modernity, major critical inquiries into the dynamics of modernity were elaborated successively from the middle of the nineteenth century up until the 1940s. This is what I call the *grand critiques of modernity*, the second major mode of conceptualizing modernity. They were grand critiques by virtue of the fact that they identified basic problems in the practices of modernity, but did not on those grounds abandon the commitment to modernity. They all problematized, although in very different ways, the tension between the unleashing of the modern dynamics of freedom and rational mastery, on the one hand, and its, often unintended, collective outcome in the form of major societal institutions, on the other. As such, they provided critical interpretations of the self-understanding of European modernity.

The first such critique was the critique of political economy as developed mainly by Karl Marx. The second grand critique was the critique of large-scale organization and bureaucracy, as analysed most prominently by Robert Michels and Max Weber. A variant of a critique of conceptions of rationality is the critique of modern philosophy and science, the third grand critique. Weber, too, was aware of the great loss the 'disenchantment of the world' in rational domination entailed but radical and explicit critiques of science were put forward by others in very different forms. In idealist *Lebensphilosophie*, the elaboration of a non-scientistic approach to science was attempted as it was, differently, in early twentieth-century 'Western' Marxism, i.e., by Max Horkheimer and the early Frankfurt School. Synthetically, then, an argumentative figure emerged as follows: in the historical development of modernity as 'liberal' society, the self-produced emergence of overarching structures, such as capitalism and the market, organization and bureaucracy, and modern philosophy and science, is identified. These structures work on the individual subjects and their possibilities for self-realization – up to the threat of self-cancellation of modernity. The more generalized modern practices will become, the more they themselves may undermine the realizability of modernity as a historical project (for a detailed discussion of such critique of modernity, see chapter 5).

This alternative view of modernity, in all its variety, did not really challenge the idea that there is one single form of modernity, emerging in Europe and showing the tendency to transcend time and space. It is thus, despite its critical edge, more a mirror-image than a full alternative to the mainstream sociological view of modernity as the era of functional differentiation. While the critiques of modernity suggested that modernity could not fulfil its promise of increasing both autonomy and rationality in human social life, but tended to undermine both of these commitments, a third, and rather more recent, conceptualization of modernity addresses these basic modern commitments from a yet different angle.

Following Cornelius Castoriadis, modernity can be considered as a situation in which the reference to autonomy and mastery provides for a double 'imaginary signification' of social life (Castoriadis 1990a; Arnason 1989; Wagner 1994). By this term, Castoriadis refers to something similar to, in more conventional terminology, a generally held belief or an 'interpretative pattern' (Arnason). More precisely, the two components of this signification are the idea of the autonomy of the human being as the knowing and acting subject, on the one hand, and on the other, the idea of the rationality of the world, i.e., its principled intelligibility. This interpretative approach to modernity, we could say, underlines the importance of the parenthesis 'as we like to think' in Weber's definition of Western rationalism.[3]

With this view, thus, the emphasis shifts from institutions to *interpretations*. Starting out from the double concept of autonomy and mastery, even though not in precisely these terms, the sociology of modern society had thought to derive a particular institutional structure from this double imaginary signification. Sociology, for instance, tended to conflate the specific historical form of the European nation-state with the general solution to, as it was often called, the problem of life in common, or the political *problématique*, which was expressed in the concept 'society' (see, e.g., Smelser 1997, chapter 3). When assuming, however, that a modern set of institutions can be straight-forwardly derived from the imaginary signification of modernity, it is overlooked that the two elements of this signification are ambivalent each one on its own and tension-ridden between them. Therefore, the recent rethinking takes such tensions to open an interpretative space that is consistent with a variety of institutional forms. The relation between autonomy and mastery institutes an interpretative space that is to be specifically filled in each socio-historic situation through struggles over the situation-grounded appropriate meaning. Theoretically, at least, there is always a plurality and diversity of interpretations within this space (see also Skirbekk 1993).

A fourth conceptualization of modernity brought even more strongly the question of autonomy back to the centre of the analysis of modernity where it had been almost absent during the long period when concerns for functionality, rationalization and, in the critical views, alienation reigned supreme. A common view of the history of social life in Europe holds that a 'culture of modernity' spread gradually over the past five centuries. This 'is a culture which is individualist [...]: it prizes autonomy; it gives an important place to self-exploration; and its visions of the good life involve personal commitment' (Taylor 1989, p. 305). Such an emphasis on individuality and individualization is equally alien to the functionalist praise of modern society as to the totalizing critiques of modernity, but it is even quite distant from the more formalized 'modern' discourses of the individual as in rational choice theory or in liberal political philosophy. In literature and the arts, the *experience of modernity* was the centre of attention and, as an experience, it concerned in the first place the human being in her or his singularity, not an exchangeable atom of social life (Berman 1982). Michel Foucault's lecture 'What is Enlightenment?' very succinctly distinguished between those two readings of modernity. Modernity as an attitude and experience demands the exploration of one's self, the task of separating out 'from the contingency that has made us what we are, the possibility of no longer being, doing, or thinking what we are, do or think' (Foucault 1984, p. 46). This view is opposed to the one that sees modernity as an epoch and a set of institutions, which demand obedience to agreed-upon rules.

In sum, the social sciences have long theorized modernity as the attempt to grasp the specificity of the present, even though the term 'modernity' has been used only rather recently. The dominant strand in the social sciences has aimed at capturing this specificity by *structural-institutional analysis*. The modern institutions are here seen as the embodiments of the promise of freedom and reason. Against and beyond this dominant strand, different conceptualizations of modernity have been proposed. In parallel to the history of the 'modern social sciences', the critiques of modernity have provided an alternative institutional analysis, emphasizing the undermining of the promise of autonomy in and through the workings of the modern institutions. Both the institutional and the critical views have recently been considered too limited in their approach, namely in committing themselves to an overly specific understanding of modernity. The research and theory during the past three decades that explicitly uses the term 'modernity' is by and large characterized by this insight. The *interpretative approach* to modernity has demonstrated the breadth of possible self-understandings of modernity. The conception of *modernity as an ethos and as an experience* has underlined the normative and agential features of modernity. In the sense of ethos, it emphasizes the lack of any given foundations and the possibility of pushing the 'project of modernity' ever further. In the sense of experience, it accentuates creativity and openness.

Multiple modernities: multiples of what?

We cannot entirely do without the institutional and the critical approaches. But the potential to further develop the thinking about modernity and overcome its impasses lies today with the interpretative and the experiential ones. While the interpretative approach provides the ground for an understanding of the variety of possible forms of modernity, the experiential approach helps to understand why a particular interpretation may come about in any given setting.

In recent years, research on 'multiple modernities' has aimed at analysing the plurality of interpretations of the modern signification (Eisenstadt 1998). Despite all its accomplishments, however, this perspective risks merely multiplying the forms of modernity by inscribing them into cultural containers that are coherent and bounded and reproduce themselves over time. It is overall too strongly shaped by the idea that modernity has a specific and constant basic structure, formed in Europe, but can express itself culturally in different ways, on the basis of older value configurations (see, for example, Eisenstadt 1999, p. 198). To take the modern commitment to autonomy seriously, however, requires a more open conceptualization of the contexts of modernity, namely as spaces of experience and interpretation, or as 'spatio-temporal envelopes' (Latour 2000, p. 259).

This conceptual move has two major consequences. First, it loosens the grip on the 'unit of analysis'. We can no longer assume that there is something like Japanese or French or European modernity, because we need to establish first whether and how far Japan or France or Europe have indeed constituted a common space of experience giving the background to a specific and unique interpretation of modernity. Second, it demands a specification of a situation that can be analysed as 'modern'. Above, I have already introduced the idea of autonomy – and its correlate, mastery – as that which constitutes a modern self-understanding.[4] And I have added that this self-understanding recasts the fundamental *problématiques* of human social life, such as the search for rules for life in common, for valid knowledge, and the aim to satisfy one's needs. These *problématiques* – the political, epistemic

and economic ones – are not specific to modernity as such; they tra-
verse all human societies. But the view that solutions to them are not
given but need to be sought is that which the modern commitment
to autonomy, the modern way of confronting these *problématiques*,
entails.

The epistemic and the political *problématiques* have often been
regarded as closely related to one another. If modernity entails that
human beings find their own solutions to them, that is, that they give
themselves their own laws (autonomy), the beginning of philosophy
as the human questioning of being coincides with the beginning
of politics as the giving of laws for living together – historically in
ancient Greece (see, e.g., Castoriadis 1986, pp. 282–6). The relation
between these two *problématiques* defines much of the history of
political philosophy.[5] Citizens of a free polity acting autonomously
expose themselves, by virtue of their commitment to autonomy,
to high uncertainty. Devising strategies for dealing with such uncertainty, they – or their political philosophers – tend to strengthen
the idea of, and the commitment to, instrumental mastery of the
world and of themselves. As a consequence, though, certain forms
of autonomy may be constrained or ruled out with a view to enhancing mastery and, thus, predictability. This consideration provides
the background for one of the persistent tensions within the modern
imaginary signification. In the history of philosophy, this question
emerges time and again, such as in Plato, with his need for excluding
the poets from the *polis*, and in Kant, who counterbalanced his
commitment to freedom by tying the exercise of freedom to the
use of reason or, in other words, by subjecting the political *problématique* to the epistemic one. In the following analysis, this particular
conflation will be avoided by discussing the political *problématique*
separately from, and prior to, the epistemic one (in Parts I and III).
Thus, the ways of dealing with the political *problématique* will not
be subordinated to any solutions found in treating the epistemic
problématique.

In some also time-honoured but much more recent ways of thinking, a third *problématique* has been linked to these two classical ones:
the *problématique* of organizing for the satisfaction of needs, or the
economic *problématique* (discussed in Part II). This third *problématique*, not unknown to the ancients, did not occupy any important
place in scholarly thought before early modern times because it was
considered to be a private matter that had to be left within the con-
fines of the household. Its elevation to a more prominent position
occurred in basically two steps. A fundamentally Aristotelian political
ontology being left intact, the size of households tended to grow over

time, until in feudalism entire principalities could be seen as single households. With mercantilism and absolutism, the polity itself was regarded as a giant household, and 'economic' thinking thus tended to merge with 'political' thinking in the form, for instance, of the policy and cameral sciences (see, e.g., Maier 1980). If this was the first step in the emancipation of the third *problématique* from its inferior status, the second step came with political economy and the idea that the satisfaction of needs could be treated, quite like the questions of knowledge and polity, in a 'modern' manner, namely by allowing human beings to find their own ways of dealing with it, autonomously, by giving themselves their own laws of economic action and interaction.

This elevation of the third *problématique* is one of the interpretative sources of the rise of capitalism (to be discussed in chapter 6). Appropriately so, Marx's analysis of capitalism proceeded as, in the first instance, a 'critique of political economy'. However, his approach tacitly assumed that answers to the other two *problématiques* were rather unquestionably available – in principle, although not necessarily in historical actuality – as means to effectively criticize this third one. Thus, the critique of political economy proceeded by means of 'denunciation' (Luc Boltanski) or 'hermeneutics of suspicion' (Paul Ricoeur) without questioning its own validity claims (see the discussion in chapter 5). And the political was conceptualized in such a way that it could unproblematically be appropriated by an emerging collective subject, once the conditions had matured. In the view that I develop here, in contrast, the rise of political economy will be considered, first of all, in terms of bringing about a change in the relation between the three *problématiques* and, that is, as affecting all three *problématiques* at their conceptual core, not merely the emerging one.[6]

Overview

Once the overall configuration of such social philosophy of *problématiques* is grasped, the ground is prepared for re-analysing the tradition of political economy, and later disciplinary economics and rational choice theory, both in terms of their possible 'modernity' and in view of developing a viable form of critique. This is, in particular, the task of the second part of this book, devoted to a historico-sociological analysis of the experiences of changes in the ways of dealing with the economic *problématique*. It will be preceded, in Part I, by a similar analysis of the political *problématique*, its transformations in the light of interpretations of prior experiences, and succeeded, in Part III, by an analysis focusing on the epistemic *problématique*. As mentioned above, the main reason for separating the analysis of these three *problématiques* is to avoid the conflation of issues, an all-too-common phenomenon in the history of social and political thought.

Furthermore, though, there is also a rationale for the particular order of analysis. When conflation occurred, it most often entailed the subordination of the political *problématique* to either the epistemic *problématique*, as said above, or to the economic *problématique* or even to both. The argument then is that either the political form of modernity can be derived from valid knowledge about the world or that there is only a limited set of modern political forms that is compatible with 'economic modernity', that is with 'market society' or with 'capitalism'. Analysing the political *problématique* here first, in contrast, makes this particular kind of conflation and subordination impossible. The following analysis will withhold arguments about the economic and epistemic *problématique* until a later point to restore a proper sense of autonomy to the ways of dealing with the political *problématique*. After all, the 'invention of the political' (paraphrasing Christian Meier and Cornelius Castoriadis) in ancient Greece entailed a strong sense of collective self-determination, of the actual capacity of a society to act upon itself and to elaborate an explicit and specific self-understanding.

In turn, this move will allow an analysis of the economic *problématique* in the light of the challenge its rise posed to the established ways of thinking about the political *problématique*. Thus, both the argument about the functional superiority of 'free markets' and the one about the role of the state as the 'executive committee of the bourgeoisie' will be rejected as theoretical 'solutions' to the relation between the political and the economic *problématiques*.

Rather, the focus will be – across all three analyses – on the variety of interpretations that have been given to these *problématiques* and their relation in the light of specific experiences made. Finally, moving the discussion of the epistemic *problématique* into the third position allows me to make visible how proposed solutions to epistemic questions need to be understood in the context of problematic situations that were often created by particular experiences with political and economic issues. The aim is not, in inversion of known reasoning, to argue for the subordination of the epistemic *problématique* to either the political or the economic one or both. Rather, various claims to context-independent knowledge will be analysed as involving the creation and transformation of interpretative resources to situate human beings in the world. Such a contextualization does not render these claims invalid per se; it should be seen as a step towards grasping the reach of the claims and to open them up to contestation, as any truly modern understanding of knowledge would require.

Part I starts out by discussing how the modern commitment to autonomy – or freedom – was recast in the light of experiences with varieties of collectivism, including totalitarianism, in such a way that the concern with individual liberty became unduly prominent (chapter 2). Subsequently, it is argued that a comprehensive interpretation of political modernity will need to devise a balance between the commitments to individual and to collective self-determination. No emphasis on individual freedom, as understandable as it may be, can make the question of collective autonomy disappear, as a historico-sociological overview of modernity's changing political forms will show (chapter 3). Finally, the experience of '1968' and its aftermath is analysed in terms of shifting balances between individual and collective autonomy (chapter 4). This particular event is chosen because it marks one of the moments of transition from the heyday of 'modern society' to the recent concern with making 'modernity' intelligible. Part II moves towards interpretations of economic modernity by first discussing the contribution of critical theory to the analysis of capitalism and market society (chapter 5). It is argued that critical theory keeps crucial insights about the workings of economic modernity alive but that it also persistently underestimates the role of democracy in capitalism. That is why the following chapter shifts towards a discussion of the relation between the economic and the political *problématiques* (chapter 6). As in Part I, a final chapter is devoted to the analysis of the most recent reinterpretation of modernity, in this case the exit from organized capitalism in the recent emphasis on 'flexibility' of economic organization (chapter 7). Part III discusses the epistemic claims of modernity under two headings. First, a brief sketch of debates on science from the 'scientific revolution' to the 'science wars' is provided in terms of the variety of interpretations the epistemic claim of modernity has undergone (chapter 8). Second, the particular claim of the social sciences is investigated in terms of the varieties of interpretations of socio-political modernity that those sciences have provided (chapter 9).

Throughout, European examples are at the centre of the analysis, but Part IV moves explicitly to a focus on the European experiences of modernity and their interpretations. First (in chapter 10), a long-term perspective on the dynamics of European history, from the religious wars to the building of welfare states, is developed that links directly to the analysis of the forms of political modernity provided in chapter 3. These observations are complemented by a view on the transformations of the self-understanding of European modernity during the twentieth century, which in their sum lead to a relativizing of the view of Europe as the avant-garde of modernity, in particular in the light of experiences such as colonialism, world wars and totalitarianism. Subsequently, the current attempt at consolidating a specific European interpretation of modernity in the contemporary global context is discussed, with particular emphasis on the comparison with the other main 'Western' interpretation of modernity, the one of the USA (chapter 11).

Part V can be considered as a methodological and conceptual appendix to the preceding analysis. Preconditions for, and implications of, the approach within the wider debates in the social sciences will be discussed here from two angles. First, a proposal is made to reconnect the social theory of modernity to the political philosophy of modernity, two genres of intellectual work that are practised in almost perfect separation today (chapter 12). Second, with the proposed focus on experiences and interpretations, the approach needs to be constitutively historical. Thus, its social theory component needs to draw on historical sociology, and its political philosophy component needs to be based on the critical history of political concepts (chapter 13).

Part I

Interpretations of Political Modernity: Liberty and its Discontents

Overture: Multiple Interpretations of Political Modernity

As outlined above, the term 'modernity' refers to a situation in which human beings commit themselves to self-determine their lives, their relations to others and their ways of being in the world. The term 'political modernity', more specifically, refers to the self-determination of life in common with others, to the rules of life in common. During the past two centuries, much of social and political theory has assumed that there is a single model of 'modern society' to which all societies will gradually converge because of the higher rationality of its institutional arrangements. Similarly, political modernity is then equated with a single institutional model based on electoral democracy and a set of basic individual rights. In what follows, in contrast, I argue that a commitment to political modernity does not lead unequivocally to a certain institutional form of the polity. Such commitment is rather widely open to interpretation; indeed, it is profoundly underdetermined and marked by deep tensions. The commitment to collective self-determination, in other words, opens a *problématique* whose solutions need to be found in the light of political experiences. Existing polities that share this commitment are based on a variety of interpretations all of which need to be understood in the light of the histories of these polities. There is not a single scale of 'political modernization', on which the USA, and possibly the UK, would always appear at the top, continental European polities lag a bit behind, and the rest of the world be still far from achieving this objective – a picture drawn by much of Anglo-American social and political theory.

In other words, the starting point of the following reasoning is the assumption that, while existing self-understandings of political modernity may – and mostly do – contain general and universal elements, they are always specific and situated in the time and space of the social life to which they refer. The purpose of this first part of this volume is to retrieve them through a brief history of political ideas and a historical sociology of socio-political forms which will regard these ideas and the institutional consequences drawn from them in the light of political experiences and the interpretations given to those experiences.

The emphasis on political modernity in this first part of my argument begs the question of the relation between such *political* modernity and other aspects of modernity. The relation between the political, economic and epistemic *problématiques* will be discussed throughout this volume; thus, the explication in this respect is merely postponed (as set out in chapter 1 above). Beyond those aspects, however, theories of modernity also invoke *cultural* and *social* dimensions. Those dimensions are often seen as – or better: conceptualized as – that which escapes conscious human action, that which is not accessible to self-determination. In much of the history of anthropology, for instance, culture is seen as something human beings have and cannot choose. In the sociological tradition, social structure may not entirely escape human agency, but it is at most analysed as the unintended outcome of a multiplicity of actions (I return to the variety of social science traditions in chapters 9 and 12 below). In such understandings, cultural and social 'facts' would pose constraints to collective self-determination; or in other words, answers to the epistemic *problématique*, in terms of valid knowledge about the social and cultural world, limit the range of possible interpretations of the political *problématique*. Indeed, observations on cultural and social relations between human beings have often been used to 'close' the political *problématique*, which otherwise would be too widely open to contingency. Bonds of common religion or language, for instance, have been considered compelling reasons for setting boundaries of polities in Europe after the religious wars and after the democratic revolutions. Challenges to social bonds after the industrial revolution and the rise of capitalism have led to arguments about the absolute functional necessity for organized social solidarity and/or for a socialist revolution. In contrast to such reasoning, observations on cultural and social relations will in the following not be considered as providing an answer to the political *problématique* of human life. They rather raise specific questions that themselves need to be understood against the background of the particular way in which the project of political modernity gained shape in Europe.

Any alternative political theory should not, however, in turn, fall into the temptation to disregard cultural or social relations as specific or 'substantive' in the sense that any general political theory would need to gain distance from such historical-empirical contaminations. This move was precisely taken in the history of political thought, first with the rise of social contract theory and the hypothesis, *avant la lettre*, of an 'original position' (John Rawls), then with the development of liberalism in its individualist form over the past two centuries. Again, though in a different way, this is an attempt at closing the political *problématique* by epistemic means, here by means of the abstractions of individualist political theory. The following analysis starts out, in chapter 2, from a discussion and critique of individualist liberalism, aiming to show both the reasons for its dominance and its basic insufficiency for understanding political modernity. Subsequently, chapter 3 attempts to reconstruct a broader view on the history of political forms, which works with a fourfold set of criteria that can be applied in arguing for a certain form of the polity rather than another. It demonstrates that each one of those criteria arose in response to an experience defined as problematic, but it also shows that none of them is superior to the others in absolute terms, that is, in abstraction from the context. Rather, what can be shown is that any one-sided emphasis of any one criterion over all others leads to normatively undesirable political solutions.[1]

Conceptually speaking, there is, thus, a double challenge – individualist abstraction versus socio-cultural determination. In our current period, the latter is strongly out of favour in the light of highly social-collectivist experiences of the twentieth century (see chapter 2 as well as chapter 11 for some more detail on this condition). However, the former remains as deficient as it always was in grounding the modern polity. The problem is how to argue for substantively significant ways of collective autonomy without imposing any political order that unduly constrains personal liberties. This problem was encountered by that recent attempt at reconstructing political modernity that has remained alive in collective memory despite its almost complete political failure: the events known as '1968'. Chapter 4 will aim to demonstrate how these events can be analysed in terms of an experience of shortcomings in the West European (and North American) political modernity of the 1950s and 1960s and a reaction towards those shortcomings, but also in terms of a failure to elaborate a convincing alternative interpretation that could lend itself to political reconstruction (this argument will be taken up again later, in chapter 11 for the current situation of Europe in the world, and in chapter 12 as a key issue in the relation between social theory and political philosophy).

2

Modernity and the Question of Freedom

Roughly in the middle of his famous lecture on 'Two concepts of liberty', Isaiah Berlin discusses the danger of 'confounding liberty with her sisters, equality and fraternity', which would lead to 'illiberal conclusions' (Berlin 1971 [1958], p. 154).[1] He then subsumes those two sisters of liberty under the notion of 'search for status and recognition' and appears to come to a clear verdict: 'It is not with individual liberty [. . .] that this desire for status and recognition can easily be identified. It is something no less profoundly needed and passionately fought for by human beings – it is something akin to, but not itself, freedom; [. . .] it is more closely related to solidarity' (p. 158).[2] And later he suggests that goals such as equality and fraternity 'appear wholly, or in part, incompatible with the greatest degree of individual liberty' (p. 161). Four decades later, the European Union chose to ignore this insight by one of the great liberal thinkers of the post-Second World War period when it committed itself to freedom and solidarity as principles of equal rank in its Charter of Fundamental Rights.

With his essay, Berlin contributed to a long tradition of concern in political thought about the proper separation of concepts and commitments. Berlin indeed seems to have seen this lecture as an exercise in the liberal 'art of separation', as Michael Walzer (1984) would put it a quarter of a century later. 'Everything is what it is', Berlin claims, 'liberty is liberty, not equality or fairness or justice or culture, or human happiness or a quiet conscience. [. . .] It is a confusion of values to say that although my "liberal", individual freedom may go by the board, some other kind of freedom – "social" or "economic" – is increased' (pp. 125–6).[3]

Berlin cautiously avoids concluding his reasoning bluntly in favour of individual liberty, in terms of what he called 'negative liberty', understood as 'non-interference' or 'liberty from' (pp. 126–7). Instead he emphasizes pluralism of value commitments (p. 171). Nevertheless his assessment of the relation between individual liberty and other goals is asymmetric, and as such characteristic for much of the liberal tradition of thought.[4] And among those other goals that are discussed as legitimate, but ultimately relegated to a secondary rank, is solidarity.

The objective of this chapter is to demonstrate that such a conceptual separation, and subsequent hierarchization, of freedom and solidarity is ill-founded, and this in a twofold way. First, the liberalism that proceeds in such a way – in the following to be referred to as individualist liberalism – does not achieve its purpose, namely to provide a general and unequivocal grounding for the safeguarding of individual liberty. In the unsuccessful pursuit of this end, though, second, it unnecessarily delegitimizes other political values and commitments, among which, significantly, the commitment to solidarity. Importantly, it is unable to consider the possibility that commitment to some such values may be necessary to safeguard liberty.[5]

The demonstration will proceed in three steps. First, the argumentative strategy on which the priority of individual liberty is based will be reconstructed to see how far a consistent and sufficient position is developed. This will be done, in all due brevity, by recourse to one key author and text from each of the past two centuries of liberal thought, John Stuart Mill's *On Liberty* and Isaiah Berlin's abovementioned 'Two Concepts of Liberty'. Second, it will be shown that both of these authors are aware of alternative arguments that share the concern with liberty but reject the conceptual priority of individual liberty. Suspending the two liberals' worries about 'illiberal conclusions' for a moment, I shall aim at identifying the core argument of those alternatives – which for the sake of clarity may be referred to as varieties of non-individualist liberalism. Without unduly forcing the argument, it will become recognizable that this core can be characterized by the commitments to democracy and solidarity in addition to liberty. The third step, then, is devoted to making the full contours of this alternative liberal tradition visible, and this will be done again by reference – much more briefly – to one key author for each of the past two centuries, in this case Alexis de Tocqueville and Claude Lefort.

The priority of individual liberty

John Stuart Mill's treatise *On Liberty* – in fact co-authored with his wife Harriet Taylor, whose name appears as a partial author in the dedication – is rightly recognized as a key statement of the liberal credo. It lends itself to the purposes of this chapter not least because of the precision in its basic definitions of concepts and problems. Mill offers the following definition of freedom in the sense in which he wants to discuss it: 'The only freedom that deserves the name is that of pursuing our own good in our own way, so long as we do not attempt to deprive others of theirs or impede their efforts to obtain it' (Mill 1956 [1859], pp. 16–17). Let us note in passing the use of the first person plural – an issue to which I shall return soon. The basic idea is very clear: freedom, to be truly freedom, does not need to be discussed with others, and should not be interfered with by others, except in the case that others are interfered with by the use of one's freedom. The meaning of freedom is unequivocal, and there is only one problem that derives from the commitment to it: the possibility that one person's freedom constrains another person's freedom.

This latter possibility requires the introduction of means to limit the use of freedom at the point at which it would interfere with others. This problem is accordingly the issue to which the entire treatise is devoted: 'The object of this essay is to assert one very simple principle, as entitled to govern absolutely the dealings of society with the individual in the way of compulsion and control' (p. 13). The search for such a principle, in the view of the author, is successful: 'That principle is that the sole end for which mankind are warranted, individually or collectively, in interfering with the liberty of action of any of their number is self-protection' (p. 13). Mill's treatise has been widely discussed ever since its publication, and its inconsistencies are well known.[6] As plausibly as the question appears to be posed, there is just no way to generally legitimize constraining intervention on the freedom of a member of society by theoretical fiat alone. For present purposes, it is rather the structure of the argument that Mill uses for legitimizing constraint that is important.

Mill's reasoning apparently knows only two core elements, and the connection between them determines the argument: the one is 'power [. . .] rightfully to be exercised', the other is conduct by someone that may 'produce evil to someone else' (p. 13), and the latter provides for the only case in which power may be exercised over the individual. Implicitly, this entails that solidarity concerns are not a legitimate reason of any society to exercise power over any of its members. However, Mill cannot state his case without reference to something else that remains undiscussed. When he refers to 'self-protection', for instance, the self that is to be protected appears to be mankind, syntactically at least, not any individual's freedom. If this were indeed the meaning, Mill would need a concept of humanity and its relations to the individuals of which it is composed, a concept that, if it existed, would spell out how the 'self-protection' of humanity protects at the same time the liberty of the individuals. None of this, though, can be found in the treatise.

Similarly, Mill's notion of 'society' is intriguing – and this relates back to the 'we' that he probably unreflectedly but revealingly uses. From a Millian perspective, the agent that interferes in a constraining manner when one individual violates the liberty of another clearly cannot be just a third freedom-seeking individual him- or herself. To surely fulfil its task, the agent of protection of individual liberty must in some way stand above the exercise of liberty. Contextually, nineteenth-century liberals mostly had no problems in identifying these agents in the existing states. However, here the argument comes full circle. Mill aims at determining the limits of 'our', of 'society's, of the state's interference with individual liberty, but he does not offer any consideration of the nature of this 'we' that would plausibly allow the conclusion that the collective agent would indeed be bound by such reasoning.

Almost exactly one hundred years later, Isaiah Berlin restated the question in rather similar terms when he defined 'negative liberty' as the answer to the question 'What is the area within which the subject – a person or group of persons – is or should be left to do or be what he is able to do or be?' (Berlin 1971 [1958], pp. 121–2). Unlike Mill, to whom he indeed refers as the key source for such a concept of freedom, Berlin is not exclusively orientated at the objective of enhancing individual liberty. In a note of caution towards the end of his lecture, he states explicitly that he does 'not wish to say that individual freedom is, even in the most liberal societies, the sole, or even the dominant, criterion of social action' (p. 169). This note is needed, though, precisely because he had used formulations earlier that are reminiscent of Mill's way of reasoning: 'If I wish to preserve my liberty, [. . .] I must establish a society in which there must be some frontiers of freedom which nobody should be permitted to cross' (p. 164).[7] Liberty is here described by means of a spatial metaphor: as a territory around which a fence is erected so that trespassing cannot occur.

Contextually, it is clear that Berlin's guarded defence of 'negative liberty' is informed by the historical experience with the widespread and radical suppression of liberties during the decades preceding his writing, an experience that Mill did not know in that form. What separates Berlin from Mill as well, though, is the experience of collective mobilizations against the impact of the application of the 'liberty principle' during the nineteenth century, many of which can be seen as mobilizations for solidarity, in terms of both solidarity among those concerned, that is, most importantly, workers' solidarity, and organized solidarity within the frame of a polity, that is, the welfare state. One could say that the view of what kinds of action could cause harm to others in liberal market society changed considerably between 1858, when Mill wrote,[8] and 1958, when Isaiah Berlin's worries about spaces of freedom could not simply mirror those voiced by Mill, but had to take those concerns about solidarity explicitly into account. Surveying roughly those hundred years in his treatise on 'the rise and fall of market society', Karl Polanyi (1985 [1944]), for instance, talked in almost Millian terms, but contra Mill, about the historical need for self-defence of 'society' against a certain form of individual liberty. Intending to show that 'negative liberty' remains a central concern even after those experiences, Berlin, in turn, spends a considerable portion of his lecture rejecting a notion of 'positive liberty' and, as mentioned at the outset, aiming to demonstrate that other values, such as the ones related to 'search for status', have little or nothing to do with liberty.

The continental deviance and the insufficiency of 'negative liberty'

The authors of both texts – though Berlin much more so than Mill – are aware of the fact that their case is not as compelling as they state it and that they cannot fully ignore the existence of alternatives to their ways of conceptualizing the issue. Their modes of presenting these alternatives, accordingly, become significant for understanding the limits of the individualist-liberal project.

Mill notes the existence of two particular strands of 'European liberalism', namely 'the last generation' and 'the Continental section', whose positions deviate in one important respect from what, by implication, he must consider as the British liberalism of his time. According to Mill, namely, proponents of those strands held that 'too much importance had been attached to the limitation of the power itself' (Mill 1956 [1859], p. 5) in liberalism, and that this concern had become much less pressing with the increasing diffusion of the idea of collective self-government, of democracy. It is worth quoting Mill here in full:

> Men ceased to think it a necessity of nature that their governors should be an independent power opposed in interest to themselves. It appeared to them so much better that the various magistrates of the state should

be their tenants or delegates, revocable at their pleasure. In that way alone, it seemed, could they have complete security that the powers of government would never be used to their disadvantage. (Mill 1956, p. 5)

This reasoning refers to a major politico-historical transformation, the advent of the idea of popular self-government, and translates it into politico-conceptual concerns. Conceptually, the watershed reads as follows: Individual liberties had to be fought for as long as political power came from elsewhere. As soon as political power is based in the people, this struggle is no longer necessary, or at least much less important.

This reasoning sounds broadly plausible, even to our ears. A major reason why Mill nevertheless rejects it is the experience with democracy itself:

In political and philosophical theories as well as in persons, success discloses faults and infirmities which failure might have concealed from observation. The notion that the people have no need to limit their power over themselves might seem axiomatic, when popular government was a thing only dreamed about, or read of as having existed at some distant period of the past. (Mill 1956, p. 6)

With the rise, in particular, of democracy in America, however, those apparent axioms have shown not to hold. Drawing heavily on Alexis de Tocqueville (see also Mill 1994), Mill discusses dangers of democratic rule and then concludes: 'The limitation, therefore, of the power of government over individuals loses none of its importance when the holders of power are regularly accountable to the community' (p. 6), adding that this is an insight by then well accepted, with the exception of 'the Continental section' of European liberalism.

Continental thinkers – such as Spinoza, Rousseau, Herder, Hegel, Fichte, Marx – also loom large in Berlin's discussions of erroneous approaches to liberty, occasionally accompanied by 'British Idealists' (Berlin 1971 [1958], p. 148) and 'neo-Conservatives [!] in English-speaking countries' (p. 170). He discusses their conceptualizations at much more length than Mill, though, because he knows, a hundred years later, that their views will not simply wither away in the course of 'the progress of human affairs', a term Mill could still use (Mill 1956, p. 4).

Mill, as we have seen, seemed to think that a convincing statement of the principle of liberty was the most important task that political theory had to accomplish. The political form of the society in which individual liberties were to flourish seemed to matter rather little to him, at least in this text.[9] Berlin went beyond this view on two grounds: first, he recognized that human beings could legitimately hold other political values to be of similar importance. On those grounds he commits himself to a pluralist understanding of the polity – within which he, though, would always emphasize 'negative liberty'. This is an understandable stand but it, too, refrains from addressing in detail the larger political setting of liberty and plurality as a comprehensive political philosophy would need to do.

Like Mill, second, Berlin is aware of the fact that the argument for collective self-determination could interfere with the argument for individual self-determination and limit the commitment to the latter. He, too, though, prefers not to tackle the question of democracy in its own right at all, but only in so far as commitments to it are either seen as commitments to freedom or as risks for infringements on individual freedom. As shall be shown, the peculiar place of solidarity in his reasoning can only be understood by tracing his understanding of self-government in its relation to individual liberty.

Claiming that 'there is no necessary connection between individual liberty and democratic rule', Berlin (1971, p. 130) separates the former from the latter in two respects, logically and historically: 'The answer to the question "Who governs me?" is logically distinct from the question "How far does government interfere with me?"' (p. 130). Furthermore, he suggests, in agreement with Mill, that there are substantive tensions that do not fail to materialize historically: 'The connexion between democracy and individual liberty is a good deal more tenuous than it seemed to many advocates of both' (pp. 130–1). Moving from those general assertions to a diagnosis of his time, he concludes that these commitments are so different 'as to have led in the end [!] to the great clash of ideologies that dominates our world' (p. 131).[10] While one may today consider Berlin's starting observations as a useful reminder that 'co-originality' of the commitments to liberty and democracy cannot easily be claimed,[11] his latter move leads Berlin to erroneously equate a highly ideologized concept (and practice) of 'popular democracy' with the general concept of collective autonomy and can only be understood in the context of the time. Any more thorough investigation of the latter is, as a consequence, so much postponed in the lecture that it hardly takes place.

The following four sections of Berlin's lecture, namely, are devoted to characterizing in more detail and great nuance the positive concept of liberty but they are dominated by the idea that such a concept ultimately needs to be understood as a 'doctrine of liberation by reason' (p. 144). While it is true that varieties of rationalism have been a problem in the history of political thought, and maybe they are to some extent still today,[12] the concentration on this topic leads Berlin to lose the question of democracy almost completely out of sight.[13] Rather than criticizing (rightly) the alleged rational underpinnings of democracy, he might have dealt in more detail with the argument about social underpinnings of political forms. To those, though, he moves only oddly – and rather indirectly – when discussing 'search for status' (section VI, pp. 154–62) as a political commitment. In this section of the lecture, which our introductory remarks used as a start-ing point for relating freedom to solidarity, Berlin gets completely entangled in the web of meanings he had himself spun. Indicative of the difficulties an advocate of negative liberty will have with soli-darity, his reasoning can also be read against the grain to show how solidarity is connected with liberty.

In line with the professed art of separation, Berlin first continues to evoke 'the danger of calling any improvement in his social situation favoured by a human being an increase of his liberty, and [asks whether this] will [...] not render this term so vague and distended as to make it virtually useless' (p. 159). Readers who followed him up to this point are almost obliged to agree. Liberty 'in this sense' – a formula repeated many times in the lecture – is certainly something different from recognition, solidarity, social status, mutual under-standing (Berlin varies a large number of terms to characterize this other, social commitment). But, being somewhat at a loss in his rea-soning, Berlin now acknowledges that an excessive practice of the art of conceptual separation may not be fruitful: 'Social and political terms are necessarily vague. The attempt to make the vocabulary of politics too precise may render it useless' (p. 158). This is in prepara-tion of his admission:

> And yet we cannot simply dismiss this case [calling an improvement in social situation an increase in liberty, PW] as a mere confusion of the notion of freedom with that of status, or solidarity, or fraternity, or equality, or some combination of these. [...] We may refuse this goal the title of liberty; yet it would be a shallow view that assumed that analogies between individuals and groups, or organic metaphors, are mere fallacies [...] or simple semantic confusion. (p. 159)

In this world of necessarily vague concepts, Berlin makes use of terms with sociological inclination, such as 'group' or 'organic meta-phor', as indeed already before with 'status' and 'recognition'. The attempt at identifying what those analogies and metaphors truly are does not lead to any conclusion within this terminology but requires him to make a significant (re-)connection to a question of political philosophy, namely 'to the question "Who is to govern us?"'. Since the answers to this question 'are logically, and at times also politically and socially, independent of what extent of "negative" liberty I demand for my own or my group's activities' (p. 160), one needs those other concepts to provide answers. At first sight, Berlin here seems only to be restating that 'negative liberty' is something different from anything else discussed here. But with the same move he asserts that these other commitments – that is, 'status, or solidarity, or fraternity, or equality, or some combination of these' – are highly significant and that they cannot be addressed from within a political theory of individualist ('negative') liberalism.

At this point, Berlin significantly suggests that whenever such an answer can be seen as '"my own", as something which belongs to me, or to whom I belong, I can, by using words which convey fraternity or solidarity, as well as some part of the connotation of the "positive" sense of the word freedom [. . .], describe it as a hybrid form of freedom' (p. 160). In other words, the question 'Who governs us?' cannot be answered by exclusive resort to negative liberty because it is an 'independent' question. At the same time, it tends to be answered by resorting to 'social' bonds between human beings, or to solidarity broadly understood. If such social bonds can be referred to as 'one's own' and are evoked to answer the question 'Who governs us?', then we have a mode of self-government that can be described as a form of freedom.

We have done nothing here but reword Berlin's statement. In the light of his starting profession to talk about everything as that which it is, and 'liberty is liberty', this conclusion must be considered as a total failure. For the purposes of our argument, in contrast, we see him arriving at an important insight: solidarity is, or at least can be, a form of freedom, and it can be so via the idea of collective autonomy, or democracy.

Alternative liberal views

Textually, this observation is incontrovertible. However, it is equally certain that the link between freedom and solidarity was not the author's main intention in this lecture; and one may even doubt whether he would have considered to have established such a link.[14] To further understand the nature of the linkage, he and other liberals who emphasize individual liberty are therefore not a useful source.

What we said at the outset remains valid: individualist liberals relegate solidarity to a secondary rank; and it is only in writings of the most sophisticated of them that one finds acknowledgement of greater complexity.

Both Mill and Berlin refer, explicitly or implicitly, to other authors from the liberal tradition in their support. Most prominent among those resource persons are Benjamin Constant and Alexis de Tocqueville. The former's *De la liberté des modernes comparée avec la liberté des anciens* may have a justified place in this tradition, as he draws a distinction that rather well corresponds with the one Berlin makes between negative and positive liberty and he emphasizes individual liberty in a way that is very close to Mill.[15] The case of Tocqueville, though, is different. Rather than fitting within this tradition, his *De la Démocratie en Amérique*, flanked by the later *L'Ancien régime et la Révolution*, provides a possible starting point for reconstructing an alternative, rather neglected, liberal tradition.

Tocqueville's key concern in both these volumes is the historical transformation in the nature of the polity that was brought about by the American Revolution and the founding of the United States, on the one hand, and the overthrowing of the *ancien régime* in the course of the French Revolution, on the other. Even though the latter did not bring democracy about, it, too, was such a profound change that it put a society basically committed to egalitarianism onto the horizon, and thus made democracy the inevitable reference point for an entirely 'new political science' that Tocqueville saw as urgently needed.

Tocqueville talks at length about individualism and certainly is highly concerned about individual freedom, threatened in particular by the possible 'tyranny of the majority' under conditions of democracy, as witnessed in the US in the form of a societal tendency towards conformism rather than as political oppression (two issues of whose equal importance Mill was also very well aware). Nevertheless, it is not individual liberty that provides the starting point of his reasoning, but democracy as a novel 'form of political society', and furthermore, it is this form of political society that institutes the individual in a particular way (Lefort 1986a, p. 208) – rather than the other way round, as social contract theory and, following it, individualist liberalism would have it.

Tocqueville shall here just be read briefly in the light of the preceding interpretation of individualist liberalism, focusing on four observations of basic agreement and difference. The two points of agreement are important but they are easily stated. First, Tocqueville agrees with Mill that the question of individual liberty did not find an automatic and self-evident answer after the advent of democracy; rather, in his view, it needs to be posed with urgency and in a new way. Second, he values personal liberty certainly as highly as Berlin and would not want to have seen the commitment towards it replaced by concern for other values.

Thirdly, however, Tocqueville does not conclude from these two assumptions that political theory should start out by posing the question of individual liberty. Rather, he sees democracy as that political form in which the individual is posited as 'unit citizen' – as Stein Rokkan should later say – and thus asks for a 'new political science' that analyses the fate of freedom under conditions of that political form. For Tocqueville, this novel form of political society is creative both of the individual and their space of freedom and of the infringements on that freedom by general opinion or by majority legislation. Where Mill and later also Berlin see 'society' dualistically as either a threat to liberty or as the hypothetical agent that could protect the liberty of individuals, and in each case as exogenous to individuals and their strivings, Tocqueville sees the political form of society as constitutive of individuals, thus he 'sociologizes' – as we may want to say; without, though, falling into sociological determinism – the analysis of political life. From this angle, he could not consider a defence of individual liberty a plausible or even compelling starting point for political analysis as it would have led to rather empty normative claims dissociated from the mode of social life.

After having embarked on his strategy of analysis, rather, a novel kind of question emerges, and this leads to the fourth and final observation to be made here, the one that is crucial for the link between freedom and solidarity. The question is: what kind of 'social' life makes democracy a sustainable political form and, in particular, maintains and creates conditions for individual liberty under conditions of democracy? To answer this question, Tocqueville investigated the specific relations of 'association' within (American and French) society with a view to their enhancing or constraining liberty. The concept of associative relations comprises everything – and more – that Berlin was characterizing as matters of status, recognition, mutual understanding and solidarity. Berlin discusses those relations in their distinction from liberty, and this, as we have seen, rather incoherently. Tocqueville opens up another perspective by seeing them as always underlying those freedom-endangering or freedom-enlarging features of democratic society as general opinion and majority will.

As Berlin's example shows, associative relations are not easily introduced into any formal reasoning of political theory. Most versions of individualist liberalism prefer to cast a veil of ignorance over them, with a view to arriving at generalizable propositions about the political. In other words, most political theorizing prefers to ignore 'the social' by introducing a sharp divide between things political and things social and then practising a well-intended but ill-conceived 'art of separation'. However, as Tocqueville has shown for American democracy, social relations are 'political' in the double sense of being constitutive of political forms (as prior conditions for the forming of political society) and as being, in principle, alterable by political intervention. Self-government, given that it cannot rely on external sources for its legitimacy, includes the search for a common understanding of the way of living together. Rather than limiting government from the beginning in the face of possible abuse, as individualist liberals try to argue, the challenge of democracy, as a situation in which human beings give themselves their own law, is to address all issues of the life in common in a comprehensive way.

How, though, does Tocqueville's notion of associative life relate to the concept of solidarity? Applying a Tocquevillean perspective to the individualist liberals' concern for liberty provides an answer to this question: solidarity is a specific form of associative relation, and it is the one that permits the combination of personal liberty with democracy, individual self-determination with collective self-determination.

A comparison with two alternative modes of thinking the political under conditions of democracy will make the significance of this statement clear. On the one hand, individualist-rationalist thinkers, many of whom embrace individualist liberalism, would arrive at decisions about the common by aggregation of preferences. They have no view of social relations between the individuals, except those revealed by statistics. There is no safeguard at all against the tyranny of the majority in this conception; thus individual liberty is at great risk.[16] On the other hand, collectivist-interpretativist thinkers, now mostly known as communitarians, stipulate that freedom is exercised within interpretative frameworks, and that it is therefore best secured by establishing polities around common frameworks. Such frameworks can be thought of as a structure of social relations that is internally congruent and demarcated from its outside. As a cultural-linguistic theory of the polity, such a view was most forcefully expressed in the liberal nationalism of the nineteenth century. Its social ontology contains valid assumptions but as a political philosophy it is subject to the liberal criticism voiced, among others, by Isaiah Berlin.

The idea of opening up the question of associative relations to empirical observation allows the overcoming of the dichotomy of individualist aggregation or interpretative commonality. It draws on eighteenth-century ways of thinking the social bond. Then, the two dominant ways of thinking associative relations focused on communication and commerce respectively; and in each version, one can find authors who hold that communication or commerce support domestic peace and well-being in liberty and those who see them as destructive of either. In Mill's words, this was the thought of 'the last generation' before the advent of democracy, and the assumptions about the effects of association were rather speculative. The experience of democracy transforms the question by making the consequences of association, and its absence, in various modes observable, at least in principle.

Rather than permitting an empirical turn only, however, the conceptual issue has also been sharpened. If political modernity is expressed in the double commitment to individual and to collective self-determination, to personal liberty and democracy, then the analysis of the associative relations between the members of a polity would search to identify the ways in which the former can be combined with the latter, beyond assumptions about aggregation or prior commonality. Human beings in democracy inevitably have the power 'to declare to each other their humanness in their existence as individuals and in their way of co-existing, of being together in the polity' (Lefort 1986b, p. 54).[17] To be in relations of solidarity would precisely mean that there are relations between the members of a polity that recognize the other as a member of the same, self-governed polity and as a free singular human being. The relations between individual liberty, democracy and 'status and recognition' – read solidarity – may be 'tenuous', as Berlin held. But they are tenuous precisely because a democracy of free citizens is a fragile entity, and it is only if the questions of freedom and of solidarity are addressed at the same level of significance that one can hope that it can be sustained.[18]

Two concepts of liberalism

There may be one, two, three or even 'more than two hundred senses' (Berlin 1971 [1958], p. 121) of the term 'liberty' – this debate may go on, but whether it will bring significant new results seems doubtful. In contrast, it seems necessary to more clearly distinguish two basic understandings of liberalism.

The past two centuries of theorizing political modernity have shown a strong bifurcation of two distinct modes of thinking. On the one hand, individualist liberalism persistently – and this means, importantly, across marked historical experiences of suppression of liberty – argues for the liberty of the individual, but does so by renouncing the elaboration of any comprehensive political theory that addresses the question of the nature of the modern polity. On the other hand, approaches that situate the 'liberty of the moderns' in the socio-political contexts of its emergence, reaching from the religious wars to the democratic revolutions and emerging class struggle, recognize the need for a comprehensive political philosophy, including a 'particular social and economic theory' (an insight shared but not followed up by Berlin, from whom this quote stems: p. 123), to sustain any concept of liberty, and thus start their reasoning from an understanding of the society and polity in which human beings can be free, rather than from those individuals themselves.[19]

Some approaches within this latter strand have tended to treat the question of individual liberty too lightly and that is why the concern of authors such as Berlin arose. By now, however, we should be able to recognize two problematic asymmetries in the politico-intellectual constellation that has resulted from this concern. First, not least as a conclusion drawn from historical experiences, the worry about 'illiberal conclusions' is, in theory, so pronounced that any alternative to such liberalism appears unsustainable from the start, and this despite the fact that the insufficiencies of individualist liberalism are widely recognized.[20] Second, more specifically, the emphasis on individual liberty as the alleged primary commitment of political modernity has entailed the neglect of solidarity and democracy, even though these commitments cannot fail to be evoked in any comprehensive political philosophy of the modern polity, as the analysis of even authors such as Mill and Berlin has shown. As one step towards finding a remedy to these asymmetries, the political tradition of non-individualist liberalism needs to be given proper status in the history of European political thought.[21] It is to this that the preceding reasoning aimed to contribute, and the brief observations on Tocqueville and Lefort were meant to serve as illustrations for the case of the existence of such a tradition.

Individualist liberalism clings to a tradition of thinking that aimed at defending 'frontiers' beyond which intervention by authorities into the lives of human beings should not go. It is based on a highly significant normative commitment; and even though the concern emerged in periods of unjustified external rule, there is no reason to assume that its relevance will ever decrease. Confusion in political theory, however, was created when such liberalism started – justifiably – to address the dangers to individual liberty that could emanate from forms of collective self-government. From this moment onwards, the defence of individual liberty became a conceptual battle against anything in society, anything 'social', from which political commitments could emerge. This move has, at best, limited the capacity of political theory to address important issues of the life in common. At worst, it has contributed to weakening ways of being together in the polity that rely on solidarity.

In contrast, what I have called non-individualist liberalism takes collective self-government as its starting point. Under conditions of political modernity, there is no other source for legitimacy than collective self-determination, with all the risks that this 'adventure' (Claude Lefort) may entail. There may be good reasons to conclude from historical experience that any democracy should commit itself to guarantee extended spaces of individual liberty, as Berlin and other individualist liberals argue. Unlike other forms of non-individualist political thought, non-individualist liberalism takes this commitment to be of a specific kind and not subsumable under any prior notion of reason or substantive collective commitment. But for this liberalism there are reasons of no lesser importance, and not less strongly suggested by historical experience, to make solidarity with others a basic commitment of the polity as well.

Following Mill and Berlin, many contemporary political theorists hold that any such equivalence of solidarity and liberty has potentially dangerous political implications. They see the former as a substantive commitment that no pluralist polity can embrace without endangering freedom. Here, in contrast, some continuity within the 'continental section' of European liberalism was defended, in which political philosophy always aimed to address questions of the life in common in a comprehensive way, including its 'social' features. The constitution of a polity, in this view, should not be limited to a bill of rights plus an institutional architecture, a conception many individualist liberals could find satisfactory. It should commit the polity to freedom and solidarity at the same time – as the EU Charter of Fundamental Rights does, rightly defying the wisdom of much of contemporary political theory.

3

The Political Forms of Modernity

In the preceding chapter, I discussed the understanding of the modern polity that gives priority to individual liberty, a currently widespread belief that I referred to as individualist liberalism. I demonstrated that it is both insufficient and misdirected as a theory of political modernity and pointed out in particular that it inappropriately and unnecessarily relegates to secondary importance the political commitments to democracy and solidarity. The current chapter aims to widen the analysis by looking historically at the variety and transformations of political commitments in the history of – predominantly European – political modernity.[1] It will show that institutional changes are the consequences of changes in political commitments that arise as interpretative insights from historical experiences.

One of the tensions between political commitments has recently been widely debated, the one between liberty and democracy, or between human rights and constitutionalism, or between individual and collective autonomy. On the level of public debate in Western polities, the main conviction is that human rights and democracy go naturally together and form the basis of the self-understanding of these polities. Sophisticated defenders of political modernity such as Jürgen Habermas (1992) claim that these two commitments are 'co-original', leaving it somewhat open whether they consider this to be a normative or a historical argument. In turn, critical thinkers such as Chantal Mouffe (2000) speak about a 'democratic paradox' and claim that there is a fundamental tension between these commitments. Where the one side constructs a too harmonious relation between these two commitments, the other side overemphasizes their opposition. With Berlin, I hold that the link is 'tenuous', but insist that the historical attempts at strengthening it need much more attention than any formal political theorizing was ever willing to grant. Such a return to historical experiences and their interpretations will then also reveal that there are more than two fundamental ingredients to the self-understanding of political modernity. The history of modernity can indeed be told in terms of four rather separate narratives, and it is from such separate narratives that the following reconstruction shall start out.

Four familiar narratives: liberty, statehood, democracy, revolution

First of all, there is the *liberal* story, the story of the gradual extension of civic rights. It normally starts with the Magna Carta (1215) and then the Habeas Corpus Act (1679) as early indications of the recognition that the reign of rulers over the inhabitants of their territory could be formally limited. Even though the position of these two bills remains supreme in the textbook version of the liberal story, historical research has found many more instances of the recognition of such rights in Europe.[2] Often, though, these rights were themselves limited to certain groups of human beings on a territory or to rather small and narrowly confined polities, such as the merchant cities around the Baltic Sea and the North Sea or the city republics on the northern rim of the Mediterranean Sea.

This story then makes a leap to the *Déclaration des droits de l'homme et du citoyen* in revolutionary France in 1789. It is a leap in several respects: the declaration applies to a large European polity, and it even has explicit universal leanings. Furthermore, it clearly refers to the singular human being, and it does not make the rights it contains dependent on any qualities of this being, beyond being human. The history of political modernity in the one and a half centuries succeeding this declaration can nevertheless only with difficulties be read as the gradual realization of the aims of that declaration. It needed the United Nations Universal Declaration of Human Rights in 1948, after the end of Nazism and the Second World War, to add a further chapter to the liberal story. But from this moment on, the narration appeared to proceed smoothly again. It then turns into a story of local European origins, some limited and partial institutionalization in this local context, then a giant step towards universalization of the normative claims, followed by a long and difficult process of globalization, that is, the actual spreading of the claims around the world.

The second narrative of political modernity has at first sight very little relation to the first one; it is the story of the development of the modern *state system*. It has two clear starting points. In intellectual history, it starts with the elaboration of the concept of sovereignty, first in Bodin, then in Hobbes; in political history, it starts with the Treaty of Westphalia (1648) that marks the end of the Thirty Years' War. The former establishes the idea that a state should have full control over its territory and its population; the latter applies this idea to end the religious wars in Europe. From now on, to idealize the story considerably, religious unity and its connection to state authority should secure domestic peace, whereas the establishment of clear territorial boundaries together with the principle of non-interference should secure peaceful relations between states.

Clearly, though, the principle of sovereignty was a suitable means to domestic peace at best, since the principle of non-interference was hardly accepted and, in the perspective that has dominated much work on international relations, the new state system is better characterized by inter-state anarchy, that is, the absence of any regulatory principle. Ways to more firmly establish 'eternal peace' kept preoccupying political thinkers and the gradual elaboration of international law was seen as the most promising route, meant to ultimately lead to a cosmopolitan political order, turning the story of state development, like the liberal story, into a narrative about gradual globalization. Unlike the liberal story, though, it gets halted at a certain point. While a cosmopolitan political order is currently often – not always – seen as desirable, many observers regard it as unrealistic at the same time.

The third story about political modernity is the narrative of the rise of *democracy*. It has the longest roots, but also the largest gaps. It starts in the Greek *polis*, with the moment of the simultaneous invention of politics and philosophy, as some theorists put it,[3] then undergoes significant transformations in the Roman Republic and, much later, the Florentine and Venetian republics, without, though, entirely subsiding. Its full reassertion, however, is an event of the eighteenth century: in the history of ideas, with the transformation of the concept of state sovereignty into the one of popular sovereignty, most clearly by Jean-Jacques Rousseau; and in political history, with the American and the French Revolutions, marking the age of the 'democratic revolution' (Palmer 1959).

As with the related moment in the liberal story, the chapter on the late eighteenth century did not really mark a breakthrough, onwards from which the story could unfold smoothly. Perceptive observers, like Alexis de Tocqueville, recognized early on that there would be no final halt before universal suffrage had not established the concept of the 'unit citizen' (Stein Rokkan), and the late nineteenth century witnessed gradual extensions of the suffrage in many European states. However, the Old Regime proved to be persistent, and it was only the end of the First World War that brought about what one would now call a first wave of transitions to democracy. And one would need to wait for the end of the Second World War to witness the consolidation of some of these democracies and for the closing decades of the twentieth century to observe further waves of democratization in Southern and Eastern Europe.

A fourth story about political modernity is partially implied in the descriptions above but it is today much less recognized as a constitutive component of modernity. The narrative of politics as *revolution* focuses on the use of conscious collective action to create a normatively superior state of the polity than the existing one. The idea of revolution resonates with some core features of modernity, as they have been discussed over the past two centuries, such as reflexivity, historicity and agentiality. Reflexivity refers here to the human ability, by means of imagination, to step out of the immediate present and to imagine other possible worlds, or partial worlds. Historicity refers to the translation of such imagination into time, by means of which the present can be distinguished from a past that was different and from a future that may be different. Agentiality refers to the belief that human action may contribute to bringing about a particular different future (Wittrock 2003). Any quick look at European history would identify this conception with eighteenth-century Enlightenment and, importantly, the Romantic reaction to it, and the nineteenth-century translation of these ideas into particular political programmes. One could easily arrive at a model – almost in the form of a caricature – of revolutionary activity by intellectuals based on insight into the essence of the world, as it formed in nineteenth-century Europe in an amalgamation of idealism, class struggle and the formation of an avant-garde.[4]

However, it seems more fruitful to conceive of the idea of revolution more broadly, one starting point for such broadening being the debate about the so-called axial age, a synthetic term for parallel major socio-political transformations in Eurasian civilizations between the seventh and the fourth century BCE (for more detail on the following see Arnason et al. 2004). This debate has often seen that era of world history as the one inaugurating the separation of the transcendental and mundane, and has thus not only tended to emphasize the rise of monotheistic religions but has also put the idea of radical change between the existing world and another world into a religious framework. Given that the socio-political transformations in question occurred in contexts of political crisis, often of deep dissatisfaction with the existing political regime, however, the recourse to the 'transcendental' most broadly refers to the conviction that, to use a slogan of our time, 'another world is possible'. Thus, rather than emphasizing the religious connotation, one should take from the observation of the axial age the broader insights that the faculty of imagination allows human beings to consider states of the world as possible that differ from the actual one and that the communication about such different possible states may support collective action to bring about such states. By introducing this element, the notion of revolution is not only broadened beyond the common understanding, the emphasis is also placed on – for want of better terms – *substantive* rather than *procedural* aspects, on conscious collective action towards a *significantly different* society and polity rather than merely on a *rapid* institutional transformation.

In this broader sense, a narrative of politics as revolution has indeed informed much of the history of political modernity, even though it has subsided and been revived several times. It can be traced to the Judeo-Christian eschatological tradition. The millenarian movements in the early second millennium CE then are another major case in point, before a secular version of such thinking arose in the Enlightenment, preparing the democratic revolutions with which the term 'revolution' acquired the meaning of a forward step in historical time. A critique of those revolutions as insufficient then inspired the socialist and communist reinterpretation that informed the nineteenth and much of the twentieth century. Today, in contrast, the revolutionary narrative is often seen as having finally subsided, be it in the affirmative philosophy of history that considers our era as the one of the 'end of history' (Francis Fukuyama) or be it in the competing post-modernist interpretations that consider all emancipatory narratives to have been refuted (Jean-François Lyotard) or the 'last conceptual revolution' in political thought as having already occurred (Richard Rorty).

All of these stories point to European origins of the political developments they emphasize. But none of them remains confined to the territory of Europe. In some cases, the principal location where the story unfolds seems to shift in the course of time, mostly to North America, and Europe has to re-enter the narrative at a later point. In the case of the liberal and the democratic story, furthermore, there certainly is a universal prospect and promise, even though it is not globally accepted in all places and at all times. In as far as such promise is projected onto historical evolution, as it often is, these stories are also essentially linear stories, even though it remains to be seen whether they will keep unfolding. They can be connected to the revolutionary story in some periods, namely when liberty and democracy are revolutionary aims. But they are entirely disconnected from the revolutionary story, even turn into its antagonists, when the claim is made that liberty and democracy have already been realized. As to the state story, as briefly mentioned above, its precise continuation is also in normative doubt. Even committed cosmopolitans have most often constructed their global utopia as a confederation of free republics rather than as one global polity.

The state story is also central in this account as it is a focus of tension between the narratives. The liberal and the state stories, namely, can be easily connected in a narrative of the 'rise of liberal institutions and customs', as it is sometimes put nowadays (Rorty 1989, p. 63). The basic political theory adopted here is individualist liberalism, fully compatible with the narrative of liberty, and the modern state is then nothing but the 'container' that holds those free individuals together and gives their freedom a legal form. One can just as easily connect the democratic story to the one on state sovereignty, but then the emphasis would shift to the commitment to collective self-determination.[5] This would essentially be the democratic story, but with an added sense, again, of the 'container' in which, in this case, social life and political action unfolds.

While in both cases, the story of state development appears to provide nothing but an empty shell, a container of formal procedures, the importance of this question – the question of the political form – needs to be emphasized.[6] The meaning of this form changes considerably when one connects it to the democratic story instead of the one on liberty. In this context, the questions of the substantive aims of a polity and, in direct connection to the former issue, of the boundary of the collectivity that self-determines its destiny arise. Contemporary political theory in its mainstream version holds that questions of the good life should not be answered by means of political organization because there will be divergent views about them, and thus their realization within a pluralist society is likely to infringe on the liberties of those who hold minority views on the good life. For the same reason, the revolutionary story is not in current favour because revolutionary aims – in our times of alleged realization of liberty and democracy – propose views of the good life that are not necessarily shared by all members of a polity. Thus, in the mainstream view, such substantive aims need to be confined to the private lives of the citizens.

The matter, though, cannot be settled so easily. The briefest of all looks at the historical dates suffices to see that the link between the democratic story and the liberal story, which is often claimed, occurs through the revolutionary story. The declaration of human rights – in France, and in the form of the Bill of Rights in the USA – co-emerges with the democratic revolutions at the end of the eighteenth century. And the re-emergence of the former after the dark middle of the twentieth century appears to be historically connected to the late twentieth-century waves of democratization. It seems indeed difficult to entirely sever the right to individual self-determination from the right to collective self-determination. Once one links the two, however, considerable ambiguity over the appropriate political form arises. An overemphasis on individual self-determination has often concerned political theorists, at least from Edmund Burke onwards (but it is not at all confined to the conservative tradition, since both Right and Left Hegelians share this concern) who worried about the viability of the polity when individual liberty asserts itself too strongly. Inversely, an overemphasis on collective self-determination brought the commitment to democracy in the vicinity of totalitarianism, or at least to the possibility of the 'tyranny of the majority' (Tocqueville). Given such tension, it is striking to see the absence of a serious concern for the political form in the heydays of both movements for freedom. It is as if freedom and democracy are self-evident and uncontroversial if one only believes in them.

In the recent past, only some, so to say, republican critics of totalitarianism, such as Hannah Arendt or Claude Lefort, were able to see that there was a version of the connection of (bourgeois) liberalism with (nationalist) democracy that was more destructive of freedom than any other political regime of modernity, and that the neglect of political form was crucial for this destruction of freedom. Significantly, these authors are among the few that have shown an interest in seriously rethinking the concept of revolution, instead of either discarding it for the contemporary era, as liberals tend to do, or of embracing it in a standard way, i.e., as the solution to all political questions, as neo-Marxists were inclined to do. For Arendt, the success of a revolution was to be judged against its achievement in creating a framework for free political action and this was for her a task that remained to be accomplished, as her remarks on the Hungarian revolution of 1956 show. For Lefort, the democratic revolutions, if successful, create the emptiness of the political space. But for him this emptiness is not a final institutional result, as a procedural liberal would hold, but the beginning of a new form of political contest, namely over the temporary filling of this space by substantive issues.

Therefore, the discussion of the tensions between these narratives is not just a historical reflection on the times before the consolidation of democracy. These tensions reside deep at the core of political modernity, and not only of its European experience. They are very alive in much of the current reasoning about the political theory of European integration which for this reason serves as a useful illustration for our argument. The two main ways of thinking politically about contemporary Europe are precisely selective combinations of those narratives, trying to reason away the tensions between them.

First, European integration is often – and affirmatively – referred to as a combination of the liberal story and the story of state development. In this account, the existing European polities, the nation-states, have indeed provided a viable combination of liberty and democracy, but this combination is challenged by the socio-economic transformations of our time, mostly known by the shorthand of globalization. The solution to the current problem, in this view, is an extension of the reach of state action while safeguarding the guarantees for civic liberty. The actual process of European integration is then seen as rather precisely following this maxim. Of the only two truly European institutions, according to this interpretation, one, the European Court of Justice, mainly serves to protect civil liberties: indeed it even extends them beyond the limits of some national arrangements. The other one, the European Central Bank, expands the reach of state action where it was most crucially needed, namely in guiding the economy by its most basic parameter, the money supply (see chapter 7 below for some analysis of this issue). In between, the European Commission fulfils its work best when it accepts the fact that it is not democratically legitimized and concentrates its efforts exclusively on enhancing the efficiency of state action (for such views, see Scharpf 1999; Majone 1996). This account, thus, combines a commitment to civil liberty with one of state efficiency at the expense of collective self-determination.

In contrast, second, other contributors to the debate on European political integration combine the democratic story with the story on state development at the expense of the liberal narrative. In this case, the European nation-state has provided a combination of democracy, trust and solidarity that is unlikely to be improved upon. The nation is the form in which rather large-scale societies have become able to act upon themselves. It stands out positively both in comparison to 'traditional' societies marked by illegitimate forms of hierarchy and to any future post-national society that can only compare negatively with the nation-state in terms of its ability to act upon itself (for the most sophisticated version of this view, see Offe 1998). This reasoning provides the background to all versions of Euroscepticism, not merely the British one. Normatively, it prefers to halt political Europeanization sooner rather than later, but it also takes quite some distance from any liberal multiculturalism within the existing nation-states, since the undermining of historically constituted relations of trust and solidarity is seen as an ever-present danger in our times.

The normative standpoints taken in these two positions are opposed to one another. Nevertheless, both positions share an important background assumption about the current political condition. This assumption can briefly be characterized as follows: the current political condition is marked by a rather strong pressure towards continuation of the liberal story, as indicated by moves towards extending the freedom of movement of people, goods and capital, often being described as the economic and cultural dimensions of globalization. There is very little space for normative resistance against such tendencies. At the same time, such continuation of the liberal story is often seen as requiring a continuation of the story of state development beyond the point where it was halted, since it is states and their attempts at boundary control that are impediments to a further increase of individual liberties. Such continuation of the state story in the direction of a cosmopolitan order, in turn, appears difficult without interrupting, or at least considerably retelling, the story of the rise of democracy.[7]

Significantly, the revolutionary narrative has no place at all in either of these two common views of European integration. In other views, however, it has, even though some effort is needed to identify it. Scholars such as Richard Bellamy and Dario Castiglione (2003) speak of a 'normative turn' in the study of European integration, and Jürgen Habermas underlines the need for 'normative impulses' (2001, p. 103) in this process. These are indicators for the presence of significant substantive concerns, and thus one can recognize that the (re-)founding of a polity should also be seen as an attempt to go beyond the normative limitations of the existing polities and, as such, as an effort at conscious collective action that stands in the revolutionary tradition, even though defining its place within that tradition in the light of the experiences of the past two centuries. In turn, Ralf Dahrendorf (2001) has recently both denigrated and warned of the view of Europe as 'the last utopia for the leaders of the Left'. In the conceptual terms used here, he thus discards any useful significance of the revolutionary narrative for contemporary politics. While such view is common among post-totalitarian liberals, it draws rather one-sided conclusions from the historical experience with revolutionary politics. To expect the solution to the question of the good life directly from radically transformative political action would indeed mean to give priority to the story of revolution over the stories of liberty, statehood and democracy. Given its potential – and, historically, often enough actual – disregard for the protection of liberties, also by formal means, this view indeed needs to be rightly discarded. However, liberals such as Dahrendorf today tend to give priority to the story of individual liberty over all other stories, and this view is normatively untenable as well; only its neglect of other political exigencies is much less recognized in our time.

The brief look at the current European political condition and the normative consequences that are drawn from it (to be taken up again in Part IV below), in contrast, supports our intuition that political modernity needs to be conceptualized in terms of persistent tensions between different exigencies of the political *problématique*, rather than in terms of an available, only not yet quite achieved, solution. While not at all adverse to the idea of a political narrative, political theory and political science have mostly devoted their energy to further refining the separate stories of liberty, sovereign statehood and democracy, often as linear, even though temporarily interrupted, accounts of evolutionary progress. The underlying assumption was that these three stories unfold unproblematically in parallel fashion, or even that they converge over time until full political modernity is achieved. The fourth story, the revolutionary one, has a legitimate place only during those historical times when barriers to the unfolding of the other three stories still needed to be overcome. The observation, though, that a given political condition can more fruitfully be seen as a compromise reached in balancing the tensions between the exigencies of liberty, statehood, democracy and quests for a normatively superior political order than the existing ones leads us to shift gear and to look at a variety of such conditions as chapters in a more comprehensive story which contains elements of some or even all of the four separate narratives.[8] A brief outline of such a more comprehensive narrative will be provided in what follows.

Re-narrating European political modernity

From Greece to Christian Rome: the particular soul and the universal individual

Greek democracy is mentioned as a matter of obligation in accounts of European political modernity, but it is most often accompanied by remarks about the highly different kind of polity and conception of politics, both of which make the Greek understanding of democracy untenable for contemporary purposes, or even for the leap to the idea of popular sovereignty in so-called early modern Europe. While this is true, it is so only in a narrowly constructed story of the rise of democracy. In a broader view, there are other political issues at stake in the ancient heritage of European politics, and even though we are here not able to fully write up this chapter in the narrative of political modernity, we may indicate some of its contents.[9]

The Greek *polis* at its apex created a strong relation between the idea of democracy and the concern for the self such that the care for the soul inspires the rules of the polity and guides political behaviour (Patočka 1983; see also Patočka 1996, pp. 81–2). One of the consequences of such view was the limitation of political action to free men. Such restriction certainly had to be lifted under conditions of political modernity, as we now understand it. Once all members of a polity participate in it freely and equally, though, any strong substantive relation between the individual member of the polity and the participation in the fate of the polity would also often be found incompatible with political modernity, on grounds namely of the – 'negative', as it should later be called – freedom of the individual, which entails the possibility of choosing a self and 'soul' that is largely unrelated to the polity. This, at least, is the reasoning that was to stand behind individualist liberalism – after devastating experiences with strong commitments of the political self to substantive issues.

Nevertheless, the question of the relation between self and polity, which was cast in specific terms in the Greek polity and into which substantive views of the good life were inscribed, should never entirely disappear from the agenda of political modernity. In a transformed version, romanticism in much later European history also both had a strong view of the self and linked it to the cultural-linguistic conception of the polity that stood in the background of (at least, some version of) the European nation-state. In contemporary debate, the attempt at reviving 'civic republicanism' and a concept of *virtù*, in explicit contrast to individualist liberalism, reiterates the same theme in different form. Despite all differences, thus, the Greek polity contained a tension that has stayed with modern polities to the present day.

The emergence of the Roman Republic and then Empire displaced Greek political power, but elements of the latter's politico-philosophical orientations were appropriated – and transformed – by the former. Significantly, the Christian religion emerged from an encounter of Judaism and Greek thought and became, after having first been combated, the 'state religion' of the later Empire. It has often been argued that this fusion marks indeed 'the birth of Europe in the present sense of the word' (Patočka 1996, p. 109, also p. 83; Meier 2002, chapter 3). In politico-philosophical terms, the Roman Republic contained ideas of the person, of law, of universalism, all the while being unstable as a polity and much more uncertain of the ground on which it stood than any of its religious-political components had been on their own.[10]

From the Holy Roman Empire to the Westphalian state system: progress or disintegration?

The decline of the Holy Roman Empire and the emergence of the European state system after the Thirty Years' War is often interpreted in terms of the impossibility to hold large empires together because of both their size and their diversity. The creation of a well-ordered system of smaller and more homogeneous states is then seen as political progress. Unlike linear evolutionism in political thought has it, however, the long-term transformation of the European polities from the universalistically inclined, yet weakly integrated, Roman Empire to the plurality of religiously homogeneous, sovereign states seems to spell in at least two respects a decline in political history. Even though, first, as briefly mentioned above, the background to the Westphalian agreement was precisely the search for stable peace, there was less of a common orientation in the relations between rulers than before, the principle of non-interference being the only firm ground to stand on. In domestic terms, second, the commitment of the new polity was less universalist than the one of the Empire. The principle of *cuius regio eius religio* let the rulers apparently decide about the value commitments of their subjects in the name of domestic peace (see, for instance, Galli 2002, pp. 47–8).

Despite this character of an imposition, the latter feature of the polity is sometimes seen as the first 'modern' version of the idea that there needs to be considerable value commonality between members of a polity, an idea that was constitutive for the later cultural-linguistic idea of the polity and that has currently acquired generalized form under the heading of 'communitarianism'. Nevertheless, one should not overlook the fact that multi-religious and multilingual empires did not face any particular legitimacy problems during this period. The novelty of this period was the form of the state rather than its substantive underpinnings. To avoid ambiguities in matters political, the state should be sovereign, i.e., have firm boundaries on the outside and to control the population on its territory. As such, and increasingly based on a formal bureaucracy often for fiscal purposes, this emerging modern state, although not liberal at all, could become the container in which claims to liberty could unfold.[11] Or in other words, the origins of the particular relation into which formal sovereign statehood and rights-based individual liberty enter can be traced to this period. The fragmentation of Europe into several neatly divided polities, in contrast, is often overlooked when the accomplishment of sovereignty is underlined.[12]

From the religious wars to the revolution, or from state sovereignty to popular sovereignty

Furthermore, the 'early modern' configuration of state and society is often only regarded as an interim between the feudal order and modern society, as it should emerge after the democratic and industrial revolutions. The state is seen as having already reached its modern form but it is still lacking democratic legitimacy. Thus, the remaining problem on the way to political modernity is the tension between sovereign statehood and democracy. And the solution to it is the move from state sovereignty to popular sovereignty, or in terms of the history of political thought, the move from Bodin via Hobbes to Locke and Rousseau. Once that solution is reached, liberty, sovereignty and democracy are connected and full political modernity is accomplished.

This interpretation, though, strikes immediately as one that focuses exclusively on domestic issues, whereas interstate issues had certainly been at least as central as domestic ones in political thought. Since Enlightenment cosmopolitanism stands at the threshold between the Old Regime and the revolutions, a look at its way of dealing with these issues can elucidate the problem. Enlightenment political thought, most clearly exemplified by Kant, recognized not one but two main problems in the old order, namely internal restrictions to liberty and interstate anarchy. The answer to these problems was equally clear-cut. The internal restrictions were to be overcome by the combined commitment of the polity to liberty and equality; and interstate anarchy would be overcome by a cosmopolitan order composed of democratic republics. Furthermore, these two solutions could be regarded as connected: democratic republics would be less inclined to warfare than autocratic regimes, and civic liberties could thrive better under conditions of peace.

While the *problématique* was well recognized, the requirements for a solution were more demanding than Enlightenment theorists expected. The move to popular sovereignty went along with a stronger understanding of membership in a polity than the 'early modern state' had known. As long as it was the state that was sovereign over a territory and a population, it mattered very little to the rulers who the members – more precisely, subjects – were over whom they ruled. When, however, the people themselves were to exercise sovereignty, the idea of an unproblematically emerging *volonté générale* soon ceased to have plausibility. Because of the closer connection that democracy introduced between those who govern and those who are governed, membership became an important issue. The French revolutionaries were still optimistic and aimed at granting membership to everybody who adhered to republican ideas. Very soon after, and not least due to the failure of the Revolution to spread across Europe and establish a European republic or federation of republics, the cultural-linguistic theory of the polity gained ground, offering itself as the solution to the problem of value diversity under conditions of democracy.

For these reasons, then, the empires also started to lose legitimacy from the moment of the democratic revolutions onwards. It is insufficient to regard them as just another form of Old Regime that could not withstand the calls for liberty and democracy. If that had been the only issue, then something like a Habsburg or Ottoman Revolution should have been as conceivable as a French or Polish Revolution, whereas in historical fact it was not. Unlike in the French case, the viability of the form of the state was as much in question as the form of government – and the reason for this was found at the time in the diversity of the population, containing several cultural-linguistic entities rather than one.

National liberalism, social solidarity and the persistence of the Old Regime

Thus, some tension between Enlightenment and romanticism as founding inspirations for political philosophy emerged during the period of the institutional onset of political modernity, the era around the French Revolution, that was to shape European political history for the following one and a half centuries. The opposition between the two approaches is often exaggerated, both as general philosophies and as political philosophies. The national liberalism of the first half of the nineteenth century, ideational support of the movements for collective self-determination, combined rather well the exigencies of both democracy and liberty with the quest for republican statehood. As such a compromise, it accepted and expressed 'the difficulty that the modern ideology has in providing a sufficient image of social life' (Dumont 1983, pp. 130–1).

With hindsight, however, one has to recognize that such viable compromise may have existed in the form of political ideas, and to some extent in the practices of the national-liberal movements, but that it hardly anywhere achieved durability as a political form. By and large, '1848', the symbolic date for the heyday of the national-liberal aspirations, marked a failure in the history of political modernity. The polities that were established in its aftermath, even though some of them included elements of those aspirations, signalled the 'persistence of the Old Regime' (Mayer 1981). Subsequently, the struggles during major parts of the nineteenth century can only be discussed in terms of the increasing inability to live politically with the ambiguity that the founding tension between an individualist-liberal and a cultural-linguistic self-understanding of the polity created.

At this point of the exercise in historical retrieval, it is useful to explicitly point to two conceptual-historical components of the account provided that come into stark relief only when recognizably 'contemporary' political events are presented. First, it needs to be underlined that the narrative of political modernity presented here is a narrative of *struggle*. True, the question guiding this account has been the one of the viability of a normatively desirable polity, and it may have presented itself more often in terms of order than of conflict, to use a standard distinction between varieties of perspectives in political sociology. At the same time, however, the emphasis was placed on the inability to conceive of any single superior political order, in contrast to major traditions in political and social theory. Thus, historical transformations can only be regarded as the outcome of struggles based on different justifications, with the outcomes themselves being in all likelihood a compromise between two or more of those justifications.

While such a view most broadly understood applies to all of European political history, the eighteenth century marks an important divide in two respects. In terms of the history of political thought, it witnesses the sustained attempt at conceptualizing the normative foundations of political modernity. As such, it explicates criteria for justification as much as it increases the stakes for any general justificatory attempt. In terms of political history, despite the existence of mass revolts at many other times, the 'democratic revolution' marks the entry of 'the people' into legitimate political debate and, thus, changes the terms of political struggle.

Second, as a combined result of the increased emphasis on normative justification and of the view of political history as a struggle over such justification, historical events came to be interpreted as *possibilities* for the realization of certain self-understandings of a polity or, in other words, as possibilities for casting a certain mode of justification into institutional form. It is in this sense that '1848' can be regarded as the *missed possibility* of giving institutional shape to the national-liberal compromise as a normatively desirable interpretation of political modernity under the circumstances of mid-century. It was to be followed, about half a century later, by a second, and in important respects closely related, missed possibility (for further exploration of such 'logics of European history', see chapter 10 below).

From the middle of the nineteenth century onwards, namely, it was increasingly recognized that there was a second founding tension at the heart of European political modernity. With its commitment to fraternity, beyond liberty and equality, the French Revolution laid the basis for what was later to be called either class struggle or the social question.[13] In France, this issue was discussed early on as a biased interpretation of the revolutionary commitment, namely one that overemphasized (individual) liberty and equality of civic rights at the expense of the possibility to organize collectively for the achievement of substantive equality by means of social solidarity.

The background to this interpretative dispute over the revolutionary commitment was the 'market revolution' and the subsequent rise of capitalism.[14] The granting of the freedom of commerce should be regarded as a shift in normative justifications in the political orders of the time, rather than straightforwardly as a victory of the interests of the bourgeoisie as a rising class in the power struggle with the Old Regime. It was based both on the acceptance of individual autonomy as a strong guiding principle of modernity, even though immediately criticized as 'abstract freedom', and on a novel political understanding of the impact of *le doux commerce* on domestic and international peace (Hirschman 1977). During the first half of the nineteenth century, though, the opinion prevailed that the consequences of the acceptance of these novel justifications could be contained within the framework of the existing polities. While the likelihood of a rise in social inequality was recognized early on, the social ties and institutions of those polities were deemed sufficient to deal with the transformation.

Not unlike the growing tension between the cultural-linguistic and the liberal commitment, however, the relation between the social and the liberal commitment was increasingly conflict-ridden when the social question was repressed rather than solved in many countries and when in response the collective movements for solidarity grew rapidly and increasingly demanded radical social transformation in response to that question. Even though in some countries, most importantly the French Third Republic and its idea of *solidarisme*, considerable attempts at arriving at a viable articulation of the individual-liberal and the collective-solidary commitment were made, by and large the ruling elites of the still only very reluctantly liberal European societies did not accept fully either of these principles and counted on the solidity of their insufficiently legitimized power position in established state structures to deal with both increasingly international markets, an effect of economic liberties, and the rising workers' movement, an organized expression of the quest for solidarity. Thus, they turned the issue into one of power and interest rather than one of a reinterpretation of political modernity.

In this constellation, around the turn of the nineteenth century, the cultural-linguistic and the socio-economic theories of the polity came increasingly to be regarded as alternatives to, rather than complements of, an individualist-liberal theory of the polity. As liberalism was widely seen in deep crisis, economically because of recurring depressions and precisely the inability to deal with poverty and misery, and politically because of the advent of 'mass society' and large-scale social organization, both of these alternatives found increasing plausibility and support. Since their modes of reasoning, though sharing the critique of individualism, were also opposed to one another and their support came mostly from different groups in society, nationalism and socialism, later communism as well, were often seen as opposing 'liberal society' – which mostly was not very liberal at all – from different directions. The resort to these political theories, thus, opened the space for increasingly aggressive nationalism, on the one hand, and for almost equally intransigent class struggle, on the other. It is important to add, though, that these theories remained committed to a form of democracy, of collective self-determination (see, for instance, Manent 1995, p. 117). Unlike liberal theories, however, they made strong presuppositions as to the nature of the *demos*.

The loss of political language and the advent of totalitarianism

These tensions exploded with the First World War and its aftermath (see chapter 10 below). The failure or – in the best of circumstances – the short-lived nature of post-war reconstruction on novel terms, which ideally would have been both more inclusive (as it often was in some respect, given the extension of the suffrage) and more reflective and explicit in its interpretation of the contemporary condition of political modernity, marks another missed possibility in the history of political modernity. The rupture was so deep that, as a consequence, the inter-war period was marked by a loss of political language and by desperate, mostly ill-fated, attempts to regain such language or to re-create one. Nazism and Stalinism remain insufficiently understood as long as the attractions that both projects, and later regimes, found among large groups in society, and not least among intellectuals, are only denounced but not addressed in terms of the questions the sympathizers with these projects were raising (Lefort 1999). In this sense, the loss of political language incurred by the combined experience of two world wars and totalitarianism, which were interpreted as the failure of any constructive response to liberal capitalism, persists to the present day.

The intellectual outcome of such interpretation was a bifurcation of social and political thought which emerged in direct response to totalitarianism, but which basically still characterizes our contemporary period. In political philosophy proper, the advent of totalitarianism was interpreted by thinkers from the European continent, such as Isaiah Berlin, Karl Popper and Jacob Talmon, as demonstrating the inescapability of some form of individualist liberalism as the founding philosophy of modern societies with a commitment to human rights and values (see chapter 2 above).[15] It is important to note that many of these thinkers, Berlin and Talmon in particular, had affinities to more substantively rich alternatives of political philosophy and that they did not abandon those alternatives lightly. Historical experience had demonstrated though, in their view, that all more substantive political philosophies, once they served as underpinning for political orders, were prone to produce catastrophic results, all worthy intentions of their intellectual originators notwithstanding. After a number of such experiences had been undergone, no further such experimentation seemed permissible. The next generation of political theorists, with John Rawls as the towering figure, accepted those findings, but lacked the historical experience and the awareness of the questions that were still raised in the middle of the twentieth century. For them, rights-based individualist liberalism was the only ground to stand on.

In broader social philosophy, the conclusions drawn from the experiences of the first half of the twentieth century took a more radical shape. Social philosophy tended to refer to the attempted annihilation of the European Jewry in particular, rather than to totalitarianism more generally. And from this specific event in human history it concluded on the loss of all language of representation. This is Adorno's intellectual trajectory from his remark on the impossibility of poetry after Auschwitz to the *Negative Dialectics* and similarly Lyotard's path from his early writing about Auschwitz to the idea of the historical refutation of all narratives of emancipation. In political terms, doubt about the possibility of representation led directly to scepticism with regard to grasping that which human beings may have in common – and thus the very possibility of politics. For fear of hypostatizing or essentializing community, as pre-totalitarian critical thinkers tended to do in the face of the damage inflicted by individualism, recent post-totalitarian political thinkers see community as 'inoperative' (Nancy 1991) and justice and democracy as always yet 'to come' (Derrida 1997).

Les trente glorieuses, *or the post-disaster compromise*

The reconstitution of polities in post-Second World War Europe, however, was initially but little informed by such debate. Certainly, political reconstruction was marked by a stronger emphasis on civil liberty and the rule of law than during the first half of the twentieth century. A closer look at the post-war polities, however, will also reveal that the relatively stable West European political orders of the 'thirty glorious years' (Jean Fourastié) were indeed not based on the pure proceduralism of rights-based individualist liberalism. Domestically, as liberal-democratic nation-states with increasingly developed welfare policies, they rather showed signs of a compromise between liberal justifications and both those of a linguistic-cultural and a social nature. They, thus, combined a rational-individualist, a cultural-linguistic and a structural-functional socio-political theory – in common political terms known as liberalism, nationalism and socialism – into a viable arrangement, which was not theoretically consistent on any terms, but was seen as satisfactory by a large majority of the population, as increasing 'mass loyalty' (Narr and Offe 1975) seemed to demonstrate until the late 1960s.

At the same time, this compromise – beyond inevitable inconsistency – fell short of normative requirements of political modernity in numerous respects. In light of the basic commitments of political modernity in terms of equal liberty, one can identify violations of the commitment to equality as non-discrimination as well as violations of the commitment to individual autonomy. To give just some examples: based on its 'cultural' component, the post-Second World War polities often justified gender inequality in law and limited the right to cultural expression for 'minorities'. Furthermore, they made moral standards compulsory, as with regard to divorce and abortion, that are in fact contested, so that their inscription into law can be seen as violating the right of the individual. Claiming to be in a warlike situation, called the Cold War, they often justified restrictions to political expression, in particular to socialist/communist groups. Vaguely aware of the inconsistency of this liberal-cultural-social foundational compromise, furthermore, these polities tied those justifications together by recourse to an empirical science of politics and society, using the tools of behaviourism and statistics, which was to guide the way on a path of wealth and loyalty and the employment of which was never free of technocratic undertones.

On grounds of such observations, the liberal-democratic welfarist nation-state in Europe, in the shape which it had acquired by around 1970, should less be seen as the hitherto highest accomplishment of human history, but rather as a temporary compromise between different requirements. This form of the West European polity from around 1970, with all differences that existed between the nation-states, had achieved a quite inclusive democracy within a bounded state, which derived the justification for its boundary from a cultural-linguistic theory of the polity and used the existence of limited membership for developing thick relations of trust and solidarity as well as of a relatively comprehensively defined, although culturally heavily circumscribed, concept of liberty. It certainly was overall relatively successful in balancing the tension between those exigencies; as a compromise without firm and consistent solution, however, it was bound to be only temporarily stable and to be challenged by future developments.

Liberal challenges, democratic misconceptions, or from '1968' to '1989'

From the 1960s onwards, this polity was shaken not only by what is now referred to as processes of globalization, in contrast to what much public and political-science opinion currently holds, but also by internal critique and demands for liberation from the constraints imposed by that socio-institutional configuration. In this sense, '1968' in Western Europe and, under significantly different conditions, '1989' first in Central and Eastern Europe and then in all of Europe mark the most recent period of struggle over the foundations of the European polities.

Both of these observations are significant for rethinking political modernity, thus they shall briefly be considered separately. First, it is erroneous to see 'globalization' as an external shock to which an accomplished political modernity needs to react and in the face of which it tries to safeguard its achievements. Rather, it is a component of the interpretation of modernity that has gradually, even though often very reluctantly, prevailed in Europe, starting with the

liberation of economic action as an expression of individual autonomy, in most countries during the nineteenth century, as discussed
earlier, and leading to the first strong period of 'globalization', then
known as imperialism, and the violent and often highly oppressive
reaction against it during the long European war of the twentieth
century, 1914–45. The new globalization of our time, in both its
economic and its cultural meaning, again emanates from inside the
European societies (as well as others, of course) and is thus part of
their modernity. If its effect is to unbalance the existing institutional
arrangements, then this, theoretically speaking, does nothing but
show the temporary nature of what I have here described as a compromise in contrast to an accomplished form.

Second, this compromise was not only unstable over the long run,
it was also normatively deficient. Hardly anybody denies that the
complex processes that led to the fall of Soviet socialism, even if they
meant many other things as well, were also about liberation from
constraints, thus in some sense related to a struggle for freedom. It is
nowadays more contested in Western Europe but equally valid to say
that the social and political activities often described by referring to
the date '1968' were similarly a liberating struggle against those constraints mentioned above. The challenge to the European nation-
state across the past three decades, thus, can normatively be described,
as Jürgen Habermas would put it, as expanding normative horizons,
or as an integral part of a struggle about political modernity.

A political analysis of this recent past, though, cannot stop at this
point. Both '1968' and '1989' fit rather easily into a narrative about
(individual) liberty, as suggested. The question whether they fit into
a narrative about democracy is already much more difficult to answer.
'1989' is commonly analysed as one of the recent waves of democratization by political scientists. At the same time, though, it was also
connected to terms such as 'anti-politics' by its own proponents, and
collective self-determination, while it figured strongly as an objective
of the protest movements, proved elusive when the initial protest
coalitions fell apart after the existing institutions had been successfully challenged. In this respect, there is some striking similarity
between '1989' and '1968'. The latter movement clearly had an initial
view of a new collective subject that was announcing its arrival in the
streets of Paris, Berlin and elsewhere; a new quality of collective self-
determination and democracy was at stake. However, this project also
fell apart into two quite diverse components, one that focused on the
liberty of individual expression and another one that emphasized
collectivism without much regard for the actual collectivity it was
addressing. Given their ambition and potential for a profound,

normatively enlarging reinterpretation of European modernity at their outset, the outcome of both movements, '1968' and '1989', both individually and seen in their articulation, cannot but be regarded as another major missed possibility in the political history of Europe (for a more detailed analysis of '1968', see the following chapter).

The ambivalent nature of the democratic commitment of the West and East European protest movements can be better understood by introducing also the third and fourth of the basic partial narratives about political modernity, those about statehood and about revolution. Even though the existing limits to individual self-determination may have been their most important driving motive, both 'liberating' movements, often referred to as ('velvet', 'student') revolutions, included some component of collective self-determination in their ambitions. However, they can be taken to have implicitly assumed that collective self-determination, i.e., democracy, is the natural concomitant once individual self-determination is achieved. Or, in other words, they underestimated the importance of a viable political form; they neglected the question of statehood.

At the same time, their revolutionary leanings showed a procedural bias that is peculiarly reminiscent of the one of individualist liberalism. The call for direct democracy to replace representative democracy, for instance, a central issue of the 1968 movement, is clearly a procedural one. With regard to substance, the activists can be taken to have assumed that the free and direct expression of the will and desire of the people will unproblematically lead to a substantively novel social configuration. The substantive void thus produced was later filled by dogmatic interpretations of Marxism-Leninism, again in an uncanny affinity to the role technocratic social science has often played as a complement to the substantive void of individualist liberalism. The 1989 movements, in turn, have often been seen as mostly wanting to have their societies 'catch up' (Habermas) with the allegedly more advanced West. As a result, while both movements can be regarded as highly successful as unsettling experiences, they were much weaker, if not outright failing, in terms of reconstructing the political form of their societies and of reinterpreting the substantive commitments of European political modernity.

My analysis of the political *problématique* of modernity will continue and conclude, in the following chapter, with reflections on '1968' precisely because the events summarized under this label mark the last attempt at a conscious transformation of political modernity, that is, at a profound reinterpretation of the political *problématique* which is more or less clearly concluded, one towards which we can look back from some distance. It is not least the failure of this attempt, in terms of providing a novel articulation of personal and collective autonomy, that requires a radical reconsideration of the nature of our modernity, as temporarily expressed in the diffusion of the term 'postmodernity'. This reconsideration will proceed further in this volume by means of an assessment of the economic *problématique* (in Part II), because it is the strength of a particular version of economic modernity, namely capitalism, that is often invoked as the main reason why a return to a strong understanding of collective self-determination is not possible. My critical discussion of this idea will find it significant but also insufficient as an explanation for the current condition of modernity. It needs to be complemented by an analysis of the knowledge claims that are made to underpin both explanations and transformations of the social and natural world. For this reason, Part III turns to an analysis of the epistemic *problématique*, in terms of the claims of the sciences in general, and the social sciences in particular, to provide a generally valid answer to this *problématique*. After these digressions, as they may seem to some readers, I will return to the political *problématique* of modernity in a more comprehensive way and will analyse it in terms of what I see as a current attempt to reinterpret it, at least on a regional basis, namely the process and project of European integration (Part IV).

4

Modernity as a Project of Emancipation and the Possibility of Politics

'1968' was seen by many of its participants as a beginning: 'This is only a beginning...', as one said in Paris in May, and what was referred to was a struggle for emancipation, even if often of a yet diffuse, ill-defined kind. Later, when the tides had turned, many rather looked back at it as an end – the end, most importantly, of some political project of change, or more precisely, and more devastatingly, of the possibility of any political project of, in whatever way, progressive change, of some form of collective emancipation. '1968' and its aftermath will here be looked at in this light – '1968' itself will be read as a project of emancipation, trying to interpret retrospectively that which was strangely both clear and opaque at the time; and societal developments in its aftermath will be investigated in terms of the fate of emancipation.[1]

Emancipation from what? The philosophical answer

To do so, it is useful to first gain more distance from the events by enlarging the temporal horizon. If '1968' was in important respects a movement for emancipation, it could not but refer to a two-to-three-century-old tradition in European intellectual history, the Enlightenment. Immanuel Kant's 'Answer to the Question: What is the Enlightenment?' (1965 [1784]) famously starts with a definition of Enlightenment as emancipation: 'Enlightenment is the exit of the human being from self-incurred immaturity'. Despite – or because of – its clarity, this claim begs further questions. What is the meaning of 'from'? What is the state of the human condition before emancipation, what is the 'immaturity' human beings strive to exit from? And where will they find themselves after the exit? The precise meaning of this assertion has remained rather widely open to interpretation.

First, and most commonly, Kant was read as having pointed towards the end of immaturity that was brought about by the so-called *democratic revolutions*. Those revolutions started in Kant's own era but remained a long time in the making until they led towards what was widely regarded as the full advent of modernity, of a modern society and a modern political order. In this interpretation, emancipation had largely been accomplished in these revolutions, at least as a matter of principle, and was only in need of completion there where reality still fell short of the Enlightenment promises (see chapter 3 above). '1968', then, would be at best a catching-up, a step towards completion there where the Enlightenment promise was not yet fulfilled. This view on its own, however, does not describe well the self-understanding of the *soixante-huitards*.

Indeed, second, Kant's view was also often seen as superseded by a later critique, namely the Marxian one, that suggested that, in the way in which it had occurred, the advent of political modernity – the *bourgeois* revolution – had resulted in an *illusion*, in an emancipation that resulted in a new kind of immaturity, of serfdom. From then on, critique had to be directed against capitalism (for a discussion of this kind of critical theory of modernity, see chapter 5 below). One had to move from political emancipation to human emancipation, as Marx had said earlier. '1968' marked the beginning of an albeit short-lived revival of Marxian thought in Western societies, and this not least because of the conviction that those societies were in a rather fundamental sense falling short of realizing human capacities and were thus in need of another revolution.

Thus, two ways of reading Kant on emancipation had been established by the time of 1968, after the history of the nineteenth and of most of the twentieth century. Emancipation was either basically accomplished, only in need of completion – and the liberation from colonialism or women's emancipation, important struggles during the 1960s, could easily be interpreted in this perspective. Or emancipation could be seen as only having taken the first of several steps. The obstacles to its accomplishments were then more deeply rooted than all political thinking that traces its origins to the Enlightenment had envisaged. Both these interpretations are part of the discourse of '1968', although both were elaborated much earlier and were rather revived with '1968'. But there is a third reading of Kant, of which we may more properly say that it emerged with '1968'.

Michel Foucault's (1984) interpretation of Kant's essay places the emphasis on the word 'exit'. If Enlightenment is the exit from self-incurred immaturity, then it is neither the state before nor the one after, it is the in-between, the moment of leaving. Thus, Foucault sceptically reviews conceptions of Enlightenment as an era, and prefers to see it as an ethos. There is no accomplished new phase or state, the one of emancipation, after leaving immaturity, exiting from it. Such state does not *actually* exist, as an epoch of political modernity. Nor is it even *thinkable*, in any normative way, as the state after the overthrow of capitalism. Emancipation rather is an ongoing demand, an exigency, precisely, an ethos.

Regardless of the actual importance of *la pensée Foucault* for '1968' (as widely debated in France after Luc Ferry and Alain Renaut's *La pensée 68*), this reading of the Enlightenment seems to capture much of the specificity of '1968', that is, of that which makes it distinct from other protest movements. There were, for instance, new forms of political events, like the sit-in or the happening, later to be helplessly described by political scientists as 'unconventional political participation'. There was the (re-)creation of a connection between artistic expression and political expression that was later often denounced as 'the aestheticization of the political'. The direct link was provided by situationism, but surrealism and the whole tradition of artistic modernism in literature and the visual arts stood in the background (Bohrer 1997). More broadly, one can identify here an 'artistic critique' of capitalism that always co-existed and in 1968 merged with the 'social critique', as advocated in the mainstream of the workers' movement, to form an explosive mixture (Boltanski and Chiapello 1999). There was a connection between the lives of the activists and their political ideas in such a way that the realization of one's own self was to mean the accomplished fusion of the two. Feminists problematically referred to this aspect as the personal having become political; sociologists derogatorily related it to the youthful lack of realism in '1968' (thus, in absolute incomprehension, to the immaturity of its protagonists). And there was a refusal to define and determine the political forms that were to issue from the contestation. The political was the revolt, the contestation, as exemplified in interminable assembly meetings, based on the rejection of exclusion and of representation. Emancipation was the 'exit from'; every attempt to define the path to follow was subject to a critique of power. In turn, such a conception of the political can be – and has been – subjected to critique. At the end of my observations I will return explicitly to the question of the political and its forms 'after 1968'. First, however, and against the frequent attempts at prematurely discarding the political perspectives that emerged from '1968', the protest has to be located in its own socio-historical context.

Emancipation from what? The sociological answer

In other words, the philosophical answer to the question 'emancipation from what?' needs to be complemented by a socio-historical answer to the same question. Every reader of Kant's 'answer to the question' will immediately recognize that his philosophy retained its vitality, his observations on how to translate it into political maxims of the time though much less so. A political interpretation of the Enlightenment, thus, requires an analysis of the specific, historically concrete forms of 'self-incurred immaturity' (for the following, see also Wagner 1994, pp. 141–5; Boltanski and Chiapello 1999, pp. 241–90; Stråth 2002; and Boltanski 2002).

If there can be little doubt that the idea of emancipation was a key element of the discourse of '1968', this idea, however, appeared from the beginning in two distinct forms. On the one hand, protest was directed against conventions and institutions that appeared firmly and unchangeably established, against the rules and regulations of that 'organized modernity' that had been established over the preceding decades in the course of often violent conflicts and oppression.[2] The older generation, that is, those who had experienced the rise of totalitarianism and the Second World War and who were in fact administering the 'administered society' (Adorno) of the 1960s, tended to see those conventions and institutions as accomplishments that were gained during the difficult first half of the century and that should not be endangered without good reason.

This basic attitude explains a number of features of the societies of post-war restoration: the denial of the earlier deep divide between supporters and opponents of authoritarian and totalitarian regimes; the integration of the latter even in top administrative positions in post-war institutions; the ban of 'extremist' parties in some societies and the long-term exclusion of the opposition parties from power as well as their increasing pacification, i.e., their unwillingness to underline points of disagreement with the governments; the return to cultural models of hierarchy and domination in personal and work relations, even though some of these models had already been shaken during the inter-war period; the elevation of Soviet socialism to the status of an – external as well as internal – enemy and the alliance with authoritarian regimes in alleged defence against that enemy; the emphasis on economic development as the primary objective of politics and, concomitantly, the elevation of private well-being, *les petits bonheurs*, over 'public happiness', i.e., substantive political goals; clear preference given to the stabilization of a societal situation, which prominently included broad-ranging attempts to provide income stability by means of Keynesian demand management, generous pension reforms, agricultural protectionism and subsidies, and the expansion of the welfare state, over any reasoning about profound reform needs or even any wider opening of political debate.

Current historical revisionism tends to reopen the question whether some of these conventions and institutions were indeed justifiable under the conditions of the time. The question is, from a democratic point of view, a truly open one at best for some of the practices under consideration, certainly not for all of them. Regardless of that matter, though, for the purposes of analysis here it suffices to state that, all variations notwithstanding, it is precisely this configuration of conventions that was considered by the activists of 1968 as unbearable. As a result of a constellation in which that which was plainly self-evident and not open for debate for much of the older generation was self-evidently intolerable any longer for much of the younger generation, an apparently irreconcilable opposition between protesters and 'the establishment' formed quickly. In this antagonism, the protesters argued in the name of a new freedom, of the right to a diversity of life-forms, of doubt as to the necessity of many rules and conventions. Even though it was directed against existing political forms, the institutions and conventions of the various nation-states, emancipation in this sense did not head in any direct way for new political forms. Rather, it meant the right to realize one's own idiosyncratic self, thus predominantly the emancipation of the individual from constraining rules and conventions.

This, however, was only one aspect of the events. On the other hand, the protest against the established conventions and institutions also elaborated conceptions of new forms of social and political organization, thus of an alternative to the existing social order. While this alternative included the idea of individual emancipation, it nevertheless was a project of collective emancipation. Drawing on the tradition of critical theorizing that had developed since the middle of the nineteenth century, the idea of a collective subject resurfaced. Such a subject in a new form would re-found and drive forward the project of collective emancipation, after its earlier incarnation, the workers' movement, had – as the view was – been integrated into bourgeois society. The most highly organized expression of such thinking was the founding of groups that referred in their practice to traditions of Marxism and saw their own interpretation – disregarding the ideas of plurality and diversity – each as the only viable one. However, references to a collective subject as the actor in a political transformation can also be found in other areas of activities related to '1968', such as in feminist debates or in action-oriented sociologies like the one Alain Touraine proposed.

If it is true, then, that an emphasis on emancipation from conventions that appeared as oppressive co-existed in '1968' with the desire for a collective reorientation after those conventions would have been successfully challenged (as captured in Passerini 2002), the awareness that there was a considerable tension between these two longings was but little developed among the activists. Such lack of awareness can possibly be understood against the background of two features of '1968' consciousness. First, as discussed above, the oppressive features of contemporary society were seen as self-evident. The intellectual activities around '1968' consisted in revealing ever more forms of oppression that had remained concealed before but that appeared clearly once critical consciousness – generalizing the 'hermeneutics of suspicion' – had been gained. The main and overwhelming task, thus, was the identification and destruction of those forms of oppression. Secondly, in this light, '1968' consciousness was marked by some kind of unexplicated Enlightenment faith as regards the aftermath of effective critical action, of the practice of reason. Implicitly, the view was that autonomous, reason-endowed human beings will unproblematically organize a free society once the obstacles are removed that stand in the way of such a project. Certainly, the removal of the obstacles was a task that was increasingly seen as difficult. The founding of avant-garde parties and the resort to terrorism were – misguided – conclusions drawn from such insight. But even in those highly organized expressions of '1968', the views about society after successful liberation were either weak or even non-existent or they were very – sometimes grotesquely – remote from the conditions prevailing in Western societies.

The tension between the two elements of a political project, critique and reconstruction, was thus de facto resolved by a strong neglect of the latter element. Saying this does not – or, at least, not necessarily – lead into a revisionist criticism of '1968'; the positive significance of the effective challenging of the conventions of organized modernity remains, in my view, beyond doubt. Those who judge '1968' negatively either in terms of practices that emerged from it (such as limitations to free speech at universities during the 1970s, or terrorism) or in terms of deplorable long-term consequences (see below as well as Ginsborg (2002) and Offe (2002) for critical discussions) have to bear the onus of the argument. They would need to respond to the question whether the maintenance of the conventions of organized modernity, if it had been possible at all, was to be preferred to the struggles and new kinds of problems from the 1970s and 1980s up to the present. In this sense, the normative assessment of the structure and conflicts of pre-1968 European societies is the hidden central theme in the recurrent debates about '1968' in France, Germany and elsewhere. As in other realms of contemporary political debate, such as about the creation of a European polity, nostalgic longings assert themselves in a new form and with a new target period, the 1950s and early 1960s – when society was coherent, when families were intact and when the nation-state was strong (and also when there was still a working class as a political subject). Beyond the rejection of such nostalgia, however, there is also a need to point to the shortcomings of any political critique that disregards the issue of political reconstruction.

Emancipation of whom?

The interpretation of '1968' that I have proposed up to this point echoes in certain respects earlier debates. Thus, it has been quite common to argue that '1968' was the conjunction of a political revolution that failed with a cultural revolution that succeeded (see, e.g., my brief discussion in Wagner 1994). This formula also underlines the tension between a collectivist project and an individualist one. More radically, Luc Ferry and Alain Renaut have suggested that '1968' was never really about anything else than the assertion of a new individualism, with self-realization as the absolutely highest commitment. The political element, the existence of which is not denied by these authors, was nothing but a subordinate aspect, though one which was functionally necessary to achieve individual liberation. Without a critique of the reigning conventions – thus, a socio-political critique – the freedom of the individual towards new forms of self-realization would not have been possible. In Ferry and Renaut's own words:

> The passage from the 1960s to the 1980s can be understood without difficulty once one recognizes that the 1980s are basically nothing else than the individualism of May, minus the utopian projects into which the latter had been translated, not to realize them at the political level, but merely to accomplish the social critique of which [this individualism] had been the carrier. (Ferry and Renaut 1987, p. 59)

In theoretical terms, one of the problems of this assertion is the distinction between the 'basic' features of a phenomenon and those others that are only contingent or ephemeral. In a different passage, the authors even dare to speak about the 'essence' of the events: 'The essence of May resides more in the *critical claim* for social autonomy than in the attachment to those utopian *political forms* into which such autonomy could (?) have been inscribed' (Ferry and Renaut 1987, pp. 70–1. Italics and question mark in the original).

There are two ways of reading such assertions. It is possible that the authors intend to maintain a philosophy of history that distinguishes between essences and appearances, although they reveal very little about it in this treatise. In the light of the brief remarks on the history of political thought in the first part of their volume, it appears as if they see indeed the full assertion of the individual and of individualism as the *telos* of history, at least since the French Revolution. In the passage following the one just cited, they indeed say that 'the truth of May' emerges in the expression of individualism in its 'pure state' during the 1980s (Ferry and Renaut 1987, p. 71). Like many teleological theories of history, this one would then see the end-state reached, or at least close, in its own time. Although such forms of reasoning are nowadays widely and justifiably discredited, a serious and unresolved issue is raised in them. Contemporary debates in sociology and political science, for instance, mirror such a concern by employing terms such as 'individualization' and 'democratization' to describe major socio-political trends of our time. Even though these terms are mostly used in conceptually irresponsibly unreflective ways, the question remains open as to if and how Western history of the past two centuries needs to be read in terms of the irreversible and inescapable imposition of these two themes (for more detail on this issue see chapter 5 below and Wagner 2001a, chapter 5).

Before returning to this question, a more modest reading of Ferry and Renaut's analysis may lead further. They may just want to offer an explanation of medium-term historical change. If this is the case, then the main problem may be that they have succumbed to the widespread fallacy known as *post hoc ergo propter hoc* reasoning: '1968' was a major event with a probably significant impact on society. The realization of their lives by individuals was important in '1968'. After 1968, society became more individualistic. Ergo, '1968' was essentially about the assertion of individual autonomy. Obviously, too many alternative explanations have here been discarded prematurely (see Offe 2002). It is not only that other events and processes may have 'caused', if this is a proper way of speaking at all, 1980s' individualism. Even if '1968' were at the roots of the later individualism, it could have been so inadvertently, as an 'unintended consequence' or, to use the French sociological formula as coined by

Raymond Boudon, as an *effet pervers*. In this case, there would be a causal relation but not one of expression of the true nature, as Ferry and Renaut maintain. Most interestingly, '1968' may well at core have been about the assertion of individual autonomy, but 1980s' individualism could nevertheless signal in an important sense a 'failure' of '1968' – a possibility against which Ferry and Renaut (1987, pp. 56–7) argue explicitly, criticizing in particular Cornelius Castoriadis's interpretation.

The decisive issue is contained in the question mark that Ferry and Renaut inserted in the sentence quoted above. They here do agree that there was a concern for political forms in '1968', not just for individual autonomy. And unlike the earlier quote, this concern does not just appear as subsidiary here (though it does this as well). The question mark signals that the critical claims of '1968' possibly could not be translated into viable political forms – and this apparently not for accidental but for systematic reasons. Translated into my terms, Ferry and Renaut seem to be suggesting that there was no collective subject of emancipation in '1968', or in other words, that the claims for individual self-realization could not be added up to the claim for a political form that places self-realization of the individual at its centre. In the light of this reading, the reduction performed in their analysis becomes visible. Rather than arguing that '1968' was 'really' about individual autonomy, the claims of its protagonists notwithstanding, they should have investigated the claims of the protagonists and, if they were not realized, the possible systematic reasons for this shortcoming.

The question about the subject of emancipation, thus, needs to be posed differently. Even a cursory look at the debates demonstrates easily that the concern for such a subject was strongly present. The problem, though, that was already visible at the time was a lack of plausibility in the ways in which it was formulated combined with a lack of consensus about the appropriate formulation. Very schematically, three conceptually different ways of approaching the question can be distinguished, all based in some way on the identification of a historically novel societal situation. First, after the *embourgeoisement* of the working class, the revolutionary subject was located at the margins of society, in marginalized groups in Western societies as well as among the oppressed of the Third World. This way of thinking adopted the Hegelian strategy of locating the force of Reason in the empirical world with the Marxian twist of expecting it by negation of the logic of the actual, rather than at the centre of the actual as Hegel did (for a new version of such thinking today, see Hardt and Negri 2000). Denying such reasoning any empirical plausibility, second, some sociologists, most prominently Alain Touraine, reoriented the theory of society such that the students themselves, as an emerging technical intelligentsia, were the driving force of change in 'post-industrial society'. This reasoning was not widely believed among the activists; and it certainly underestimated the 'transitoriness' of the social situation of an educationally defined group (as Claus Offe (2002) also points out) as well as the heterogeneity of socio-professional positions later in life. Thirdly, and maybe most characteristic of the current appreciative memory of the events, some strands of the movements doubted the possibility of any theoretical determination of such a subject and insisted instead on the permanent production of a political subject in one's own practices. Such orientation was most visibly taken up in the women's movement and in attempts at self-organization in all walks of life, as characteristic of the *mouvement autogestionnaire* in France and the *Alternativbewegung* in West Germany, experimenting both with new forms of 'family' life and with new forms of economic organization (see Ginsborg 2002 and Stråth 2002).

Of those three positions, the first two arrived at the construction of a collective subject more by theoretical and/or political fiat than by an actual assessment of the situation. It was the insight into the necessity of such a subject that drove the analysis. Under this aspect, individualism was not at all at the centre of '1968'. However, the political theorizing that emerged out of '1968' largely failed to address the situation of the time because of the employment of facile notions of the collectivity. The third position, instead, can be seen as factually addressing the difficulties of constructing a collective subject after the critique of pre-existing collective forms, which precisely include the conventions of organized modernity against which '1968' was in the first instance directed. Its fate, though, was that those difficulties could most often then not be overcome.

To talk about failing in the face of difficulties of constructing and maintaining political forms, however, is something entirely different from asserting that individualism is the authentic, only initially concealed truth of '1968'. This individualism rather emerged by default, as a consequence of the failure to construct a viable political form: '1968' was quite successful in dismantling the conventions of the post-Second World War restoration societies of 'organized modernity'. Because of the de-collectivizing implication of such a dismantling (see chapter 6 below and Wagner 1994 for a more detailed conceptualization), it contained individualization as a *possible* outcome. However, in as far as such individualization actually occurred, this should not be seen as the direct and necessary outcome of such challenging of conventions but rather as a result of the inability to successfully address the question of rebuilding social and political forms. Who the actors of emancipation are and how far they have to act in common to construct such forms, not only to dismantle them, remained an open question (which could be cast as the quest for a 'political individual'). And it is in the absence of an answer that individual solutions followed. It is thus this latter question that finally needs to be considered – in the terminology proposed here, this is the question of the objective of the struggle for emancipation.

Emancipation for what?

While there may be agreement that some idea of individual emancipation, or liberation, was central for '1968', did the events also stand for some collective idea or arrangement, or were their terms primarily directed against the existing ones? In contrast to other interpretations of '1968', in my view this question cannot be answered by merely looking at the aftermath of the events, not even if one could precisely distinguish those aspects of European societies over the following decades that were 'caused' by '1968' from those that were not.

The recognition of the substantive project of collective emancipation in '1968' is made difficult by the plain fact that, if there was any, it was not accomplished. Like every other historical actor, even the most powerful one, the protagonists of '1968' were not the masters of their own socio-historical situation. This means that, on the one hand, the direction of '1968' was to some extent pre-shaped by the forms of social analysis and criticism that were available to the actors. In the history of European thought, the two registers introduced above predominated. Either, in the Enlightenment tradition, critique was seen as fully preparing the ground for action, which was entirely unproblematic under conditions of autonomy, or 'maturity'. Or, in the romanticist tradition, the subject of critique was unproblematically seen as an authentic collectivity (see Löwy 2002). Limited to these two registers, the substantive collective project, while certainly not absent, remained either largely unspecified or lacked plausibility.

Faced with an only weakly formulated alternative, on the other hand, the powers-that-be reassert themselves relatively easily, and the project of autonomy and emancipation disintegrates under the pull of societal forces. Such a perspective allows a critical analysis of the consequences of '1968' without falling into revisionism. It is then possible to say that the commitment to individual autonomy is a fragmented part of the '1968' heritage – without claiming that individualism was its true nature. It can even be maintained that there is a connection between the '1968' form of critique, if separated from its specific societal context, and the recent transformations of capitalism – without maintaining that strands of '1968' promoted the 'new spirit of capitalism' (see Boltanski and Chiapello 1999 and chapter 7 below). The protagonists of '1968' made history, but they did not make it under circumstances of their own choosing, and they did not control the outcome of their actions.

Contemporary ways of reappropriating the heritage of '1968' require, on the one hand, a critical analysis of our contemporary socio-political situation, of our capitalism and our modernity, in analogy to the critique of organized capitalism and nation-state-based modernity provided during '1968' and in its aftermath. On the other hand, however, such ways also require a renewal of normative political philosophy; and this task may more clearly need to go beyond '1968' (Part V below will discuss this demand in theoretical and methodological terms). While I share the emphasis on the 'utopian surplus', as expressed by Varikas (2002) and Passerini (2002), without which the endeavour would be without point, this emphasis alone is insufficient.

Under conditions of a weakly formulated collective project and strong countervailing forces, the power of imagination, as forceful as it may be at any moment, persists only with difficulty. As much as the commitment to autonomy and liberation in '1968' can be considered as the move to an 'instituting' mode of societal imagination, to use Castoriadis's terms, to a re-founding of the imaginary signification of autonomy, as much is there a need for endowing such movements with 'instituted' moments to sustain their impetus. To put the issue in Foucault's terms: while the critical ethos is persistently necessary, a political project cannot remain purely in the situation of 'exit'. In the absence of such instituted moments,[3] the events of '1968' either fade into the distance or they are reinterpreted beyond recognizability – such as by Luc Ferry and Alain Renaut.

While my analysis claims to restore a broader analytical perspective on the historical meaning of '1968', the politico-intellectual conclusions from it still need to be drawn. In current critical debate, much emphasis is – rightly – given to the question of an alternative to a neo-liberal understanding of economic organization (the following part of this volume, Part II, is devoted to this question). The weakness of intellectual and political alternatives to individualist liberalism and to the thin approach to democracy that accompanies it is, in contrast, much less the centre of attention, although this question is at least as important. Post-1968 individualism emerged to some extent as a reaction to insights into the difficulties with many of the available 'thick' approaches to democracy, some of which were adopted by political groups that sprang from the '1968' experience. It is a resigned, fatalist reaction, however, that mirrors the insufficient understanding of the question of the political form of critical practice in '1968'. If this was the major weakness of '1968' as a political project, the conclusion that follows is then to make this question central for current debate.

A political form constitutes the relation between singular human beings and the collectivity under specific socio-historical conditions, including power relations. The predominant such form was the democratic-capitalist nation-state, the existing varieties of which were strongly and partly effectively criticized by '1968'. Afterwards, however, the whole question was lost, and never seriously taken up again. It is striking, for instance, that the process of so-called European integration, nothing less than the founding of a polity, has – some exceptions notwithstanding – mostly found benign disinterest at best among the former *soixante-huitards* (Part IV below will address this issue). One of the consequences of this loss is that we now hardly even have the realm in which to discuss and assess the consequences of '1968'. To constructively relate to '1968' means to keep alive its 'utopian surplus' but to combine it with a thinking of the political that aims at remedying for the future the weakness of the historical events.

Part II

Interpretations of Economic Modernity: The Endgame and After

Overture: Capitalism and Modernity as Social Formations and as Imaginary Significations

Evoking the terms 'capitalism' and 'modernity' is usually understood as an attempt at representing a societal configuration, most often the contemporary societal configuration, but sometimes including a notion of the historical development up to the present. In those terms, the last few decades have witnessed a significant intellectual change. The 1970s and at least the early 1980s were marked by a clear opposition. On the one hand, modernization theories referred to (post-) industrial society and emphasized the basically smooth development of societal configurations once they had embarked on a course of modernization, by which they mainly meant a successful accomplishment of both an industrial and a democratic revolution. On the other hand, neo-Marxist critical theories continued to refer to (late) capitalism and insisted on the basically unstable, contradiction-ridden nature of contemporary societal configurations. They devoted most of their efforts either to elaborating new explanations for the surprising persistence of capitalism despite the allegedly profound class antagonism or to detecting signs of novel forms of crisis and imminent breakdown of the politico-economic order.

By the late 1980s, both accounts had lost much of their – anyway already limited – plausibility. Modernization theories contained too much of an implicit idea of a stable social order to cope with, on the one hand, the weakening of the external boundaries of social entities, mostly now discussed as 'globalization' and 'the decline of the nation-state' and, on the other hand, the dissolution of the internal structures, discussed as 'individualization' under conditions of 'risk society'. Neo-Marxist theories, in turn, suffered from the blow of the fall of existing socialism. Not that many of those theorists had shown much allegiance to those politico-economic orders; what was profoundly shocking was the fact that (the elites of) those societies hastened to embrace capitalism as a constitutive part of the new kind of modernity they were intent on entering. From then on, there seemed to be no barrier to the globalized, neo-liberal variety of capitalism any longer. More than most of the proponents of capitalism, its critics talked endlessly about *la pensée unique* and the ideology of there being no alternative.

Social theory responded to the double crisis of the theorizing of 'capitalism' and of 'modernization' by embracing the term 'modernity'. While there is without doubt a great variety of uses of this term (see chapter 1 above), almost unknown in social thought before the end of the 1970s, it appeared to provide a new common ground precisely in terms of representing the present societal configuration. At the same time, however, and despite the coinage of such proto-conceptual terms as 'reflexive modernity', 'second modernity' and 'another modernity', the move towards such a common reference term was sometimes seen as entailing the loss of all possibility of critique. Traditionally, critique used to embrace modernity (even without using the term) and to denounce capitalism because of its inability to complete the project of modernity – or, rather, because of the obstacles it posed towards such completion. To use the term 'modernity' for a contemporary reality that was without doubt capitalist as well made such a conceptual strategy impossible.

Once this situation was recognized, scholars who see themselves as critical theorists started to lament it. The move towards speaking about modernity, even with a critical tone, is said to have the effect of 'naturalizing capitalism' (Wood 1999, p. 115), of indeed making it appear as inevitable. As a response, at least some of those theorists returned to conceptualizing capitalism as if a quarter of a century of debate had not happened. In my view, in contrast, there is a potential gain in the debate around the term 'modernity', even though only in some versions of theorizing modernity. To consciously go through the intellectual as well as the socio-political transformations since the 1970s means that both capitalism and modernity will need to be reconceptualized and a novel understanding of critique needs to be elaborated.

Capitalism and modernity are mostly used as terms to characterize a social formation, at the very least pointing to its dominant aspect, thus meaning more precisely 'capitalist society' or 'modern society'. This is the kind of institutional approach and its critical, but similarly institutionalist, alternative that were discussed above (in chapter 1) as the two most time-honoured ways of understanding modernity. On this basis, the relation between capitalism and modernity can be conceptualized in a limited variety of ways. First, and most common in the classic Marxist tradition, capitalism can be seen as the dominant – or original – aspect of a social formation. Then, modernity contains a greater promise, but it remains necessarily incomplete, precisely because of the dominance of capitalism. Alternatively, modernity can be seen as the dominant aspect. In the most widespread version of this thinking, the development of a capitalist market economy is a functional aspect, and a functional achievement, of the development of the more broadly conceived modern society. Under the conditions of liberty created by modernity, capitalist markets demonstrate their superiority with regard to the efficient production and distribution of goods and, as a consequence, tend to eliminate other forms. Modernization theory provided the most comprehensive version of this thinking, although it overall contributed little to economic research specifically. In turn, neo-classical economics is built on the assumption of market superiority rather than on any effective empirical demonstration.

Thirdly, the development of capitalism and modernity can be analysed as being inextricably intertwined. This occurred in the classic writings of the Frankfurt School, most notably in Adorno and Horkheimer's *Dialectic of the Enlightenment*. Capitalism is seen as the result of a one-dimensional elaboration of the Enlightenment promise, thus as a particular version of modernity that has become dominant (see chapter 5 below for a detailed discussion). Because of the conceptual fusion of the economic, the political and the epistemic *problématique* into one conglomerate that imposes itself onto social life, such theorizing tends to become totalizing, often inadvertently so, as the frequent attempts to reopen the analysis demonstrate. More within the mainstream of Marxist thinking, the so-called social relations school openly advocates a totalizing theorizing, claiming that all social relations are pervaded by capitalism, once the latter reigns (see, e.g., Jessop 2000).

Fourthly, capitalism and modernity can be analysed as co-existent but as analytically distinct features of a societal configuration. Then, capitalism refers more or less clearly to the economic *problématique*, when interpreted in terms of an alleged endless need for accumulation and instrumental mastery, and modernity is about the political *problématique*, as traced back to Enlightenment and Revolution, and thus rather directly connected to democracy and critique. The work of Cornelius Castoriadis is an example of such thinking. Castoriadis diagnosed contemporary Western societies as being based on what he calls a double imaginary signification, namely on the ideas of autonomy and of mastery. On the one side, 'democracy is the regime of self-limitation, or in other words the regime of autonomy, or of self-institution' (Castoriadis 1997a, p. 150). On the other side, the 'unlimited expansion of the so-called rational so-called mastery' is 'the central capitalist imaginary' (Castoriadis 1997a, p. 166; here qualified by the historicizing formula 'ever more'). These statements assert the double character of the imaginary signification of modernity, and both elements of that double signification are seen, at first sight, as independent from each other. The search for a relation between them leads to the idea of a parallel emergence, linked by a common historical context, namely the struggle against the Old Regime. This struggle is seen as 'combining the tendency towards the realization of the project of individual and collective autonomy with the capitalist transformation' (Castoriadis 1997a, p. 149). Historically, it is this co-emergence indeed that justifies bringing the two imaginary significations together as the double imaginary signification of modernity. Theoretically, this perspective entails a concept of modernity (as the broader term) as consisting of two basic components, one of which supports the development of capitalism (as the narrower term, included in modernity), the other one the development of democracy. There is, however, no subsumption here of capitalism under modernity, unlike in modernization theory. Rather, the two components of modernity are seen as mutually irreducible and in persistent tension (see Arnason 1989, pp. 327 and 330).

Even though arguing from a more traditionally Marxist position, Ellen Meiksins Wood (1999, pp. 105–13) arrives at quite similar conclusions, based on more detailed historical analysis. Wood criticizes any conflation of modernity with capitalism and sees even – unlike Castoriadis – two entirely different origins. In her analysis, England is the site of the origin of capitalism, whereas France is the one of (political) modernity, in the form namely of the Enlightenment and the French Revolution. Thus, modernity and capitalism appear not only as analytically distinguishable but even as purely contingently related.

Both Castoriadis's and Wood's versions of analytical separation of capitalism and modernity allow the elaboration of a conceptual approach that is open to historical-empirical observation. Or, in Bernard Yack's terms (1997), it avoids, at least at the start, any fetishism of modernity, or for that matter, of capitalism. Let it just be added at this point that most recent analyses of historical and contemporary capitalism confirm such a perspective. Analyses of capitalism that actually bother to look at the empirical world find little trace of *la pensée unique* (see, e.g., Crouch and Streeck 1997; Hall and Soskice 2001; Hollingsworth and Boyer 1997; Salais and Storper 1993; Sabel and Zeitlin 1997; Kitschelt et al. 1999; Whitley 1999). Thus, to give only two examples, Peter Hall (1999, p. 160) talks about an important 'interpretive dimension' in institutional change, providing for a variety of arrangements. And David Soskice (1999, p. 133) underlines that the differences between European economic policies cannot be explained as merely various degrees of resistance to globalization but should rather be seen as different actively pursued strategies in a changed environment.

While such findings are significant, a strong emphasis on the empirical refutation of linear and totalizing assumptions misses an important point in the debate about capitalism and, to some extent, modernity, namely the question of whether there is a *dynamics* of capitalism that drives the history of modernity in a certain direction. Approaches that focus on diversity and contingency tend to presuppose the absence of any such dynamics and thus fail to address that very question. It is the merit of the approaches that analyse capitalism and modernity as co-existent, but as analytically distinct and complexly related, to permit an exploration of this question while maintaining a focus on contingency and historicity.

Castoriadis and Wood share the ambition to *both* accept historical contingency *and* grasp the historical development of capitalism. This ambition leads them to devise strategies to deal with contingency. For them, social change over the past two centuries is driven by capitalism; modernity – 'on its own', so to say – is not seen as endowed with a similar dynamics. For Castoriadis, the driving force is the striving for 'unlimited expansion of rational mastery', which is the dominant imaginary signification of capitalism. Under its power, the imaginary signification of modern democracy tends to wither away. Although human beings, because of their radical imagination, can always seize back their autonomy, in Castoriadis's analysis we have no way of saying when and how, under which circumstances. Analytically, such assertion means a *bracketing of contingency*, its exclusion from analysis. In contrast, Wood proceeds by *historicizing contingency*. As both Marx and Weber did in different ways, she argues that once capitalism happens to emerge, for contingent reasons, it tends to impose itself, basically by asserting its productive superiority in market competition.

Despite the merits of both approaches – the anti-determinism in Castoriadis's case, the historical perspective in Wood's – one would like to be able to say more than they do. One would have had to ask Castoriadis about the nature of that ontological gap between the sociologically grounded observation of the withering of autonomy and the ever-existent possibility of its re-emergence. And one would need to ask Wood about the ways in which such imposition of capitalism precisely works, why it is that there have been no historical alternatives (or were there?) and, finally, how this view ultimately differs from a totalizing perspective, if imposition is that which apparently unavoidably happens.

If even the more subtle approaches to understanding capitalism and modernity leave such crucial questions open, one may wonder whether the issue should not be confronted in a different way. Theorizing in this area is imprisoned in the idea of representing a societal configuration in terms of a social formation. This idea demands that basic principles be identified that penetrate the social world and shape its institutions in a specific way. As a result, monolithic representations of society tend to emerge, subsuming a multifarious social world under a very limited set of laws and reasoning away epistemic obstacles to social knowledge. Even the separation of different aspects of the social world, and thus the rupture of any overall assumption of coherence, as practised by Castoriadis and Wood, does not solve the problem if those separate aspects are then viewed in the same manner as the overall society before. However, the elements required for developing an alternative conceptual perspective can be found in those two authors. With his concept of imaginary significations, which refer to what I here call basic *problématiques* of human social life, Castoriadis, on the one hand, opens the way for an interpretative approach to analysing large-scale societal configurations. Merging this approach with Wood's historical perspective, on the other hand, one obtains the possibility of investigating the historically changing ways of dealing with such *problématiques* in the light of experiences.[1]

In this light, my further exploration will proceed as follows. The subsequent chapter will critically analyse the critical theory of capitalism, focusing on Adorno. The double purpose is to grasp both the shortcomings of this approach and its lasting contribution, the latter being at least a partial explanation for the persistence of such critical approach despite its shortcomings. The conclusion of this analysis is the call for a historical-comparative sociology of capitalism focusing on the variety of ways of dealing with the economic *problématique* in relation to the epistemic and political ones. Such historical comparison will need to focus on experiences with capitalism in different societal settings and the interpretations given to such experiences. The broad contours of such a historical-comparative sociology are sketched in chapter 6. Chapter 7, finally, will provide a contribution to the analysis of the most recent transformation of capitalism, focusing on the concept of 'flexibility' and its interpretations.

5

The Critique of Capitalism and its Impasse

In the analysis of capitalism, critical theory constitutes a distinct intellectual tradition. Inaugurated by Karl Marx, it reaches from the Frankfurt School to the neo-Marxism of the 1970s to the recent debates about the inevitability of neo-liberal globalization. While the conceptual weaknesses of this mode of thinking are well known, at least from Max Weber and Karl Polanyi onwards, critical theory nevertheless shows a remarkable persistence. The objective of this chapter is to analyse the tradition of critical theory in the light of its failure to grasp the inevitably political constitution of frameworks for economic action, but by doing so this chapter ultimately aims at understanding the strong reasons for the persistence of this intellectual tradition. Selecting Theodor W. Adorno's work as a key example for both the neglect of the political and the persistence of the critical perspective, it will be shown how – despite a general insight into the possibility of discussing the economy politically – the place of political philosophy was evacuated in favour of a reasoning that emphasized epistemic obstacles towards analysing capitalism instead. From such an angle, then, any embedding of capitalism appeared impossible, and the well-known apocalyptic tendency of critical theory emerged forcefully – in the following to be captured by the notion of the 'endgame' (as set out in chapter 1). In a second step, however, the chapter proceeds to demonstrate that the dimension of political philosophy in the critical analysis of capitalism can be restored. If Adorno and other critical theorists are read in this light, their observations on the developmental tendencies of capitalism gain new meaning and provide insights that cannot be found in current debates about 'varieties of capitalism'.[1]

The idea of an endgame that is already being played is constitutive for critical theory. In Marx, it appears in the form of the self-overcoming tendencies of capitalism, as a combined result of competition and class struggle. In Lenin's view of imperialism as the highest stadium of capitalism, the idea of self-overcoming has been discarded and replaced by the emphasis on the voluntarism of a revolutionary avant-garde that will spell the end of capitalism. In Adorno, as will be shown in detail below, a totalizing vision of a society in which everything is dominated by a single logic leads to profound pessimism. The debates of the 1970s and of the 1990s are less focused but the idea of a terminal state of the social configuration is similarly central.

The persuasiveness of this idea of an endgame can – very broadly – be related to the respective historical state of capitalism itself. Marx himself was writing at a time of liberal ideology and rapid growth of world trade and was thus led to uncover the hidden dynamics of capitalism in terms of commodification, exploitation and alienation. He did not live to witness the nationalization of European societies with the building of social policy institutions from the late nineteenth century onwards, during which a revisionist Marxism emerged that indeed saw a prospect for social change due to reformist collective action in nation-states. The world economic crisis of 1929 and the rise of Nazism provided the context for the renewed plausibility of a totalizing view of the dynamics of capitalism, whereas the return to democracy after the Second World War shifted the emphasis again to significant varieties of political possibilities. This 'cycle' is reflected in Adorno's work, as will be discussed below. In the more recent past, the rise of 1970s neo-Marxism, after the student revolt and during the first post-war recession, was followed during the 1980s by a return of the political, this movement being usefully illustrated by the names of Louis Althusser and Elmar Altvater for the first period and the renewed interest in the works of Claude Lefort and Hannah Arendt for the second – the latter being authors who always were or became critical of the critical tradition precisely for reasons of neglect of the political. Finally, the rise of neo-liberalism was easily accepted by critical thinkers as a hegemonic *pensée unique* to which 'there is no alternative' in an era of globalization, while there are currently signs that this intellectual fashion nears its end.

From this ultra-brief contextual history of critical theory, one may easily conclude that the central ideas of this tradition swing helplessly in and out of fashion with the economic and political tides. The main tenets of the theory are seen as refuted by the next historical transformation, only to be re-instituted a historical moment later. This, however, would be too simple a view of the mirroring of intellectual and socio-economic change. As shall be demonstrated in what follows, it is more fruitful to try to reconstruct the main argument of critical theory, to some extent inevitably against the intentions of its proponents, to see more clearly what is dead in this intellectual tradition and what is alive and can still serve us in our attempt at understanding the development of capitalism. Such a reconstruction will be attempted here focusing on a single but central contributor to critical theory, Theodor W. Adorno.

Samuel Beckett's *Endgame*, first performed in 1957, seems to have anticipated and joined together two diagnoses of our time that should emerge in their explicit forms only much later: on the one hand, the post-modernist notion that all meta-narratives of emancipation have been exhausted, and that words have lost all of their meaning; and on the other hand, the conviction that global capitalism based on neo-liberal ideology effectively rules the world. The two protagonists of the play, Clov and Hamm, are individuals of the kind presented in those diagnoses. Even though they still speak, they are highly alienated both from one another and from the world. Almost any social bond between them, and towards their parents, Nell and Nagg, the only other two persons on stage, seems to be severed. The references to the other address only needs that emerge from damaged lives, and those needs remain unsatisfied. The memory of an earlier, richer social bond is still on the mind, but it can no longer be retrieved in communication. What dominates, in contrast, is the wish to leave the other, a wish that remains unfulfilled because nobody is in fact able to leave. And this is a condition that is no longer going to change. The endgame does not lead to an end; it is going to last.

Theodor Adorno (1974) recognized the force of this representation immediately.[2] A text from 1958, titled 'Attempt to Understand the Endgame', discusses the play as a representation of the human condition 'in the face of permanent catastrophe', of 'infinite catastrophe' and in light of the 'fact of damage' (pp. 292, 319 and 289) as well as a further, and presumably higher, step in the history of modernism, the one in which modernism turns into 'that in modernity which has come of age' (p. 281). The exploration of these themes, in turn, is grounded in a broader reading of *Endgame*: 'The misery of the participants in the endgame is the misery of philosophy' (p. 295); and the misery of philosophy stems from its inability to grasp 'historical tendency' and 'social truth' (pp. 287 and 289). Philosophy always has to be social theory at the same time, according to Adorno, and in our times such social theory will importantly have to draw on an analysis of capitalism.

Individual, rationality, capitalism: rise and fall of the autonomous subject

Adorno reads *Endgame* as a diagnosis of the present. In its centre, he identifies the 'liquidation of the subject',[3] which leaves only 'asocial partners' in unintelligible interaction (pp. 287, 290 and 309). He tries to understand this condition first philosophically, namely in the light of the history of the subject as it was conceived across one and a half centuries of history of philosophy from idealism to existentialism (pp. 290–1). The 'hypostasis of the individual' emerges in idealism, finding its full form in 'Fichte's free deed' (pp. 293 and 310).[4] In existentialism, the relation between individual and context, recast as the person who experiences her/himself aspiring towards harmony with the situation, is philosophized suprahistorically as the 'once and for all of Dasein' – at a moment, though, that turns out to be precisely the 'point of history that breaks' (p. 288).[5] This 'historical moment' is the one in which 'the individual has revealed itself as a historical category, as a result of the capitalist process of alienation and as a stubborn protest against it, as something again perishable' (pp. 285 and 290).

At this point, thus, Adorno connects the history of the philosophy of the subject to the history of capitalism, and he does so by suggesting a historical process that comes full circle. The positing of the all-powerful subject corresponds to the moment of the rise of capitalism whereas, at the advanced stage of mid-twentieth-century capitalism, the transitory nature of this positing becomes evident when the subject turns out to be a historical phenomenon, at the point of withering away. For a fuller discussion of capitalism by Adorno, one would have to turn to the *Dialectics of Enlightenment*, but even in this text the main contours are clear. In terms of its material effects, capitalism is seen as objectifying the world and as annihilating everything natural, everything that precedes capitalism.

Capitalism produces these outcomes because the radical positing of the subject eliminates constraints on human autonomy and enables the hubristic thought of human omnipotence to emerge. This tension between the modern commitment to freedom and autonomy, on the one hand, and its outcome in the form of world objectification and destruction, on the other, leads to what Adorno calls the irrationality of rationalization, in line with other twentieth-century social theorists such as Max Weber and Cornelius Castoriadis. In the context of his discussion of *Endgame*, Adorno links this insight to the concept of absurdity, seeing the latter as precisely the 'contradiction between the rational façade and the unalterably irrational' (p. 308).

Thus, the emergence, or so it seems during the 1950s, of the absurd as a world-view does not mean the overcoming of the rational world-view, rather 'the latter comes to itself in the former' (p. 310). Mobilizing the Hegelian motive of *Aufhebung* (sublation), but turning its meaning around, Adorno, again in affinity to Weber, proposes a concept of self-annihilation of capitalist modernity, and sees the endgame as the period in which the contradiction between the rational and the irrational moves towards resolution in accomplished self-annihilation.

At close reading, Adorno's position on the terminal nature of this endgame is unclear. In the phrase: 'ratio, having become completely instrumental, bare of any self-determination and of any determination of that which it disqualified, must ask for the meaning that was cancelled by itself' (p. 319), for instance, everything hinges on the meaning of 'must'. If it refers to a mere normative demand, then this demand can be seen as finally unrecognized after the cancellation of meaning, and the game is over. If there is something in the rational, though, that compels it to sustain the quest for meaning even under those conditions, then the contradiction stays alive. In the broader context of Adorno's writings, the former interpretation finds more support. In the analysis of Beckett's play, for instance, he links the analysis of objectification and alienation to core concerns of language and philosophy. The disintegration of language leads to illusions of communication (pp. 306–7), and truth threatens to disappear from sight as the 'possibility of something true that cannot even be thought anymore' arises (p. 319).[6] In conclusion of such line of thought, Adorno states the inescapability of 'negative ontology' (p. 319) and notes that the contemporary world is in such a state of regression that it disposes of 'no counter-concept anymore' that could be held against that regression (p. 289).

Extracting from these notes Adorno's perspective on capitalist society, we can see that he links a very basic conceptualization of *capitalism*, which focuses on alienation and reification and was readily available for him through the Marxist tradition, with a social *epistemology* that draws on the Enlightenment quest for truth and freedom but is employed here to assess the intelligibility of capitalism from within a given capitalist society, and combines both with a long-term view on history – or rather with a rudimentary *philosophy of history* – that links the advance of capitalism with the decreasing persuasiveness of the concept of the autonomous individual and the decline in the intelligibility of the world.

This combination of an analysis of capitalism with epistemology and philosophy of history shaped Adorno's approach to a theory of society. Already in a lengthy discussion of Karl Mannheim's *Mensch und Gesellschaft im Zeitalter des Umbaus*, written in 1937,[7] Adorno appreciates Mannheim's attempt at providing a diagnosis of the contemporary social transformations but identifies as its major problem its specific epistemic claim to provide a 'value-free' analysis of society. In his critical review, Adorno diagnoses an 'overestimation of appearances' as the consequence of that stand, and this overestimation in turn entails the neglect of the more important underlying reality of capitalism. In such light, most significantly, major political changes, such as what Mannheim calls 'fundamental democratisation', are seen as a 'phenomenon of mere façade' (Adorno 1986a, p. 17; see again pp. 43ff.) that can only be properly understood on the basis of a fuller theory of capitalist society that does not depend for its conceptualizations on the observation of appearances.

Such a view, though, places a gigantic burden on the 'genuine theory of society' into whose context the findings of social research have to be placed, according to Adorno (1986a, p. 44). To see how far his own social theory lived up to this exigency, a look at his writings about those same phenomena, related to 'mass democracy', of which he claimed that mainstream sociology was unable to grasp them properly, is necessary. Adorno, namely, even though these aspects of his work are largely forgotten, was interested in political institutions, in the actual running of public affairs, and was able to make distinctions within the same totality of 'capitalist society'.

Democracy under conditions of capitalism: Adorno as a political scientist

Rather than insisting on considering 'fundamental democratisation' as a mere 'phenomenon of façade', as he did in 1937, Adorno acknowledged in 1949 that the 'idea[s] of democracy' can be given 'a more concrete meaning' if and when democratic leadership takes the place of the prevailing forms of mass manipulation: 'Today perhaps more than ever, it is the function of democratic leadership to make the subjects of democracy, the people, conscious of their own wants and needs as against the ideologies which are hammered into their heads by the innumerable communications of vested interests' (Adorno 1986b, p. 268). In the position Adorno takes here, significant differences between empirically existing varieties of democracy exist; and no theoretical insight imposes the conclusion that under conditions of capitalism the idea of democracy will always only be applied 'in a merely formalistic way' (Adorno 1986b, p. 268).

This observation is confirmed when Adorno in 1951 explicitly addresses the 'difference in political climate between America and Germany': 'The American state, namely, is well recognized by its citizens as a societal form of organisation, but nowhere as one that flows above the lives of the individuals, that commands them or forms even an absolute authority.' In the US, according to the returned exile, large parts of the population do not have 'the feeling that the state is something other than they themselves', and Adorno goes as far as claiming that this nuance of difference between McCarthyist USA and post-Nazi Germany entails 'a more felicitous relation between the supreme form of societal organisation and its citizens' in the former (Adorno 1986c, pp. 290–1).

A year later, Adorno continues his reflections about the state of democracy by addressing a theme that would gain much more prominence in the work of Jürgen Habermas rather shortly afterwards, the formation of public opinion. His observations on opinion research contain elements of the critique of a merely aggregative mode of empirical social research that were at the centre of his articles on sociology and empirical research. However, he not only insisted that richer forms of opinion research – 'in closest context with the most advanced knowledge about society as a whole' – are possible (and indeed experimented with in Frankfurt), he also praises the 'democratic potential' of opinion research that 'in consciousness of the contradictoriness of our societal state' can develop towards the fulfilment of its 'genuine democratic function' (Adorno 1986d, pp. 300–1).

One can again recognize here Adorno's concern for varieties of democracy, some of which are normatively more desirable than others, and the attainability of which needs to be assessed with the help of a social theory that does not preclude by theoretical fiat any of those possibilities but that is interested in the analysis of the state of the 'societal play of forces': 'In a society in which democracy is meant to be neither an empty slogan nor a merely formal principle, it will at least be necessary to assess, ever again, from below, all institutional claims to represent public opinion' (Adorno 1986d, p. 295).

One may want to question the value of these of Adorno's writings. The comparison of political organization in the USA and Germany may today resonate with those strands in the revival of republican political thought that claim continued existence of that political tradition in the history of the USA, but it will sound at least crass and surprisingly one-sided from the pen of this very European intellectual (Adorno 1986e, p. 394), and is rather devoid of any more sophisticated insight from historical political sociology. And in the light of Jürgen Habermas's analysis of the structural transformation of the public sphere, Adorno's hope for a democracy-sustaining version of opinion research appears unfoundedly optimistic.[8]

As weak as the analyses are in substance, however, these political writings demonstrate that there were elements in Adorno's thought that lent themselves to the elaboration of a social theory in which political organization gains significance on its own and accounts for important varieties of societal configurations. These elements, however, appear as a rather minor thread in Adorno's work, they do not add up to any sustained component of his theorizing, and accordingly they have never altered the underlying social ontology of his social theory.

Theorizing the present: the task of social theory

Adorno's social theory remained firmly anchored in the totalizing 'critique of bourgeois society' (p. 284). And, overall, the elements of a more subtle nature, some of which were retrieved above, can hardly be seen as providing the 'concrete mediation' (Adorno 1986a, p. 25) between the basic theory and the appearances that Adorno himself had called for. The reason for this lack, however, should not be sought primarily in Adorno's difficulty to relate the theoretical to the empirical. If these aspects and elements of his work have remained rather undeveloped, substantive reasons for such neglect must be taken into account.

Returning to Adorno's interpretation of *Endgame*, the suspicion arises that he himself, while being able to formulate the key criteria for a needed philosophy and social theory, was aware of the fact that such philosophy and social theory remained still on the horizon and were far from being accomplished. Shortly after having stated that 'the irrationality of bourgeois society in its late phase is resistant towards attempts to be grasped; those were good times still, when a critique of bourgeois society could be written that took that society by its own ratio', he adds, slightly hesitatingly, the call: 'One could almost turn that into a criterion for a necessary philosophy: that it shows itself at the height of this' (p. 284).

The precise meaning of this call depends on the referent for the final 'this', which, however, remains unclear. It could be that Adorno demands of philosophy to analyse bourgeois society critically by demonstrating that its irrationality has taken on such a form that it can no longer be grasped. This would be in line with his reference to a 'negative ontology' in the same text and with the gist of the later *Negative Dialectics*. But it would also mean abandoning philosophy altogether, which thus would not show itself 'at the height' of this situation at all but would declare itself defeated by the hegemony of the irrational. And, furthermore, it would mean accepting the performative contradiction that arises when a quite ordinarily intelligible analysis of capitalism is mobilized as the foundation for identifying the utter unintelligibility of society. Another interpretation seems much more fruitful. The necessary philosophy would show itself 'at the height' of the situation in as far as it places into the centre of its attention not the irrationality of contemporary bourgeois society – for which 'late phase', by the way, has not proven to be a useful term – as such, but its resistance to being grasped, and to do this by analysing the specific nature of the contradiction between the rational and the irrational under contemporary conditions.

If Adorno did not entirely make up his mind about this choice, this indecisiveness seems to stem from a dilemma that critical social theory faces up to the present day. On the one hand, the longing of critical theory since Marx has been the identification of a dynamics that could be denounced as driving societal development towards normatively ever more undesirable states. To fulfil this longing, a theoretical argument had to be deployed that was applicable with a considerable degree of generality: such dynamics would need to exist across all capitalist societies and it would need to unfold over time.[9] Critique would gain its power in proportion to the generalizability of its denunciation. On the other hand, such an approach, if taken to extremes, disarms itself in as far as it tends to present an insurmountable dynamics, in the face of which all human action is futile. And it risks losing plausibility whenever and wherever societal developments are too varied and too complex to sit easily with any sweeping generalization. Adorno's early attempt to declare 'fundamental democratisation' of European societies after the First World War as rather insignificant succumbs to such a verdict, but his later writings on democracy try to remedy the earlier misjudgement, even though never in a fully convinced way. The interpretation of *Endgame* consciously combines the radical version of the argument about an underlying dynamics of capitalist society with a historical diagnosis that situates the present at 'the nadir' of the history of the subject and, we may say, of modernity. This, precisely, is Adorno's Hegelianism in reverse.

This theoretical attitude, however, can much more easily be criticized than it can be entirely discarded. The strong alternative, which would emphasize the contingency of historical developments and, thus, the plurality and diversity of existing varieties of capitalist societies, both across time and across space, risks replacing the problematic overconfidence in theoretical presupposition and teleological reasoning with mere observational detail and/or flat presentism (see Arnason 2005 for a constructively critical discussion of this debate). Adorno's way of theorizing, in contrast, preserves a sense of long-term transformations, and of some direction of such transformations, that indeed can be experienced – even though during some periods more than others. The critical rendering of such an experience is the one of loss; and in Adorno's version this loss is not conceptualized in a conservative way, as the loss of a more harmonious past, but as a modernist critique of modernity, a critique of modernity's tendency towards self-cancellation. At this point, the distinction between the two ways of interpreting Adorno, as introduced above, becomes crucial.

If Adorno needs to be read as seeing modernity's self-cancellation as accomplished, then no rise from the nadir of critical theory is thinkable. History has unfolded in such a way that it entirely confirms the critical theoretical presuppositions. If Adorno – maybe against himself – can, however, also be read as offering a diagnosis of a specific present, marked by a particular – historically prepared, but not determined – articulation of the tension between the rational and the irrational, then his theorizing can offer elements upon which an appropriate recasting of the relation between a historical-empirical analysis of societal developments in the recent past and present and a social and political theory of capitalist modernity can be built – elements that exist neither in standard versions of Marxism nor in the presentist expressions of the debate on the varieties of capitalism. To see how Adorno's work can be put to such use, I need to redescribe it first in terms of the sociology of modernity I aim to put forward here.

Critical theory, political philosophy and the theorizing of modernity

Recasting it in such terminology, Adorno's theoretical position entailed a view of modernity as focused on a certain conception of the economic *problématique*, i.e., capitalism as economic modernity, in alliance with a certain view of the epistemic *problématique*, i.e., the world to be known in as far as it is measurable and carved up into quantifiable elements. The particular nature of Adorno's approach stems from three features that we have already noted above but that can now be discussed in different terms. *First*, he takes the analysis of economic modernity for granted, namely as the critical analysis of the outcome of the liberation of economic action, basically accomplished since Marx, and recognizes the inescapable tendency of such economic modernity towards alienation and reification. *Second*, epistemic modernity, i.e., the Enlightenment tradition, while inaugurating the theme of the free subject, was misconstruing the human being as an abstract individual and thus failed to develop an adequate notion of autonomy. *Thirdly*, the historical trajectory of economic and political modernity was conjoined in such a way that the rise of capitalism accompanied the 'zenith' of the philosophy of the autonomous subject, now identifiable as a misconception and an illusion, while the full development of capitalism marks the 'nadir', the 'endgame' of any such conception.[10]

In more general, say, for want of a better expression, meta-theoretical terms, this thinking is characterized by a very strong social ontology, and this in two major respects. First, it deploys its concepts in such a way that they, and the conceptual edifices they contribute to, are 'stretched' to cover a large variety of societal situations, basically the history of the northwestern quarter of the world since the Enlightenment and since the industrial and market revolution. Second, the basic concepts are arranged in such a way that the same, static conceptual constellation determines the entire 'spatio-temporal envelope' (Bruno Latour) that the theory postulated. To speak very crudely, this constellation meant some *economic-epistemic* determinism in the light of which all other aspects of human social life fade into insignificance. Most importantly, for my purposes here, such conceptual arrangement implies that it is impossible for any expression of *political* modernity, of collective self-determination, to acquire significance for the understanding of modernity overall, or of certain historical forms of it.

By describing Adorno's social theory in such a way, a first step is made to advance the claim, to be detailed in what follows, that an alternative social theory and political philosophy is possible that retains the critical capacity of Adorno's approach, but that is able to address varieties of configurations of modernity, again both across space and over time, in a more differentiated and, thus, more adequate way. The social ontology of such an approach needs to be 'weaker' than Adorno's in two precise ways, each one leading to an opening towards a mode of inquiry that was underused in the theorizing of the classical Frankfurt School. First, it needs to accept the possibility that configurations of modernity are of such a variety that a move from one to another requires conceptual change, change in the language of interpretation. This insight requires an opening towards historical-comparative sociology, and in particular towards those – mostly more recent – strands of historical sociology that are conscious of social change being accompanied as well as brought about by reinterpretations of the human condition (see chapter 13 for more detail). This latter aspect leads over to the second ontological move. The required social ontology needs to be weak also in the sense of accepting that, even for a precisely delineated given social configuration, its concepts do not exhaustively determine the social world. Rather, it would recognize that its concepts, drawn as they always are from the social world that they refer to, are also elements of justification either of a given social arrangement or of activities to create a different social arrangement (see chapter 12 for more detail). In the history of social theory, this insight was of course not unknown, but it was translated into the opposition between affirmative and critical social theory, a dispute that was meant to be decided by epistemic means alone. Instead, the observation would need to be led to the more general insight that normative justifications, and disputes over them, are empirical components of a social configuration. This insight leads the theory then to an opening towards normative politico-philosophical reasoning, not in the sense of a separate discipline, though, but as an integral part of both the societal analysis and of the positioning of the theoretical endeavour itself.

Taking both of these elements together, an image of the 'necessary philosophy' emerges as a comprehensive, politico-philosophically sensitive historical sociology of social configurations of modernity, at the core of which the relation between social theory and political philosophy is kept open and in which the elaboration of a critical diagnosis of the time is an objective that is to be accomplished by means of situating the present within a historical horizon that is not determined by any logic of development but the interpretation of which itself is a persistent task in the present. The meaning and effect of the integration of either of these two elements will be discussed in some more substantive detail in the following, starting with the opening towards political philosophy and moving subsequently to the question of historicization.

Critical theory and the place of the political: the purposes and the common

The duo of approaches to social theory that dominated much of the post-Second World War period, critical theory and (neo-)Marxism, on the one hand, and the evolutionary social science of modern societies, on the other, shared the assumption that social configurations were shaped and held together by social processes and structures of social relations. It was, thus, jointly opposed to all thought that considered societies to be (always) politically constituted in the first place, a thinking that was for a long time confined to political philosophy and even lived there rather at the margins. In the light of the above, however, the question of the justification of collective action within a polity as well as the one of the self-understanding of a polity in its boundaries needs to be an integral part of a comprehensive social theory.

For the sake of clarity of reasoning, it is useful to pursue this issue by starting out from the perspective that takes the political, and in particular the constitution of the polity, as the primary question of social and political theory, as is the case with the approaches proposed by Hannah Arendt and Claude Lefort and to a considerable extent also by Cornelius Castoriadis. The political is here understood as all action that is concerned with determining which matters are common to members of a collectivity and with handling them in common. As already discussed above (see Overture to Part I), the question of the political can be seen as being approached in a modern way if and when a collectivity deliberates about these issues autonomously, in collective self-determination. Significantly, political action, on the one hand, presupposes a collectivity to determine both the reach of the 'common' and, under modern conditions, the right to participation in self-determination. On the other hand, the determination of the boundaries of a polity is itself a political act, a constitutive one and, thus, possibly the most important one. Only a political thinking that does not, or at least not fully, accept the 'imaginary signification of modernity' can either ignore the latter question entirely, because it sees polities as always already pre-constituted, or draw on non-political resources to find an answer to the question of the constitution of the polity, such as the assumption of a need for a common language did in nationalist political thought. In contrast, modern political thought needs to take the question of the founding of the polity as the most fundamental political question of all. Accordingly, it has, from social contract theory onwards, included a hypothesis about the founding moment in its reasoning, even though often only to keep the issue at bay and move on to consider the workings of an already constituted polity.

This latter move has contributed to obscuring the impact that founding assumptions can have on the very understanding of the political. The tradition of contract theory postulates that human beings, who are ontologically separate individuals, enter into association for a common *purpose*. This understanding paved the way for a later social science that lost the sense of the political. Sociology drew on the term 'society', which originally referred to an association for a purpose, for the conceptualization of its basic unit of analysis. Accordingly, functionalism aims to explain societal development as needs-driven, thereby obscuring the fact that such explanation resides in nothing but a prior assumption. The conceptual alternative within the framework of social science becomes clear when one compares Ernest Gellner's insistence that the functional needs of industrialism were the driving force behind nation-building in Europe, on the one hand, with, on the other, the assumption that some common world, here conceptualized as residing in the common hermeneutic engagement with the world through language, must pre-exist collective action because common purposes can only be developed or identified on such a basis.

The question whether polities are constituted over common *purpose* or by virtue of the fact of togetherness and *sharing a world* and common problems can to some degree be opened to historical investigation, including importantly comparative investigation of highly differently constituted polities. But it will not be answered by those means. Even if one takes a cautious stand, though, and accepts the existence of common needs and purposes, to be dealt with by a division of social labour, for instance, the decision to deal with such needs and purposes in common will always remain a political act. Therefore, a conceptual move that makes the political derivative of the economic is in no way justified, or, in other words, the *problématique* of political modernity cannot be subordinated to the *problématique* of economic modernity, as happened in critical theory.

At the same time, however, the gliding from a socio-economically driven social theory to a mode of political philosophy that detaches the political from the socio-economic, as a response to the above, also needs to be avoided. Such gliding has occurred both in mainstream individualist liberalism and in some more radical thinkers such as, notably, Hannah Arendt and, to a lesser degree, Claude Lefort; it is part of the general intellectual devaluation of sociology and critical theory compared to the renewed interest in individualist political theorizing and the rise of cultural studies. A more appropriate response would have to conceptually articulate the political with the economic.[11]

Such articulation could start out from a double assumption: first, rather than being asocial or apolitical, the modes of dealing with needs, in as far as they *relate* human beings to each other, create a common. The term 'relation' refers to a variety of highly different phenomena, which also have found different degrees of attention in social theory. The very *creation of community by exchange* is a theme known from at least the idea of *doux commerce*, as discussed by Albert Hirschman (1977), for instance. In such light, extension of exchange relations thus potentially also *extends community*, historically diagnosed – in sometimes overdrawn ways – as extension from the local to the national, and as extension from the national to the global today. Such extension of exchange, though, may also *disrupt existing community organization* by breaking out of existing confinements – a strong theme in Marx – and then, in turn, support arguments and, eventually, action towards *re-creation of community*, such as the conscious building of inclusive national arrangements in response to the threat of the 'dissolution of society', as analysed by Karl Polanyi (1985). In this latter case, the *relation* in question takes on the particular nature of *regulation* and becomes a conscious collective act, a society acting upon itself by political means, with varying degrees of participation – in Europe moving historically towards the internally all-inclusive, externally closed form of modern democracy – and of deliberation.[12]

The historical horizon of contemporary capitalism: the plausibility of modernity's self-cancellation

Even though the last remarks have resorted to the means of historical illustration, thus far only a general conceptual scheme has been offered. It is richer than Adorno's way of integrating the analysis of capitalism into a comprehensive social theory and thus begs the question whether there are any strong reasons why Adorno's thought did not move in a similar direction. An answer to that question was already hinted at above: his observations of society led Adorno to the suspicion that long-term historical transformations had occurred that could not be grasped by considering the relations between political, economic and epistemic modernity as an open constellation containing a variety of possible interpretations, but that, instead, a particular articulation reigned in a rather durable way over European and North American societies. We have described this articulation as an economic-epistemic determinism that erases the political, or, in terms of the imaginary signification of modernity, as a configuration in which the commitment to autonomy under the conditions of capitalism as the prevailing form of economic modernity produces reification and alienation that, in turn, undermine the search for certain knowledge and the attempts at collective self-determination, i.e., the expression of autonomy in epistemic and political terms.

In the conceptual terminology proposed here, this diagnosis describes a *historical possibility*, which is formulated in somewhat extreme form but which cannot be ruled out as a possibility, indeed needs to be taken seriously as a possibility that finds at least partial confirmation in observations of social life. Given the structure of the argument, it will never be possible to fully assert such diagnosis as an empirical given at a certain moment in history. Its force as a critical diagnosis of the present resides more in the *identification of normatively problematic tendencies* in modernity. To sustain it in a credible way, however, one would need a *historically plausible* account of a major change in the ways in which the various *problématiques* of modernity are addressed, a change that makes the self-cancellation of modernity likely. In the following, the basic elements of construction of such an account shall be sketched, even though in a very crude way. At this point, the account first of all aims to perform the two openings that were presented above as necessary for a revived critical social theory, the opening to political philosophy and to historical sociology (for more substantive detail, see the subsequent chapters 6 and 7 of this volume).

The threefold commitment to autonomy and mastery that was discussed above is often seen as finding historical expression in the scientific and philosophical revolution, in the market and industrial revolution and in the liberal and democratic revolution. Any detailed analysis will show that justifications were given in and for those great transformations that at least partly resonated with the modern commitment to – individual and collective – autonomy and mastery. However, even while neglecting all historical qualification and comparison, we can state that none of the three events determined the others and, more particularly, that none of them can be regarded as having been brought about by the consolidated interest of a rising capitalist class, the bourgeoisie. How then, one needs to ask, assuming that Adorno's view has some validity, is it possible that a certain interpretation of economic modernity cannot only prevail but also dominate over the others in such a way that self-cancellation threatens to occur?

The reasoning proceeds in three steps. First, a tendency towards self-cancellation can be diagnosed already with regard to individual aspects of the *problématique* of modernity. Thus, Marx accepted the commitment to autonomy as a background for the rise of capitalism, expressed in the liberation of economic action both as freedom of commerce and as freedom to buy and sell labour power. However, he asserted that 'behind the backs' of the actors this freedom was undermined by the transformation of human relations into relations between things, between commodities. Reification of the world and alienation of the human beings from their own selves, from others and from the world are the result (see chapter 1 for a discussion of the critiques of modernity).

This diagnosis, though, secondly, does not offer any reason why such problematic development could not be halted or reversed within the context of a societal configuration, or in Polanyi's words, by virtue of the embeddedness of economic action. A belief in the balancing between the various *problématiques* of modernity was indeed held by the Enlightenment conviction of a harmonious unfolding of freedom and reason, and it was revived in Talcott Parsons' functionalist account of modernity in which the separate workings of the subsystems of society will provide an overall beneficial outcome. Despite his insistence that under capitalist conditions false consciousness held human beings in its grip and that institutionalized political action was reduced to the workings of the executive committee of the bourgeoisie, Marx himself saw a reversal of such epistemic and political condition as possible in principle, unlike Adorno, at least according to the predominant interpretation of the latter's writings. Between Enlightenment optimism and Frankfurt School pessimism, a conceptually more open perspective would hold that the various *problématiques* of modernity, even though all based on an assumption of autonomy, are likely to express themselves in different 'rationalities', to use Adorno's terms, and that there is no a priori reason to assume that those rationalities would be balanced by the working of some higher principle. Thus, the tension between the individual rationalities may give rise to an overall irrationality, as Weber and, following him, Adorno assumed.

But still, thirdly, such lack of reconciliation does not necessarily entail the dominance of one rationality – in the case of these analyses, an individualist-instrumental one – over all the others. Conceptually speaking, the reasoning should keep pursuing the issue as one of an articulation between the various *problématiques* of modernity. In particular, any argument about the dominance of one aspect over the others would also need to give reasons for the weakness of those others. After all, it has been maintained until the 1970s, and not without practical results, that a political embedding of economic action is possible in the context of the European nation-state, on the assumption that the direction of regulatory action could be determined on the basis of rather certain knowledge about the common world that one is referring to (see chapter 6).

The forms of knowledge in question were, in particular, a political philosophy that translated its conception of justice into ideas about a political community of responsibility, and a socio-economic theory that could balance apparently opposed interests in the framework of a broader theory of society and its development. The former was a compromise between a liberal and cultural-linguistic theory of the polity, and the latter the conjoining of Keynesianism with the sociology of modernization. Such knowledge forms underpinned the democratic Keynesian welfare state of the post-Second World War period. They were never beyond critique and a detailed analysis of their operation is still needed at the time of their demise. However, their persistence and efficacity over a relatively long period demonstrates that action in common with reference to a world in common is possible even under conditions of advanced capitalism, or, in other words, that the commitments to epistemic and political modernity do not necessarily become completely subordinated to the capitalist interpretation of economic modernity.

This observation provides the key for rephrasing the question. If, and in as far as, there is nevertheless validity in Adorno's perspective, one would need to show how action in common with reference to a common world becomes more difficult under conditions of capitalism. A reasoning of plausibility for such difficulty to arise can indeed now be provided. The difficulties arise from the conjoined effect of two historical transformations in the development of European capitalism and democracy.

For the sake of simplicity, we assume that pre-capitalist, pre-democratic Europe was a rather stable world in which autocratic rulers defined the common and acted upon it as a master does in his household. The scientific and philosophical revolution, our historical shorthand for epistemic modernity, cast doubt on the stability of the world, partly in thought but more significantly in experimental action (see chapter 8 below). The market and industrial revolution, our historical shorthand for economic modernity, introduced a hitherto unknown idea of infinity into the way of dealing with needs. This idea, now mostly known as the profit motive, suggested the liberation of economic forces through formally free exchange of commodities on markets and, thus, inaugurated an accumulation-driven economy, which, in turn, found support in the means provided by science-enabled technology. In this combination of effects, persistent and rapid processes of world transformation were inaugurated.

The liberal and democratic revolution, in turn, our historical shorthand for political modernity, gradually widened the free participation of inhabitants of a territory in the deliberation about the common matters to be dealt with in common. One can assume, *ceteris paribus*, that the widening of political involvement entails an increasing diversity of views about the common and about the rules to regulate it. The attempts at organizing modernity from the late nineteenth century onwards can precisely be interpreted as a means to counteract such rising diversity while accepting the inescapable commitment to inclusive democracy (see Wagner 1994). The more individual human beings see themselves as 'unit citizens' with a stake of their own in the determination of the common, that is, the less they see themselves as tied into pre-existing networks of social relations held together by common values and beliefs (with those networks defining the boundaries of the polity itself or at least an identifiable sector of the polity), the more difficult will the deliberation about common matters become.

Considering these two processes together, the transformation of the world and the transformation of the political relations between human beings, and accepting them as by and large valid descriptions of the history of the past two or three centuries, the idea that an economic-epistemic determinism de facto reigns over the world becomes plausible. The more problematic the creation of a relation to a common world and to particular others becomes, the more compelling becomes a relation to the world that focuses on the measurable and a relation to others that starts out from the individual atom, both relations joined together by an instrumental attitude. This view of human relations is not convincing as such, and theoretically it is flawed as many discussions in social and political philosophy have demonstrated; it is compelling, however, as a default view in the absence of attainable other views (see Wagner 2001a, chapter 6).

And it becomes particularly difficult to avoid in historical moments in which the attainability of other views is extremely low. This was the case during the 1950s after life- and world-destroying deeds and events of unprecedented nature; and it may be so again at the beginning of the twenty-first century, after an era of rapid technological change and the extension of relations of exchange in terms of trade and of communication. The paradox of so-called globalization resides in the fact that, on the one hand, the world was never as common as nowadays, the extension of relations having created potential community, while, on the other hand, existing structures of communication about the common world – most importantly in the national polities, but also in the social sciences and philosophy – have been opened up, and uncertainty about the world in common has been increased as a consequence. Structures of collective self-determination at the global level, such as the United Nations, may then easily, even though erroneously, appear as a 'phenomenon of mere facade'. But globalization will need to be understood as world-making, as a dispute over varieties of possible modernities, now for the first time acted out on the global level. Such world-making takes the existing extended relations as a background and it needs to institute a frame of reference for it, as a common world, with a view to creating possibilities to act in common (see Karagiannis and Wagner 2007a).

In conclusion, then, it is important to retain Adorno's insight into the increasing difficulties to develop a valid view of the world in common, i.e., an answer to the epistemic *problématique*, and the increasing risk that collective self-determination, the answer to the political *problématique*, will have only superficial effects on the common matters. But while these difficulties indicate a strong possibility for the answer given to the economic *problématique* to dominate the other two, there is no necessity for this to occur.

Despite the reasoning of plausibility provided above, a reasoning loosely rooted in historical observation over the past two centuries, the articulation of the relation between the *problématiques* of modernity remains a matter of historical contingency. Such contingency is ultimately inscribed into the modern commitment to autonomy itself. Thus, there is no endgame in the history of modernity. The 'endgame' is a known hypothesis of social theory, as a combination of rational choice theory and individualist liberalism, but also in the post-modern liberalism of Richard Rorty's kind in its affirmative version, and in Marxism and critical theory in its critical version. But even if in the latter version the motive of alerting of an 'infinite catastrophe' that could already have occurred is understandable, such motive is ultimately nothing but the mirror-image of the complacency of affirmative social theory.

In the light of the above recasting of Adorno's position, the possibility of 'infinite catastrophe' needs to be counteracted by an analysis of the possibilities to act in common with a view to reconstituting a common reference to the world under contemporary conditions. Such analysis will require a social theory that is based on a historical sociology of changing configurations of modernity and that analyses the justifications for those varieties in terms of a political philosophy that is contextually sensitive in the sense of being aware of the empirically available justifications for each of those varieties. Adorno's position contains insights needed for such social theory that can be found neither in the rationalist-individualist and behaviourist-neo-positivist views of mainstream social science nor in the cultural studies that have taken much of the intellectual space held by critical theory in Adorno's times. But on its own, it does not yet provide an easy access way to such a 'necessary philosophy'.

6

Towards a Historical-Comparative Sociology of Capitalism

After having set out in general terms in the previous chapter that the relation between the three *problématiques* of human social life remains contingent under conditions of modernity and that any economic-epistemic determinism, to which critical theory is committed, is only one historical possibility among others, the present chapter will now discuss in some more historical detail if and how the relation between those *problématiques* may historically have been transformed in such a way that this possibility becomes plausible and probable. As a first step, we need to prepare the conceptual ground in some further, more specific way.[1]

Capitalism/modernity as changing interpretations of *problématiques*

The question of the relation between capitalism and modernity can now be recast in two steps as follows. First, the historical phenomenon known as the 'rise of modern capitalism', something that had a long gestation period but emerged forcefully in eighteenth-century England and somewhat later on the European continent and in North America, is to be explored, in theoretical terms, as precisely a shift in the relation between the epistemological and political *problématiques*, on the one hand, and the economic one, on the other. If the epistemological and the political *problématiques* had already been cast in 'modern' terms in ancient Greece, one may explore, second, whether the rise of capitalism needs to be related to something like the onset of 'economic modernity'. Kant's first two critiques, *The*

Critique of Pure Reason and *The Critique of Practical Reason*, can without doubt be read as forceful restatements of the cases for philosophical and political modernity. Are they then only coincidentally related to Adam Smith's *The Wealth of Nations*, which is often seen as inaugurating modern economic thinking? If not, what precisely is the relation between these parallel reinterpretations – or reiterations of particular interpretations – of the three *problématiques*? And why is it that the outcome of those reinterpretations appears to be – at least historically, if not theoretically – a shift in the relation between those *problématiques* themselves?

Capitalism can be seen, to phrase the issue in terms of classic thought, as a novel way of socially dealing with needs. Up to the eighteenth century, as mentioned above (in chapter 1), needs were mostly dealt with in 'private', in the household, even if a household could reach the size of a feudal principality. 'Public' ways of dealing with needs had been emerging more strongly, in particular with the markets in cities, but they had not yet become the organizing element of a social order, with the partial exception of trading polities such as the Hanseatic League, and to some extent the North Italian cities and the Dutch provinces. The radical alteration of this situation in some settings, in particular in Britain, during the eighteenth century is only insufficiently explained by the rise of a new class, the bourgeoisie, with new interests. It needed a 'spirit of capitalism' (Weber 1930) as well as 'political arguments for capitalism' (Hirschman 1977) to bring such radical change about.

The emergence of a spirit of capitalism entailed the rise in importance of 'economic' activities, of work, in human life (Zimmermann 2001a); the political arguments provided a justification for this increased importance for the collectivity, thus beyond individual salvation. They enabled the rearrangement of the basic institutional set-up of society, in particular in terms of granting the freedom of commerce, including the sale and acquisition of labour power – without a political revolution, unlike Marxists thought, since this change occurred in England rather than in France. What happened here was, in the first instance, a reinterpretation of the socio-political order, the introduction of a new imaginary signification of society, to use Castoriadis's terms, and legal-institutional changes that were intended to bring the socio-political order in line with the new imaginary signification.

At those origins, capitalism did not show any explicit commitment to the 'unlimited expansion of rational mastery', not least because not all other frameworks for social action were abolished (only some of them), and those other frameworks limited the reach of the new mode of justification. Even though Adam Smith's argument about the increase of the wealth of nations made a principled case for the functional superiority of the proposed arrangement, in terms of a better satisfaction of needs (and a pacification of social life), this did not entail historically that capitalism immediately imposed itself on other societies in competition, given that hardly any general argument that market exchange should orient *all* social life can be detected. Rather, we witness here the emergence of a new register of justification, a new *cité* in the sense of Luc Boltanski and Laurent Thévenot's *De la justification* (1991), the *cité marchande*. This register supported the institutional rearrangement, but it was far from reigning supreme. There were other justifications that *either* also played a part in justifying the change, but on different terms – such as the *cité d'inspiration*, suggesting a release of creativity – *or* that competed with the *cité marchande* – such as the *cité civique*, not least because of the predicted rise in inequality, to be counteracted by a concomitant 'rise of politics'.

In what sense then can these reorientations be related to questions of modernity? Above, the hypothesis has already been proposed that the late eighteenth century in Europe – Enlightenment cum romanticism – should not only be regarded as a period in which the claim for autonomy was revived (for this view, see Castoriadis 1997b, pp. 129–31; Habermas 1985, among many others), but also as one in which this claim was explicitly extended to realms for which it had not been seen as applicable before, such as the question of the satisfaction of needs. The claim for human autonomy is, on principle, linked to plurality and unpredictability of outcomes of the use of autonomy, as has long been recognized and indeed been taken to be the key question of political philosophy. The extension of autonomy to wider realms, thus, tends to exacerbate further the significance of this question.

Returning briefly to the preceding chapter in those terms, we can now see that the Marxian diagnosis of capitalism was already based on the acceptance of the rise of the economic *problématique* to new importance. His particular analysis asserts the structuring impact of the commodity relation, which emerges and becomes dominant in the realm of the satisfaction of needs, over the question of valid knowledge, then leading to distorted consciousness, and over the question of a normatively acceptable polity, namely as political emancipation falling short of human emancipation. In Marx's view, the liberty of commerce gave rise to an illusion of freedom, since it hid the asymmetry in the social relations of production, and this illusion infected all of social life. Nevertheless, it was not the dominance of the economic *problématique* over the political and the epistemic ones that was the fundamental issue for him. He tended to agree with such elevation of the question of needs as an essential part of the abolition of poverty and inequality, in particular in later writings. In his view, it was rather the flawed organization of the realm of the satisfaction of needs that was the source of the problem, and once this was remedied both the political and the epistemic *problématiques* could also be solved. All sophistication notwithstanding, critical theories of capitalism have ever since stayed very close to this basic conceptualization.

Assuming that a critical approach shares a normative commitment to autonomy and plurality (that is, to modernity if we accept these as constitutive characteristics of modernity), one cannot remain satisfied with this analysis. Beyond the general discussion in the preceding chapter, further specific questions need to be asked. Accepting for a moment the subdivision of realms, three major questions stand out. *First*, within the frame of the third *problématique* of the satisfaction of needs, does such standard critique of capitalism not denounce the liberty of commerce prematurely as an illusion? A fully satisfactory answer to this question is not easy, and I am very far from providing one here. However, it seems clear – in theoretical terms and not only after historical experimentation with alternative forms of productive organization – that the promise of liberation that accompanied the demand for the liberty of commerce is attractive far beyond any stereotypical bourgeoisie that had a class interest in it. The Marxian critique of commodification – in both its emphases, on exploitation and on alienation – needs to be seen as subsequent to an endorsement of 'free association' also in the realm of the satisfaction of needs. Any other approach would be non-modern in the sense of rejecting autonomy. If this is the case, though, market organization (including markets for labour power) is as a distinct possibility included under the auspices of 'economic modernity'. The projection of any 'beyond' the market as the *only* true realization of the project of modernity is not warranted as a conceptual step.

Nevertheless, capitalism does not become synonymous with 'economic modernity' by this conceptual move. Rather, it is based on a particular interpretation of the imaginary signification. Depending on how precisely one wants to define capitalism, it is based on an interpretation, first, that relies on the sale and acquisition of labour power, i.e., categorially distinct positions of human beings within such an order, as a fundamental operating mode, and second, that is driven by the need to realize profits under competitive conditions and thus shows a tendency towards 'the expansion of instrumental mastery'. Without outlining any full definition of capitalism myself, I will go no further here than claiming that these two features may usefully be taken to be constitutive of capitalism, but that they are not necessarily characteristic of any conceivable version of 'economic modernity', that is, the autonomous determination of ways to satisfy needs. The entire discussion about 'varieties of capitalism', as mentioned above, presupposes the openness of modernity, and of capitalism, to interpretation. Such interpretations become conceptually distinct by employing registers of justification in various ways. At the same time, they will be identifiable by historical-comparative analysis.

The further discussion of this first question becomes difficult, however, also because the resources needed for a fuller answer are not contained within the framework of the question alone. The suggestion, known from political economy and neo-classical economics, that the best way to satisfy needs is by unconstrained market exchanges, entails a strong delimitation of the reach of collective autonomy, namely to agreeing on accepting market rules of exchange. This act of acceptance, however, is not itself anything that occurs in a well-demarcated realm of the satisfaction of needs. Rather, it is an agreement about a rule among the members of a collectivity. As such, it pertains to the realm of the political *problématique*. This observation leads to questioning the very delimitation of realms, and thus to our further questions regarding the standard critique of capitalism.

The rejection of the idea that 'the market' could be – and, normatively, should be – separated from other social realms and be analysed according to its own laws stands at the centre of the standard critique of capitalism. This is indeed an appropriate and necessary part of any critical discussion of justifications of market-capitalist arrangements, such as currently in the guise of neo-liberalism. It remains an open question, however, how the relation between the 'market' and the 'non-market' is to be conceptualized differently – again, this entails an analytical and a normative question – and on the basis of which kind of knowledge such a conceptualization may proceed. Standard critiques of capitalism often have overly firm and distinct viewpoints on these issues. The second and the third question to be raised here address the grounds on which the standard critique of capitalism stabilizes the relation between the economic *problématique*, on the one hand, and the political and the epistemic *problématiques* respectively, on the other.

As regards the relation between the economic and the political *problématiques*, *second*, an ambivalent, not to say latently contradictory, view is often held. On the one hand, a capitalist response to the economic *problématique* is regarded as inevitably constraining the range of possible answers to the political *problématique*. These are versions of the argument about the priority of capitalism over modernity, as mentioned above (in the Overture to this Part). On the other hand, the liberation of the market forces is identified as being based on a political decision, which, in principle, can be reversed – and, normatively speaking, should be reversed, against all interest-based resistance. This view implies a principled primacy of the political over the economic *problématique*. Under conditions of modernity, with its emphasis on self-determination, this seems the appropriate view. Then, though, there is no conceivable theoretical argument why capitalism should constrain the exercise of collective autonomy. And even though a historical such argument is conceivable (as in Wood 1998, for instance), as a historical argument it would not hold under all circumstances. More precisely, it would hold either when capitalism precedes democracy (as a shorthand for the exercise of collective autonomy) or when capitalism in some situation or other has undermined existing democracy and from then onwards limits the possibilities for its reassertion. A particular set of circumstances in this respect is to be discussed below.

In this context, *thirdly*, it needs to be remembered that most – though not all – critiques of capitalism are but little interested in particular circumstances. They mostly proceed by theoretical reasoning, and they exude an air of certainty about the general claims they make that itself is at odds with modern ways of thinking about the epistemic *problématique*. The force that is seen as required of a critique pushes aside the doubt that is constitutive of epistemic modernity. It is, as mentioned in chapter 5, the 'critique of ideology' that proceeds by 'denunciation' and 'suspicion' that is at issue here. It cannot be denied that such approaches pursue a viable intellectual strategy, in principle. Some consideration of the fact, though, seems to be needed, that the entire approach was developed by Marx in a historical situation that was rather devoid of actual – epistemic as much as political – practices of autonomy and self-determination, and instead marked by strong cleavages and hierarchies that limited the access to such 'modern' practices. Since then, however, certainly West European and North American societies have witnessed the diffusion of such practices, although these fall radically short of any desired level, so that it seems difficult to maintain, if one ever could, that most human beings most of the time neither know what they are doing nor know what they want. Again, a constructive answer to this issue is difficult, but the objections to any straightforward application of 'critique of ideology' are strong enough not to pursue this path as the dominant, or even exclusive, intellectual strategy. If one did, one

would do nothing but undermine the modern commitment to autonomy and plurality with regard to knowledge practices (for more
detail, see chapters 8 and 9).

In sum, I have tried to argue that the standard critique of capitalism
does not itself live up to the requirements of modernity. Rather than
fully accepting the commitment to autonomy and, as a consequence,
the likely plurality of outcomes of the exercise of autonomy, it reasons
the issue away by establishing a conceptual hierarchy between the
problématiques of modernity as well as between the realms in which
those *problématiques* are supposed to be dealt with. This move
amounts ultimately to nothing but a rejection of these *problématiques*
– which are seen as being problematic only under capitalist conditions, but finding self-evident solutions once capitalism is overcome.
A critique that lives up to the modern commitment, in contrast, needs
to start out by accepting the *problématiques* and the variety of justifiable ways of dealing with them – with each single one of them as
much as with the arrangement of the relation between them.

This approach does not make critique impossible. This would be
the case only if all existing ways of dealing with the *problématiques*
were equally justifiable. What the approach does require, however, is
to take the justifications for certain historico-institutional arrangements seriously, rather than denouncing them as only an ideological
expression of a power struggle. What it is able to provide, in turn, is
an understanding for the conditions in which certain such arrangements – be they those that one may normatively regard as to be
avoided or those to be striven for – have become possible, or have
even imposed themselves with little choice or alternative. It is to such
a historical analysis of spatio-temporally varying interpretations of
the basic *problématiques* and their relations that I now return.

Capitalism/modernity as historical experience

Let us assume, for a start and despite the above-mentioned doubts,
that historical analysis had indeed confirmed the first radical breakthrough of capitalism as the reign of the commitment to the unlimited
expansion of rational mastery in eighteenth-century England.[2] Such
regional emergence tells us as yet very little about the likelihood of
the worldwide diffusion of such an arrangement. Certainly, politico-
economic elites on the European continent were impressed by the
rise of the English economy and they saw some need for action and
adaptation on their part. However, their attempts to promote their
economies remained long subordinated to other imperatives. Only

the free-trade agreements from around the middle of the nineteenth century can be interpreted as fully opening the door to the imposition of capitalism.[3] But then again, barriers to trade were increasingly being reintroduced from the 1870s onwards, and social policies were proposed and gradually introduced in response to 'the social question', leading to 'the fall of the market economy' during the first half of the twentieth century, as analysed by Karl Polanyi (1985).

In this light, it seems historically mistaken and conceptually misleading to analyse the rise of European capitalism from the point of view of its English origins.[4] The main intellectual source for this perspective is again Karl Marx who, however, did not live to see the full-fledged response to the first emergence of capitalism in Europe. Later, post-Second World War, authors inspired by this perspective reason against the background of indeed a much stronger assertion of capitalist rules and practices. Historically, however, they overlook the complex nature of European politico-economic arrangements during the century between 1870 and 1970. Conceptually, as a consequence, they assume a mode of imposition of capitalism that did not take place in this form and ignore the persistence of a large variety of registers of politico-moral evaluation. Thus, the actual reasons for such imposition, in as far as there were any at a later point, get obscured. I will just deal with one single, but historically as well as conceptually crucial, observation, namely the rise of America, or more specifically, of the USA.

Most contemporary critics of capitalism would admit that it is in an important sense American capitalism they refer to. The USA (still) holds the global reserve currency, is the source of many of the important technological innovations of our time, is the basis for the largest number of globally operating companies, dominates the global institutions and is the stronghold of the neo-liberal ideology of globalized capitalism. At the same time, however, America is highly anomalous in terms of theories of capitalism. In this currently hegemonic country of globalized capitalism, capitalism emerged after the constitutive democratic revolution, which it cannot be said to have guided, and without a ruling class in any Marxian sense of the term. From a Marxian point of view, this country of 'political emancipation' should have been the most likely starting point for the process of 'human emancipation'; instead, however, it became the country where capitalism developed without fetters at a time when in Europe it appeared to be somewhat reined in. At this point of the reasoning, we have to return to the theorizing of modernity, with a view to grasping how the relation between modernity and capitalism may develop under particular circumstances.

There may be some plausibility in arguing (as Wood tends to do) that England was the birthplace of a version of 'economic modernity', namely capitalism, and France the one of political modernity. In America, though, these two processes were more closely connected to one another, albeit not in terms of any dominant and overarching logic, as some critical theories of capitalism see it, but rather in terms of the socio-historical generation of the *problématiques* specific to modernity. To understand this connection, a brief look at the early history of the US is required.

With the creation of the American republic, after the Declaration of Independence and the War of Independence, a truly modern political order is founded, in the sense namely of being based on collective self-determination and the constitution of the collectivity itself being based – all necessary qualifications notwithstanding – on the agreement of its members. Initially, thus, that order worked with a rather strong concept of the political, inspired by republican ideas. By the middle of the nineteenth century, however, that strong republicanism had given way to individualist liberalism, with the latter becoming, as some observers see it, the basic political theory of the United States.[5] Such rather 'thin' foundation of a political order then eased the development of industry and commerce that made the US rise to become a leading economic power by the end of the nineteenth century. Only a few decades later, after the First World War, it had become the economy at which European observers were looking as a model, or at least as a challenge for a future that one could not escape.

Across long-standing disputes among historians of the nineteenth-century United States, nobody seems to deny the existence of such historical linkage between the onset of political modernity and the rise of capitalism in the US in those broad descriptive terms. The question then is what the implications of this observation are for our broader understanding of modernity and capitalism. It has been a matter of considerable debate whether the shift from republicanism to individualist liberalism resulted from inherent weaknesses of republican thinking in the face of a large and rapidly changing polity or whether it was a result of the assertion of business interests.[6] Rather than continuing this debate here, I will turn the question around and ask whether there are particular features of the American situation that brought about precisely such a linkage – one that did not exist in the same form elsewhere.

Jumping again to the twentieth-century outcome of these developments, one can certainly state that the American version of capitalism can, more plausibly than any European one, be interpreted as being guided by the imaginary signification of 'unlimited expansion of rational mastery'. In comparative terms, at least, it was often enough analysed as such by European observers (see, as one small contribution, Wagner 1999b and for further elaboration chapter 11 below). In terms of the theorizing of modernity that was introduced earlier, American capitalism is based on a rather radical interpretation of the double imaginary signification, autonomy and mastery. More precisely, autonomy is interpreted as individual autonomy, and mastery is regarded as the striving for rational, instrumental control. Or in other words: The reach of the idea of collective autonomy is reduced, precisely in terms of an individualist liberalism (or even libertarianism); and forms of reason or rationality other than an instrumental one are weakened.

In terms of social and political theorizing, this interpretation of modernity leads into individualist liberalism as a theory of politics and justice, on the one hand, and into economic theorizing as a theory of action and exchange, on the other. The most recent – and currently highly prominent – form of the latter is rational choice theory which, as pointed out earlier, provides a kind of default mode of social theorizing. It offers itself when other resources are not at hand, in a state of emergency. Theoretically speaking, the default situation may arise as a consequence of the exigency that all other interpretations of modernity have to make stronger social presuppositions or, in other terms, would need to assume more substantive social prerequisites, than the individualist-rationalist one. To relate this idea to the signification of modernity: *not* to interpret autonomy as purely individual autonomy requires, if not a coherent and stable collectivity, then at least socially rich ways of relating to others, that is, both singular others and networks of others. *Not* to interpret mastery or rationality in instrumental terms requires other substantive value orientations which again need to be, if not shared with, then at least be communicable and acceptable to others.

The problem being addressed is the lack of common interpretative resources – or of a common register of moral-political evaluation – to deal with a socio-political situation. Individualist rationality is then proposed as some kind of bottom-line on which everybody can agree – or at least would be willing to agree to end a dispute. Historically speaking, such absence or weakness of other resources tends to occur in situations of the founding of 'modern' socio-political orders ('modern' meaning that liberty and diversity are guiding assumptions) and in situations of breakdown of socio-political orders such as wars and revolutions, when common moral-political resources become scarce (see chapter 8 below for an analysis of epistemic debates along those latter lines).

The American situation certainly was a situation of founding a society, and as such it provides an example of the co-emergence of the double imaginary signification of autonomy and mastery and the co-generation of its *problématiques*, but this occurred under rather specific conditions. Generally, as briefly discussed above (in chapters 1 and 3), the positing of autonomy leads to the situation of tension characterized by the fact that, on the one hand, it allows human beings to *give* themselves their own laws, as radical freedom, but on the other hand such positing entails the requirement to indeed give *laws*, i.e., to master the relation to the world, to the others, to oneself. This tension, which is theoretically aporetic, may nevertheless be relatively unproblematic in situations in which certainty about the world, others and oneself is high. For a long time after the revolutions that led towards political modernity, European political thought had no particular problem in constructing substantive collectivities that should act together and form a polity.

However, the American situation is one of founding a society without strong prior commonalities (even if there were some, and not entirely insignificant ones). It is precisely on this ground that a look at the American situation may be more revealing to an understanding of both capitalism and modernity than European history. A historical analysis of the origins of modernity and capitalism provides reasons to assume, theoretically, that a rather particular – and in certain respects radical – version of both were being created there.

This short look at the American situation has thus led to two results. First, it has served to recognize more clearly an inescapable *problématique*, namely the one of the ambivalence of the modern imaginary signification of autonomy and mastery that is always in need of interpretation – and thus subject to contestation. Second, it has entailed the identification of the particular American way of responding to that *problématique*, namely the building of a society on the basis of a double commitment to individualist autonomy and to instrumental mastery. Now we have to add that, in the light of our analysis, this interpretation of modernity is not the only one possible, precisely because the modern imaginary signification is open to interpretation. The American one remains just one among others; its theoretically extreme nature, in terms of individualism and instrumentalism, in no way suggests – at least not at this stage of our analysis – that it is also the historical *telos* of human societies. At this point, this interpretation appears rather as one that is marked by a lack compared to others, one that tends to emerge under conditions, namely, of a lack of countervailing significations, of other orders of justification, that can assert themselves (see also, in slightly different terms, Baechler 1971, p. 117). Or in other words, in the American context, the onset of political modernity has led to the rise of the capitalism that we know as dominant today. This was the case, however, under conditions of poverty of common politico-moral registers that favoured a rationalistic-individualistic interpretation of modernity. There is no a priori reason why different contexts, such as the European one, should not lead to significantly different relations of modernity to capitalism.

At the same time, though, the analysis of the American situation also throws light on the hypothetical conditions that need to prevail for the successful maintenance or development of alternative interpretations of modernity. From a current point of view, the search for such conditions will immediately point to the visible difficulties in developing and sustaining alternatives. To more fully grasp the relation between modernity and capitalism we have to understand both – these *alternatives* and the *difficulties in reaching them*. The next step of my reasoning is meant to be a step in that direction.

The *problématiques* of modernity and the direction of history

To approach that question, I once again return to established readings of the history of capitalism. Both Max Weber, in *The Protestantic Ethic*, and Cornelius Castoriadis have emphasized a kind of historical self-undermining of a transformative social project. The argument works with a distinction between, to use Castoriadis's language, an instituting phase of history and an instituted one. Weber concludes his analysis of the transformation towards capitalism as follows: 'The Puritan wanted to work in a calling; we are forced to do so. [. . .] The spirit of religious asceticism [. . .] has escaped from the cage. But victorious capitalism, since it rests on mechanical foundations, needs its support no longer' (Weber 1930, pp. 181–2). And Castoriadis (1997a, p. 178) observes that the new kind of individual that capitalism produced 'has no longer any relation with [those] who created this regime on the political level, or even on the economic level [. . .]. These men and women could never have made the American or French Revolutions – nor even played the role of the great figures of the industrial revolution.'

This reasoning provides a sense of historical direction, even if only in the form of two phases. Offering a view that sees modernity/capitalism as being transformed from within, by those who adhere to the respective imaginary significations, but nevertheless bringing a transformation about that falls but little short of a complete loss of those significations, it is of great importance for answering my question. Nevertheless, this reasoning is also doubly problematic, in theoretical and in historical-empirical terms, and I will need to address its problems first before taking up its argument again. Theoretically, it invites a separation of capitalism from all other social practices and leads to a dualist social theorizing from which there is then no escape, regardless of actual developments in the social world. Empirically, it has grasped important tendencies towards the bureaucratization of capitalism and of modernity that marked the major part of the twentieth century. But it fails to understand the recent transformations in capitalist practices because it has ejected any trace of autonomy and creativity from that part of the social world.[7]

Neither Castoriadis nor Weber were entirely unaware of the kind of creativity that is at work in capitalist practices themselves. The former, for instance, argued that it may be possible to both observe and deplore that innovation in our time happens predominantly in technology, production, trade and finance rather than in politics, philosophy, culture and the arts (Castoriadis 1997a, p. 166). However, first, it seems difficult to sustain that the former kind of innovation has nothing *at all* to do with the idea of self-realization, which is an intricate part of the 'project of autonomy'. Castoriadis knew this very well as his praise, in passing, of the 'great figures of the industrial revolution' shows. And, second, it seems that whatever judgement is to be derived from the shift in fields of innovation needs further discussion; it cannot just be taken for granted.

If, furthermore, a considerable number of members of our societies are either creatively active in those areas of innovation or at least significantly attracted by the results of such creativity, the disconnection between instituting 'spirit' and actual practices, in a Weberian vein, is difficult to uphold. Luc Boltanski and Eve Chiapello's (1999) recent attempt to analyse 'the new spirit of capitalism' tried to demonstrate precisely this. And if one agrees with the latter's conclusion that such creative practices have substantially transformed the operating mode of capitalism and its justification, then one cannot even sustain without qualifications that the 'project of autonomy' has been reduced to some individualized exercise of a freedom to make insignificant choices. Rather, the observation of the new infusion of spirit into capitalism needs to be followed by the insight that there is, as a consequence, also a renewed connection of capitalism with ideas of autonomy and creativity, even if those ideas may be very specific and may in many respects fall short of any normative concept one may want to hold.

But let me here move to the sense in which one can fruitfully elaborate further the Weberian–Castoridian observation of self-undermining. Although neither the 'autonomy' of the producer in the flexible, self-employment economy nor the 'autonomy' of the consumer in the post-mass consumption era of fashion and design lives up to the modern imaginary signification of autonomy in anywhere near its full sense, the problem with autonomy in our time is nevertheless not its absence or weakness in general, as many critical theorists claim. The problem is the weakness of its connection to anything that resembles a common project or even a common world. The weakening of that connection limits the range of possible meanings of autonomy. Notions of autonomy that focus on sociality and on self-determination in common with others are marginalized or excluded. They may occur in conceptual connection with 'identity' and 'cultural expression' but are largely considered unsustainable in the realm of political philosophy.[8]

Beyond Weber and Castoriadis, elements of such a critique of 'actual autonomy' in the name of some potentiality of autonomy have long been captured by authors who were neither modernists nor just critics of modernity or capitalism, but were *modern critics of modernity*. Looking at the history of social theory, we find here a theme which unites its critical tradition from the eighteenth century onwards, in particular that strand which runs from German idealism and romanticism to the Frankfurt School, even if different explanations are attached to it, and different conclusions drawn. Strong versions can be found in Nietzsche and, in particular, in many of the inter-war debates of the early twentieth century. Its voice is comparatively weak, however, in contemporary debates. This weakness is probably due, at least in part, to the tendency of contributors to this strand to cast the argument in terms of a philosophy of history that is hard to sustain, or, more generally, in terms of a philosophizing that shows little interest in socio-historical conditions. An empirically more open historical sociology finds it difficult to relate to many of the contemporary interpretations of, among others, Nietzsche's *Genealogy of Morals*, Heidegger's 'fallenness to the they', Adorno and Horkheimer's *Dialectic of the Enlightenment*, or Walter Benjamin's 'Theses on the Philosophy of History'. It may be possible, however, on the basis of the above reflections, to reinterpret those writings in terms of some kind of a historical sociology of modernity and capitalism. Certainly, though, such historical sociology may end up neither satisfying the critical spirit of thinkers in these traditions nor the more conventional practitioners of historical and sociological research. Nevertheless it may be worthwhile to explore this possibility, as I will try to do in the following considerations.

Against this background, the view that I will try to explore suggests that the ambivalence within modernity itself has provided the possibility of the reduction in the meaning of autonomy that we currently face. There has been no necessity in this development; modernity does not inevitably breed capitalism in the form in which we know it. But our current situation can be understood by analysing the ways in which the ambivalence of modernity has historically been interpreted and actualized in social practices and institutions. To be fruitful, the idea of undermining in both Weber and Castoriadis should be read as a thoroughly historical proposition, not as an argument of a general theory of capitalist development. The reduction of the meaning of autonomy is there identified as a historical result of the working of capitalism. By implication, this means that the concept of autonomy is (always) broader than its current historical actualization. This reading allows the maintaining of a distinction between the interpretative range of an imaginary signification and its respective historical actualization in institutions. Thus, while there are contradictions between the two imaginary significations of modernity from the start, it is a historical process that has led to the dominance of the one and the reduction and retreat of the other, not an intrinsic logic of their relation.

The argument will proceed in three – necessarily brief – steps. First, the tradition of such modern critique of modernity will be re-read with regard to its view of autonomy in context. Second, these observations will be re-entered into the frame of current modes of theorizing. Finally, I return from there to a re-reading of critical theory, but now with an emphasis on the interpretation of mastery (or rationality).

The historical hypothesis implicitly contained in such modernity-critical views grounds its diagnosis of decline on the observation of some – social and/or historical – flattening of human social life, on some kind of decreasing historical depth. Regardless of the theoretical explanation (implicitly or explicitly) provided by the classical authors in this tradition, more empirically minded observers may identify the constant re-composition of societies in processes of industrialization, urbanization and large-scale migration from the nineteenth century onwards as the common source of all these diagnoses. The flattening of human social life occurs as a consequence of such processes, but neither in terms of a grand philosophy of history nor as a systemic requirement of capitalism. Under such circumstances, rather, singular human beings tend to become overburdened with the task, maybe less so of reconstructing their lives but of also reconstituting the guiding frameworks for the social world of which they have become a part. It is not that they no longer possess creative agential capacities; rather, those capacities may no longer suffice for self-institution under conditions of great mobility and of expanding social networks and the growing scale and intensity of social phenomena. In the course of 'modern' human history, it is then seen as inevitable that a 'flattening' of the temporal depths of social life and a 'weakening' of the social bonds occur.

We can easily recognize how such observations relate to the main forms of social theory and philosophy. On the one hand, individualist liberalism and rational choice theory draw the radical – and radically affirmative – conclusion from what otherwise are merely trend observations. They see human beings increasingly as left on their own, without substantive ties to others, and with reason as the only resource they could reliably draw upon, given that other resources presuppose that they are to some degree shared or recognized by others. The only polity that is viable under those conditions is a very thin one; the only rationality for action an instrumental one. On the other hand, critical theorists of the tradition referred to above take the observable trends to be merely the surface of a strong underlying dynamics that cannot be stopped. 'Capitalism' may then be the driving force of this trend; or capitalism in alignment with Enlightenment rationality (chapter 5 above dealt with this theorem in more detail); or the loss of the meaning of Being as the result of the adoption of a modernist 'world-view' in science (see chapter 8 below for more detail) and, as a consequence, the technological frenzy that transforms the human condition.

In each of these versions, however, such strong theories are not warranted. They radically divide the diagnosis of our current condition by mere theoretical fiat instead of remaining sensitive for historical-empirical observations. In the one, usually affirmative case, they insist on formal concepts of agency and rationality, or to use old-fashioned terms, freedom and reason, without considering the socio-historical context in which human life takes place. In the other, critical case, inversely, both freedom and reason are seen as completely undermined, thus denying those actually living human beings all agentiality and creativity. Even though there are, thus, basic flaws in both modes of theorizing, the latter nevertheless points to a fundamental problem that needs to be redescribed, the historical direction of human mastery of the world.

The brief analysis of the American case has shown that, under certain conditions, the modern commitment to autonomy can be interpreted in such a manner that, socio-historically, the way is cleared for an understanding of mastery as the striving for the unlimited expansion of control. Such a project of 'rational mastery' is based on the hubris of assuming that human beings are, in principle, able to master and control the world. In the tradition of critical theory, human beings are then seen with this objective in view as having developed knowledge forms – of technology and science – the power of which always creates an even greater powerlessness, in connection namely with the weakening of collective autonomy. Thus, they are subject to an 'illusion of mastery' (Castoriadis 1990c, pp. 73 and 98) – again already a Weberian theme. Such perspective underlines the signifi-cance of the two-century process of transformation of the world through large-scale application of industrial technology. The thesis of powerlessness can be read in two different, though related, ways. First, it may relate to the intervention of a techno-scientific rational-ity, itself best understood as a combined result of the opening of the epistemic and of the economic *problématique*, of modern science and of capitalism, into a differently pre-constituted world (see both chapter 5 above and chapter 8 below). Second, it can refer to the difficulties of human beings to communicate about and in the world, i.e., the political *problématique*, if the world is constantly changing and, in addition, the position of human beings in it as well (see chap-ters 3 and 4 above as well as 12 below). The loss of power because of the illusion of mastery thus emphasizes potentially both the transfor-mation of the relation of human beings to a technically reshaped world and the relations of human beings to one another in a rapidly changing world, a relation that is being transformed in parallel to the transformation of the world. The idea of a world that precedes sin-gular human beings and that will outlast them, and which at the same time unites them by virtue of the fact of having this world in common, is weakened in this process (to put the issue in the terms proposed by Luc Ferry 1989, p. 343).

Neither the commitment to autonomy as such nor the plurality of registers of justification as such are the 'root causes' of this weaken-ing. More importantly, it is the changed relation between the three *problématiques* which weakened the only sustained and unalterable concern for the common, as expressed in the political *problématique*. Accepting the modernity of the political created the possibility of the rise in importance of the economic *problématique*. The modernity of the political leaves the space of power empty, as Claude Lefort (1986c, p. 27) argues, and thus opens up the possibility of totalitarianism as a thoroughly modern regime. The same modernity of the political also allows the diminution of the range of questions that are seen as requiring deliberation in common, and thus the possibility of 'economism' as an equally modern arrangement. Such an occurrence is in the background of my 'American story' as an account of a historically specific interpretation of modernity with far-reaching consequences. At the same time, however, it is also the modernity of the political, and it alone, that opens the possibility for democracy – and thus of a reassertion of collective autonomy.

It is the combination of those two effects then that explains the difficulties of developing richer varieties of modernity than the individualist-rationalist one that suits perfectly well an expansionary capitalism. The problem of human agency and creativity to sustain a common social world in the face of rapid social change combines with the steady transformation of the material world as a consequence of the very application of human creativity in its techno-scientific form.

While there is no necessity in this development, there is a need for constant awareness and engagement against this possibility. The stakes of autonomy – to give oneself one's own laws – tend to increase historically with the successive attempts (and the – long-term – consequences of them) to exercise autonomy and mastery, since every exercise of autonomy goes along with a questioning of any certainty of a common world prior to us. Liberation may occur along with, and as, increasing loss of the world.

This is the background for the conjoined themes of the 'loss of freedom' and of the 'loss of meaning' in critical theory (see, e.g., Habermas 1981). The former theme leads to the question of the possibility of action in common, of politics; the latter to the question of the reference for action, of rootedness in the world. But this loss does not – at least, not exclusively, and not even most profoundly – occur because someone has taken freedom and meaning away; a theory of power and interest is insufficient to understand this possibility. While it would be flawed to argue that modernity leads inadvertently to the loss of freedom and meaning, as some authors do, the ambivalence of modernity – that lies in the fact of the relation of autonomy and mastery being open to interpretation – may be actualized historically in such a way that loss of freedom and of meaning do indeed occur.

Crisis and criticism

I have here proposed to analyse capitalism as a possible consequence of the imaginary signification of modernity – neither as equal to nor in contradiction with that imaginary signification but as drawing on a particular interpretation of it. After elaborating this view in general terms (starting in chapter 5), I have indicated elements of a transfer of this perspective into a historical sociology, in terms of contingency. The observations along those lines have led one step towards spelling out the conditions for the likelihood of such a particular interpretation to become actualized. And the historical fact of its actualization has, finally, opened the way for a reassessment of the idea that, more than mere possibility or likelihood, there was an element of necessity in such actualization, at least in the sense of the overpowering difficulties and obstacles that other possibilities face.

Such reasoning should, if developed, lead into a theory of capitalism that does not see the latter as, in the first instance, driven by the interest of a class or by the logic of a system. Rather, the term refers to a situation, self-created by human beings committed to the modern ideas of autonomy and mastery, in which a certain interpretation of these ideas prevails over others, and this as a consequence of the need to adjust one's interpretation to the perceived requirements of historical experiences.

In such a view, capitalism is neither naturalized nor conflated with modernity. As a consequence, there is also no end to critique; and the critique of contemporary capitalism does not become conflated with a critique of modernity. Rather, critique takes on a novel form. Since the conclusions drawn from earlier experiences were not necessary conclusions, there always was (and is) a greater range of possibilities from which those interpretations of modernity were selected. Consequently, no *pensée unique* is sustainable and critique always possible. Nevertheless, the impact of those historical actions cannot be undone; current critical analysis has to live up to the exigencies of our own modern condition and has to avail itself of the interpretative possibilities that modernity offers. Critique of capitalism now means criticizing a particular interpretation of modernity, and the ways in which it has become dominant and has shaped practices and institutions (see the following chapter for an example).

Modern social theory emerged at a moment of conjunction of crisis and criticism (Koselleck 1959). The task of criticism is to identify the nature of the crisis, at its moment, in its time. In terms of the diagnosis provided here, this requires work at (re-)constituting reference and commonality. However, critique always also needs to face transformations of its own conceptual vocabulary in the course of social transformations. Under current conditions, this means that there is no return to concepts of collectivity and political action in the form in which they seemed plausible in earlier situations. Rather, currently available resources need to be identified; instead of foundations provided by a strong philosophy of history, useful concepts need to show 'empirical' strength in the given situation. Registers of moral-political evaluation beyond individualism and rationalism are, in principle, available; contemporary critique would aim to demonstrate their significance and potential (for such attempts, see Boltanski and Chiapello 1999; Lamont and Thévenot 2000). There is no intellectual achievement on which a critique of capitalism can rest for ever. On the contrary, the failure of critique is precisely related to this belief.

7

The Exit from Organized Economic Modernity

Over more than three decades the term 'flexibility' has come increasingly into vogue in the social sciences – as well as in public debate.[1] It is now an accepted and familiar, though certainly not uncontested, concept; a piece of common parlance much like 'class' or 'nation' or, to use examples closer to our subject, 'market' and 'industrial relations'. The rapid rise to prominence of the term 'flexibility' – together with the diffuse and even confused character of the debate it has spawned – demands a form of investigation that does not merely take a concept, or a version of it, and prove (or refute) its usefulness by matching it with empirical observations. What is required is an approach that relates conceptual to historical analysis by situating the concept both within a discursive structure and within a historical context. In the following, first, the discursive lineage and the semantic relations of 'flexibility' in its current usage will be identified. Second, the term will be located in historical context by means of the tools of a historical sociology of modernity. Since the outcome of these two steps of inquiry will be largely critical, some elements of recasting the issue of 'flexibility', both in the social sciences and in politico-institutional debate, will be discussed in a third step.[2]

What is to be flexible?

Traditional as such an approach may sound, one way to start such a terminological analysis is to seek the referent of 'flexibility'. It is significant in itself that many users of the term do not give it any clear referent at all. Nonetheless the bulk of recent contributors make it clear that they are talking about *labour market flexibility*. This particular variant of the term has even acquired a technical meaning in its own right in the legal and economic sciences though this is not entirely uncontested. In this part of the literature, two approaches prevail. In one kind of investigation, the objective is to empirically assess the extent of labour market flexibility in certain markets, mostly national but also sectoral ones. The starting point is often the assumption that flexibility has – or should have – increased and the target is then to determine the degree of change. A second kind of analysis more explicitly addresses the conceptual question that always lurks in the background: it enquires what is the relation between labour market flexibility and unemployment in given markets. The assumption here – sometimes more, sometimes less critically discussed – is that unemployment rates should be lower in highly flexible labour markets.

The orientation of this second kind of analysis is doubly significant. First, it reveals the key problem that the discourse on flexibility is meant to address, namely *unemployment*. That this does not go without saying will become clear when we show later how much broader a signification the term can acquire. Second, the discussion of the relation between labour market flexibility and unemployment marks the point at which the issue relates directly to key questions and assumptions in the disciplines of the social sciences. The case in point is neo-classical economics which assumes that markets are pure and unfettered unless there are restraints upon their full workings. This assumption also entails an implicit counter-concept and counter-phenomenon to that of flexibility, namely that of labour market 'rigidities', which must be abolished. However, we shall see later that this is not the only possible counter-concept to 'flexibility', since the discourse of neo-classical economics is not the only discourse into which the term 'flexibility' has been absorbed.[3]

Within neo-classical economics, the identification of the counter-concept 'rigidity' allows us to trace the conceptual lineage of 'labour market flexibility'. The immediate predecessor of the latter was the notion of *wage flexibility*, which was much invoked between, roughly, the mid-1970s and the mid-1980s. Just like its successor, the term referred to something that was seen as desirable but not sufficiently present. The problem was 'downward rigidity' of wages, i.e., the unwillingness of workers to accept lower wages in situations in which, according to economists, the declining profitability of companies demanded this. The causes of this phenomenon were seen to be twofold. Keynesianism, on the one hand, justified state interventions which had the effect of preventing the 'natural' clearing of markets by introducing external elements of a quasi-economic (such as deficit spending) or of a plainly political nature (such as the commitment to preserve full employment). A high degree of unionization, on the other hand, impaired competition for jobs and fostered 'cartels' which put the price of labour at unsustainably high levels. It must be recalled that such interpretations were not only put forward by economists close to business circles but also by neo-Marxists whose perspective mirrored the absolute and unshakeable predominance of market analysis that is typical of neo-classical economics. The most prominent example of the time was Andrew Glyn and Bob Sutcliffe's (1972) observation of a 'profit-squeeze' into which British capitalism had fallen between international competitors on the one side and unionized workers on the other.

Let us note at this point only that the root causes of the problem of wage rigidity were identified as (national) state and union policies – socio-political phenomena largely regarded as impediments to market interaction and, as such, to efficiency. Both the choice of these two phenomena and the interpretation of their effects can only be understood against the historical backdrop of the emergence of this reasoning, as shall be shown in more detail below.

The shift towards a notion of 'labour market flexibility' in the mid-1980s basically meant a broadening of the issue under debate.[4] Rather than focusing on wages alone, the latter term brought into consideration all aspects of labour supply, such as working time, working conditions and hiring arrangements.[5] In this sense, it extended the scope of the criticism of state and union activity beyond mere wage protection to much wider aspects of the 'regulation' of work. Indeed, 'de-regulation', in as far as it related to labour issues, came to be almost synonymous with 'labour market flexibility'.

The analysis can be deepened by tracing the lineage of the concept of 'flexibility' one step further into the past. Even a cursory look at the bibliographic evidence reveals that the term had a quite different referent at the turn of the 1960s and up to the mid-1970s, namely the *flexibility of the exchange rate* of national currencies.[6] This was the period of the terminal decline of the Bretton Woods system of fixed exchange rates using the US dollar as the anchor currency (see Andrews 2005 and Stråth 2005). Amidst increasing signs of crisis, not least related to the Vietnam War and to declining productivity in US manufacturing, economists discussed the likely consequences of abandoning a system which had been seen as one of the guarantors of the recovery of the world economy after the Second World War.

It is not at all surprising to see a number of economists embracing the idea of exchange-rate flexibility. If the terms of international

trade and finance directly determined the 'price' of national currencies (as expressed in other currencies), then government strategies to
keep the value of their own currency down (for reasons of export
promotion) or up (to control inflation, for reasons of prestige or in
the interest of national finance) would become largely impossible.
Thus, another kind of market impediment would be removed. This
view is entirely within the logic of neo-classical reasoning; and the
main targets in this case are the nation as the container of an economy
partly sheltered from global speculation, and again the state as the
agent of that national economy.

What is surprising, in contrast, are two other phenomena. First, one
may note the fact that global market exchanges operating on the basis
of nationally guaranteed means of exchange, politically fixed against
a conventional standard – first gold, then the US dollar – had not
been considered as particularly problematic at an earlier juncture.
Today, indeed, there is a broad consensus that it is less the actual
'value' of a currency in whatever market terms, and more the general
acceptance of a standard and its stability, that over time is most
important for economic action across currency boundaries. The stability of a social *convention* is in such a view, at least implicitly, conceptually opposed to the market-driven flexibility of a *value*. 'Rigidity'
and 'stability' as counter-concepts to flexibility may refer to exactly
the same property in a given situation but the semantic spaces they
open are highly diverse.

And in the light of this conceptual observation, second, it is significant to see that exchange rate flexibility, though it still governs the
world economy at large (although a reversal may already be under
way), was very soon seen to hamper economic development. As early
as the mid-1970s, some countries, especially economically weaker
ones, 'pegged' their currencies to those of larger ones and thus chose
a (reversible) commitment to rigidity above exposure to absolute
flexibility. Further, the largest development of this sort has been the
creation of the Exchange Rate Mechanism (ERM) of member states
of the EU in 1978 which was more recently transformed into the
(declared irreversible) European Monetary Union (EMU). Despite
the generally negative reputation of the EU in this respect, hardly
anyone goes so far as to argue that in EMU 'political' considerations
entirely outweigh the element of rational 'economic' behaviour or
create new barriers to flexibility in the process of monetary integration.[7] Rather, European monetary integration can be seen as an
exemplary case demonstrating the limited reach of analyses centred
on an unspecified and normatively loaded concept of flexibility (I will
briefly return to this case at the end of this chapter).

Management of currencies at the national level had been a key element of global economic exchange policies up to the crisis of the early 1970s. Even though highly consequential errors of political judgement were sometimes made, in particular during the inter-war years, there appeared to be no alternative to a system of national controls and international concertation. Its most important task was to provide a stable framework for economic interaction.[8] From the 1970s onwards, global exchanges of goods and capital, however, took on such dimensions and such degrees of fluctuation that the stability of the framework itself came increasingly to be considered as an element of uncertainty. Any adjustment of currencies prone to pressure to devalue or revalue was determined by national governments and central banks, and the potential mismatch between governmental criteria of assessment and market drives became a source of instability: a controversial debate about a regime of flexible exchange rates emerged. On the one hand, 'flexibility', i.e., the abolition of one set of criteria, naturally would eliminate the tension between 'political' control and 'economic' forces. On the other hand, however, the same move would abolish all buffers between global exchanges and national production.

The semantics of 'flexibility'

At this point, tracing the lineage of the term 'flexibility' and its politico-conceptual implications can be interrupted to permit a broader look at the semantic combinations in which the term is currently employed. Some of those combinations have already been hinted at but I intend to underline four kinds of semantic connotations of 'flexibility' more systematically.[9] There is a fundamental ambivalence in the use of the term 'flexibility', an ambivalence which is expressed in the creation of counter-concepts – as well as of accompanying concepts which extend its meaning.

Significantly, 'flexibility' has a variety of such counter-concepts which, taken together, open the dimensions of the term more fully than can any single one of them alone. As discussed above, the predominant counter-term is 'rigidity', or perhaps 'constraints'. In this relation, the asymmetry is extremely pronounced and the superiority of 'flexibility' stands almost unchallenged. However, 'rigidity' can be replaced by 'stability' without any substantive loss, and the relation is repaired, becoming almost symmetric. The need for a balance of exigencies is thus underlined. We can see that the term 'stability' also lends itself to be extended to 'security' as an accompanying term;

and by implication, 'flexibility' acquires the additional meaning of 'insecurity'.

With such progression, however, the original symmetry is almost reversed and the positive connotation of 'flexibility' is in turn unclear. There is, instead, a similar accompanying concept to be encompassed, namely 'efficiency', which provides reasons why 'flexibility' should be embraced despite problematic side effects. By further extension, then, 'efficiency' relates to 'equity' and 'fairness' in terms of what is often seen as a trade-off; the furthering of one objective will be to the detriment of the other. In a less self-evident way, this latter relation echoes the issues of collectivism versus individualism and unity versus diversity. If the promotion of fairness presupposes collective action and some degree of unity, then 'flexibility' may lead to 'fragmentation' and, again, to 'uncertainty'.

By now it should be unmistakably evident that the whole terminological issue is fraught with the normative implications to which these words readily lend themselves. It is indeed part of the attraction of 'flexibility' that it is difficult to be against it as a matter of principle: in the first instance, 'flexibility' is a 'good'. It provides an opening, an exit from some closure or constraint. For example, the strongest use of these semantic connotations has been made in the literature on 'flexible specialization' of production, finding its climax in the title of a publication by key authors in this debate, namely Sabel and Zeitlin's *World of Possibilities* (1997).

It is only after reflecting on the asymmetric construction of the counterparts and extensions of 'flexibility' that the need for a balancing of different requirements becomes apparent. Thus, one can point to adverse consequences of the adoption of an otherwise beneficial orientation as 'the dark side of flexibility', 'the deficits of flexibility' or 'paying the price of flexibility'.[10] An attempt to explicitly formulate the opposed exigencies is the formula 'social protection vs. economic flexibility', which in a very dense, and certainly not unproblematic, way links the social to protection and the economic to flexibility and opposes these double terms to each other.

This very same recent publication, however, retreats immediately from the strong formula promised in its title and, after having set up the issue in this way, asks whether there is a trade-off at all. And indeed, the view that there is not necessarily a strong opposition has become a perspective of its own, finding its expression in terminological combinations such as 'sustainable flexibility' or 'offensive flexibility'. The basic idea is that flexibility can be, or has to be, embraced, but that that outlook does not need to be highly problematic, provided some conditions, which are then specified, hold true.

Most of the contributions that flag up the term 'flexibility' have in common that they see the emergence of this issue as a sign of a major socio-economic – and often also political – transformation. The connection of this concept to notions of 'post-Fordism' or 'post-Taylorism' as well as *in extremis* the idea, though critically discussed, that flexibility may have the properties of a 'magic wand' make this entirely clear. 'Flexibility' is then seen as a key characteristic of a new social formation. This idea was certainly inspired by Michael Piore and Charles Sabel's argument that a 'second industrial divide' would see 'flexible specialization' replacing standardized mass production as the dominant mode of production, but it also has broader societal connotations (to be discussed below).

The significance of this insistence on a major social transformation can be elucidated by means of contrasting it with an analysis of labour flexibility that is reasoned in terms of the further elaboration of an established model. When Archibald Evans diagnosed, for the OECD in 1973, a future of 'flexibility in working life', he argued exclusively in terms of gradual evolution and progress. Flexibility was for him a phenomenon that could without ambivalence be described as providing 'opportunities for individual choice', namely the opportunity for people to 'choose their working time [...] with as little constraint as possible'. Evans also had de-regulation – *avant la lettre*, I presume – in view when he emphasized that 'some of the existing constraints and rules' needed to be dismantled. But he saw this process as fairly unproblematic since those rules, while they 'may have been introduced in an earlier situation for what were then quite rational reasons of orderly production or social protection', 'are now upheld more out of tradition and habit' (Evans 1973, p. 11).[11] This optimistic view distinguishes itself from later writings on flexibility (even those that are moderately optimistic) principally in its assumption of an uninterrupted full-employment regime as a background condition for those opportunities. The latter insisted instead on a major rupture that could only be understood as a reaction to the persistent employment crisis since the mid-1970s.

Before I address the question of the nature of that transformation in more detail, I want to briefly point to another feature of current flexibility debates, namely their tendency to broaden the issue beyond just labour market flexibility. If the debate is conceived in predominantly economic and organizational terms, it appears as a natural extension to move from labour flexibility to 'corporate flexibility'. Just as rigidities of labour supply are seen to lead to a sub-optimal allocation of resources, large-scale, bureaucratic companies are likely to show organizational rigidities with similar consequences. The notion of the 'flexible firm' then seems to summarize ideas of 'lean production', 'just-in-time production' and 'outsourcing', amongst others.

It is a bigger step, but again not an implausible one once this route is embarked on, to go beyond the realm of what is conventionally understood as the economy to perceive a 'flexibilization' of society overall and the emergence of the flexible individual. The British debate about 'enterprise culture' during the Thatcherite 1980s is a major example of such a deliberate broadening of the issue. The desired end was a population exclusively composed of 'entrepreneurs' who would run their lives as businesses (Keat and Abercrombie 1991; Heelas and Morris 1992). While this particular debate could be seen as an extremist aberration of Thatcherite market individualism, the apparent dissolution of social collectivities and moral commitments in Western societies at the turn of the millennium has given rise to wider critical concern about the emergence of a 'flexible human being' whose key personality trait is the 'corrosion of character' (Sennett 1998; see also Wallulis 1998). Here the critique of capitalism and its cultural forms in the tradition of Weber and Nietzsche, the theorists of mass society and the Frankfurt School, finds its latest reincarnation.

At this point, I intend to leave this – quite cursory – discourse analysis of 'flexibility'. Its main purpose was not an exhaustive survey of the debates but rather an unfolding of the principal semantic connections and, through this, of the dimensions of societal life at stake. Since the term 'flexibility' on its own is so multipurpose as to be almost empty of content, some key ingredients should now be available to set the debate into a socio-historical context. In the next step, therefore, I want to put the aspects and dimensions generated in this discourse analysis to use for providing a portrait of the society that allegedly is desperately 'in search of flexibility'.

The social construction of 'inflexibility': towards a historical perspective

Many of the analyses sketched above have some historical perspective, at least in the limited sense of identifying a contemporary issue against the background of an earlier, decisively different situation. However, this historical comparison is seldom spelt out and, even where it is, the explication is rarely well grounded. The following proposal to locate the current debate in historical context will use the preceding observations of the current debate as a structuring device.

Thus, it aims at discussing the claims of the flexibility discourse on its own terms, though sometimes by drawing implicit inferences.

The flexibility discourse is organized by the argument that Western societies are currently undergoing a major transformation which has at its core the regulation of labour but whose implications go much beyond the world of work and affect the overall self-conception of social organizations and the orientations of individuals. This transformation, while widely being seen as to some extent necessary and inevitable, remains contested and appears to point to inescapable ambivalence. This ambivalence is played out in the oppositions of equity and efficiency as well as of security and employability. In both cases, the former are seen as historically having had higher priority and having been related to collective arrangements whereas the latter are the demand of the contemporary period and go with an emphasis on the individual. In particular, the collective arrangements that are singled out as hampering the required increase of flexibility are related to the state, the nation and the unions, in their combined – and partly overlapping – political, cultural and institutional-organizational connections. A look at the historical period during which the arrangements that are accused of 'inflexibility' were constructed can then be taken to possibly identify those rationales on which the construction of these systems was based.

A useful point of temporal reference is the mid-nineteenth-century period of liberalization of economic exchange that went along with rapid 'globalization' – in the sense of a growth of world trade that far exceeded the growth of world production. From the 1870s onwards, and not least in connection to that long period of economic stagnation now known as the 'Great Depression', the view gained ground that the combination of political and economic liberalism that had characterized the mid-century years had seriously underestimated the problem of coordination between actors. Societal thinking stemming from such liberalism no longer appeared to be adequate for the reality of an emerging industrial society. Several developments of the late nineteenth and early twentieth centuries can be analysed as consequences drawn from such a diagnosis.

The way in which the industrial mode of production developed led to the creation of work situations that could only be regarded as constitutively collective. As a consequence, individual workers could no longer justifiably be made exclusively responsible for the outcomes of their actions. Collective security arrangements, such as compulsory work accident insurance and unemployment insurance, were introduced and collective conventions about working conditions and pay were permitted (among recent publications, see Zimmermann

2001b; Wagner and Zimmermann 2003). Then, industrial companies, in particular in the new and rapidly developing sectors of chemical production and electrical engineering, tried to reduce their exposure to market uncertainties by vertical integration and forming cartels. The larger the share of the relevant sector was that could either be directly controlled or regulated by inter-organizational coordination, the smaller the risk of supply or demand fluctuation would be. In Imperial Germany, where next to the USA these developments were most pronounced, the term 'organized capitalism' was coined by the Marxist economic theorist and Social Democrat politician Rudolf Hilferding. It suggested that organizational growth and coordination, which included also that of banks ('finance capital'), led to a new phase of capitalism that limited its subjection to market vagaries and could ultimately be transformed into a planned economy (Hilferding 1968). Further, if cartels are seen as a mode of coordination on the business side and unions – as the 'cartel of labour' – as a mode of coordination among workers, then the institutionalization of channels of communication between workers' and employers' representation marks a third level of coordination. Given that important representations of society during the nineteenth century postulated either a basic asymmetry and hierarchy between these groups – in conservatism – or incompatibility of their interests – in Marxism – such a coordination was for a long time difficult to envisage. In many countries, it was only the national mobilization of the First World War that led to significant steps in this direction (Didry and Wagner 1999).

These few observations may suffice to suggest that the period between, roughly, the 1870s and the 1930s was marked by increasing attempts at collective organization and coordination in European societies. These efforts were seen as a means to cope with the exigencies of patterns of production and exchange that had become increasingly large-scale and extended across space. The significance of the comparison with the current situation lies in the fact that an apparently similar challenge – the loss of control over spaces of action – was met by moves that seem to point in a direction opposite to that pursued in the current debate. Rather than increasing adaptability to changes that are beyond influence or control, the objective was to extend control by fixing parameters and stabilizing situations. The more 'inflexible' an arrangement could be made, the more certain was the grip on it.

It must be recognized that, in theoretical terms, neither of the two strategies is superior to the other, and neither of the two is even feasible in its pure form. If, on the one hand, one tried to stabilize the entities of economic exchange and their modes of coordination at any given point, this would be equal to an attempt to arrest any dynamics of change. As long as there is a continual mutation of the external environment, such an attempt is unlikely to succeed. Indeed, such an experience is certainly one of the elements behind the demise of Soviet socialism. On the other hand, the opposite notion of making flexibility the ultimate criterion of economic organization amounts to the idea of a permanent need to negotiate the terms of our relations to others, without any acquisition of rules on which to base communication. Even the purest form of rationalist thinking requires some notion of a preference-ordering that is not itself part of the rational process, and thus needs to refer to resources both prior and external to the moment of rational choice itself.

If no arbitration in the abstract is possible between the argument for organization and coordination and the argument for flexibility, then such proposals must be read as being relative to a given socio-historical situation, and any judgement of their validity must consequently be based on an assessment of that situation. The difficulty of forming such a judgement becomes plain when looking again at our historical analogy. Both National Socialism and Stalinism were in some respects societal outcomes of practical critiques of liberal individualism and the consequent movement towards a greater degree of organization and collectivization earlier in the twentieth century.

Before commencing to weigh the criteria of judgement against the historical context, the conceptual issue can be pushed at least one step further. There is an asymmetry in the construction of the alternative between a 'flexible' liberal individualism, on the one hand, and its 'inflexible' organizational-collectivist alternative, at least under conditions of Western modernity. This asymmetry resides in the fact that the unit of observation seems to be self-evident in the flexibility discourse, namely the individual human being, whereas any argument for organization and coordination needs additional substantive resources to provide an underpinning for the collectivity. Now, while one can justifiably argue that this shift of the 'onus of the argument' (Taylor 1989, pp. 196 and 514) is based on erroneous and flawed reasoning, it nevertheless remains the case that a culture like Western modernity, the self-understanding of which is broadly humanist and the institutional justifications of which cannot do without some element of rights-based individualism, will show an individualist bias and that this bias is likely to make itself felt in political disputes.

Under such conditions (and if one excludes the recourse to violence and oppression), any coordination by organized collective actors presupposes some common understanding of belonging to such a collectivity, a broad acceptance of membership rules and some degree of responsibility towards other members. This is especially true for institutionalized coordination, which is expected to show a certain longevity and durability of structuring of orientations. Put like this, such stable coordination must seem a rare occurrence in a world consisting of individuals. However, it is the ability of human beings to invest 'social labour' (Luc Boltanski) in the construction of social 'things that hold together' (Alain Desrosières) as well as the availability of some substantive resources from which to build such 'things' that makes stable coordination less unlikely than it may at first seem (see chapter 6 above). It is in this light that we can try to understand the historical building of those 'inflexible' institutions that are currently questioned.

In Europe, the struggles over the containment of economic liberalism focused on the two issues of cultural-linguistic identity and social solidarity (see chapter 3 above for some more detail as well as Wagner 1994). These were struggles, we could also say, about the limitation of the socio-historical meaning of modernity, and thus about the socio-political feasibility of modernity in Europe. The form that European political societies gradually acquired during the nineteenth century was not predominantly a politically liberal and democratic one, but that of the cultural-linguistically based nation-state. Liberal ideas and national ideas were linked by the concept of national self-determination and, where this matrix for cohesion was accepted and its territorial foundation accomplished, it became possible to set the external boundaries of the modern polity. 'Flexibility' in terms of movements across those boundaries could thus be reduced – by immigration restrictions, tariffs, currency regulations and other forms of border control. And the question of 'stability' also became an issue inside national societies. This dispute was triggered not least by the experience that the dynamics of liberated economic allocation, i.e., the emerging capitalist economy, had had an adverse impact on living and working conditions of many compatriots. This is one way of formulating what became known as 'the social question'; its very formulation presupposed external boundaries to the polity. The question itself, however, referred to the internal boundaries within the polity.

The national and the social question were both linked to notions of collective identity and of collective agency, namely 'nation' and 'class'. The management of these questions through the creation of organized collective agents should be seen as a historical way and means of containing the unlimited challenges of the liberal utopia. Just like nation and nationalism, working-class and class struggle had been conceptually constructed to render possible collective action or to make members of presumed collectivities, 'imagined communities' (Benedict Anderson), relate to each other, act together, or consider themselves to be acted upon.

The means to give structures to societies that according to the liberal imagination should only be composed of individuals were the state and the law. States were indeed developed as vessels for the building of modern institutions; their boundaries defined the limits of the reach of these institutions, in territorial terms and otherwise. In economic terms, the 'unbound' Smithian notion of market efficiency was soon countered by the Listian idea of setting protective boundaries to help a national economy prosper. Cultural-linguistic terms provided the very foundation for the nation-state. Far from remaining in the discursive realm, however, these ideas were also given institutional forms by the setting up of nationally organized academic institutions, fostering national intellectual traditions, and of national networks of communication (see chapter 9 below).

If neither the prevailing consciousness of European societies nor the social sciences as their tools of self-understanding were prone to reason about such internal and external boundaries in terms of 'inflexibility', this was because those rigidities were regarded as essential components of, even requirements for, stability and social order. If one adopted a Parsonsian functionalist paradigm, for instance, those boundaries could not even be experienced as inflexibilities, since cultural identity and social solidarity were part of the socio-cultural norms of these societies and state institutions were the natural units of activity. Such a view has rightly been accused of providing an overly harmonious picture and of denying the existence of oppression and exclusion owing to such rules and institutions. In addition, this view has always been unable to reflexively develop a historical understanding of itself. In the current situation, however, it serves as a useful reminder of social reasons for avoiding a concept of flexibility that presupposes a permanently alert population.

Currently, it has become rather obvious that this historically constructed social configuration, which dominates our consciousness through the experience of the long post-war era of full employment, marked a rather exceptional period.

In retrospect, the epoch of western labour history immortalised in *Modern Times* can now be seen to have been a transitory form of organisation induced by the conjuncture of a technology that involved large numbers of workers at specific sites and an industrial economy that was still confined (with the Japanese exception) to Europe and its outposts, which set a floor to wage and working conditions. This epoch, like the technology and society that subtended it, began to come to an end around 1960. (Grantham 1994, p. 24)

This insight alone, however, does not lead us very far in assessing the current situation after the end of the era of organized modernity. There is thus a double task involved here. First, the foundational concepts and institutions of organized modernity need to be exposed to scrutiny; the 'flexibility' debate is indeed a part of such a critical investigation. And secondly, on the basis of this conceptual inquiry possibilities for a reconceptualization and re-institutionalization need to be explored; given the way it has taken shape, the 'flexibility' discourse is unable to achieve such an objective.

The first two sections of this chapter have underlined that the term 'flexibility' has come into widespread use in the current social and economic sciences, but at the same time have insisted that it is difficult to envisage this concept as acquiring a key importance in societal analysis. 'Flexibility' qualifies rather as a transitional term, surfacing during a period in which, to paraphrase Max Weber (1949 [1904], p. 112), the light of the great cultural problems moves on. The brief historical sketch of the development of Western societies through the twentieth century in the third section, however, has more concretely suggested that conceptual reorientation is necessary in the context of fundamental societal change. It demonstrated that the major 'collective concepts' (Weber) in the social sciences – such as class, state and nation – refer to particular historical phenomena, the emergence of which happened to coincide with the formative period of the political and social sciences, rather than to general nodal points of social organization. In addition, it suggested that it was precisely in response to disintegrative tendencies in nineteenth-century European societies that the coherence of such collective phenomena was emphasized and strengthened. If we take the findings of these preceding sections together, then two further questions emerge. If, first, we do not wish to use the term 'flexibility' itself, are there then *other concepts* in the contemporary social sciences from which a rethinking can start out? And, second, if the strength and coherence of important collective phenomena declines, are there then *other phenomena* that emerge in their stead – or have the questions to which their construction was addressed become obsolete and been superseded? The first question will be approached here in terms of a brief review of social-science developments, to be continued in Part III below. The second question will here only be touched upon by one aspect of the specific

European experience with, and interpretation of, 'flexibility', namely in terms of the creation of a common currency in response to 'exchange-rate flexibility'. In more comprehensive terms, the European experience and interpretation of modernity is the subject of Part IV below.

Beyond 'flexibility' (1): work at reinterpretation

From the late 1960s onwards, theoretical debate in the social sciences has been characterized by an opening up, a loosening of, strong conceptual presuppositions. Before this, structural-functionalism, and the sociological theory of modernization which accompanied it, and structuralism had provided objectivist pictures of society that rested on the idea of strong ties between human beings guaranteeing coherence and a stable socio-political order. The conceptual elements varied between the approaches, but some combination of an interest-based, an identity-based or an institution-based explanation, emphasizing structure and social class, culture and nation and procedure, law and state respectively, was always at play. In the area of social theory, this thinking was challenged in all respects. To give just some key examples: Anthony Giddens' work stands for the turn away from functionalism; Pierre Bourdieu's for the opening up of the structuralist tradition towards considerations of issues of temporality and agency; and Jürgen Habermas and Alain Touraine have tried to diagnose contemporary Western societies without fixing their institutional structures in any modernized version of a philosophy of history.

From the critical debate that was thus opened, I consider two features of particular significance in the present context. First, one strand of criticism had focused on the unacceptable ease with which 'epistemological obstacles' (as Bourdieu liked to quote Canguilhem) have been presumed to be solvable by methodological fiat alone, in particular in quantitative-empirical research. Even though there is no full agreement among the critics, an adequate acceptance of those obstacles would seem to require a focus on the always linguistic nature of the representations of the social world given in the social sciences and the inevitable indeterminacy of the relation between such representations and the social world they are allegedly about, even though such focus may render social-science research sometimes more difficult (see chapter 13 for more detail). This move, second, also entailed a more sceptical attitude towards the postulation of 'collective concepts' (Weber 1949, p. 108) without sufficient investigation into the existence of the social phenomena they referred to. This line of criticism recently ushered in the emphasizing of ideas of increased 'individuality' and tendencies towards 'individualization' in contemporary social life, including the individualizing implications of 'flexibility'. Together with the parallel debate on 'globalization', a sociological image of the contemporary world emerges in which there are no social phenomena 'between' the singular human being, on the one end, and structures of global extension, on the other.[12] This, however, is an image which at best captures some recent tendencies in the restructuring of social relations; it can hardly be upheld as the basis for a renewed sociology of contemporary societal configurations.

Despite doubts about some outcomes of these critical debates, there is, in the light of this double critique, no possibility of a return to those concepts on which the social theory of twentieth-century modernity – or, in other words, of mass-democratic industrial-capitalist society – was based. *Conceptual* debate has effectively destroyed collectivist ontology in the social sciences. *Socio-political* changes during the last three decades have undermined the historic building of social order on collectivist imaginary significations such as class, nation and state. Without doubt, the double existence of such concepts, in intellectual as well as in political life, provided considerable security, not least in terms of justifications for political action. Clinging to those concepts after the double critique, however, violates rules of intellectual integrity as much as it hampers political persuasiveness. It appears to be nothing more than a contemporary conservatism.

Such an attitude, which can be found both in sociological and in political circles, is not only looking nostalgically 'back' to times of relatively high security and bounded inclusiveness in social arrangements (or what I call 'organized modernity'), it also denies or underrates one key aspect of modernity, the emancipatory promise of liberation. The experience of modernity, or its 'adventure' (Lefort 1986a, p. 213; see also chapter 6 above), is made possible by the questioning of all foundations – of knowledge, of justice, of politics. This questioning is a liberation from the imposition of external sources of legitimacy, but it cannot but go along with new uncertainties as well, which may appear as threats and dangers.

The ambiguity and ambivalence of 'flexibility' stems from this double relation to historical forms of social organization. In relation to the arrangements of the heyday of the interventionist welfare state, 'flexibility' looks like a loss of certainty and security, on the one hand, and as the opening up of new opportunities unconstrained by collective rules, on the other. In slightly different terms, the sociological discourse on 'individualization' captures the same phenomenon, as does also the debate on 'post-modern identities', which are seen as rather less rooted in social locations than are 'modern' ones, and instead as being a matter of choice, change and the possibility of permanent recombinations.

If the overall change in conceptual debate actually mirrored changes in the social world, then this world would be devoid of social structures as well as of forms of domination. It would be inhabited by individual human beings pursuing their lives by constantly reshaping their orientations, achieving what they achieve on the basis of their abilities alone, and moving in an open world which itself would be constantly adjusting in line with the evolving orientations of the human beings that populate it. Such a picture is blatantly inadequate to describe the current social world. However, a redescription of the state of social relations under current conditions has to take the challenge that this image provides seriously. The image is based on the observation and the experience of recent changes; while it is conceptually inadequate, it thus cannot be ignored.

The social sciences are as yet quite far from providing such a revised analysis of the state of social relations. The current task can be compared to the one that now so-called classical sociologists faced when they were trying to develop conceptual tools for understanding the emergent mass-democratic industrial-capitalist society roughly a century ago. Then as now, such an intellectual project never rests on observation alone. It relates to the ongoing restructuring with its own active interpretation and thus becomes itself a part of that restructuring, part of an interpretative-interventionist effort.

Beyond 'flexibility' (2): work at re-institutionalization

The current socio-political condition of modernity is, I argued, one of major transition and transformation. In such situations, intellectual restructuring may well be partly anticipated by institutional restructuring. Political actors may respond to situations with an intuition of adequacy rather than a fully elaborated policy design, but nevertheless may arrive at insights that, in turn, may influence intellectual debate. In chapter 2 above, I argued that the Charter of Fundamental Rights of the European Union contains elements of a more adequate articulation of political commitments than can be found in the dominant currents of political philosophy. Here, I want to briefly suggest that the creation of a common currency within (parts of) the

European Union contains the seeds for a fuller response to the current challenges of economic modernity than much of economic theorizing.

Recent developments from the creation of the European Central Bank to the debate on a constitutional treaty, despite the latter's failure, have demonstrated that European political elites, or at least a majority among them, do not by and large see the process they are involved in as any full-scale institutional dismantling along the lines of de-regulation or neo-liberalism. They rather conceive of their project as one of institution-building, certainly under conditions of considerable external strain, but not without creative possibilities. It was the insight that a truly global flexibility of exchange rates would enormously increase uncertainties both for management and workers in economies with high export exposure, such as the European ones, that caused European political elites to embark on the process of monetary coordination, first, and monetary integration, second. By doing so, they cannot be seen as having generally favoured stability (or rigidity) over flexibility, or the other way round.

Rather, they have created a new kind of economic space with properties different from the established national ones, in particular a smaller degree of import penetration, but also a higher heterogeneity of economic situations.[13] At the same time, the new entity, characterized by the absence of all barriers to exchange within its space, is also of a size and weight in the global economy such that fluctuations of the latter will have less of an impact. Its rules and arrangements of monetary policy, while not entirely different from the national ones, entail a certain retreat from day-to-day politics (on the so-called *Bundesbank* model), but simultaneously reassert the responsibility of a political entity, the EU, for the stability and credibility of a currency.[14] If one wanted to use the term at all, one could probably say that 'flexibility' has increased for the movement of people, goods and capital within this new space, but that this has been achieved by stabilizing and unifying – and thus 'rigidifying' – the framework conditions for such movements.

The socio-political details and implications of this new compromise still remain to be worked out. Certainly, the European Union in its current state is at best on the way towards a new relatively stable compromise over socio-political and economic arrangements. Arrival at any such compromise with significant substantive and collective components, which could replace the dismantled post-Second World War arrangements, is made difficult and problematic by the accumulated historical experience of the asymmetric arrangements of modernity.

Compared to the building of national institutions more than a century ago, the interpretative resources available to current actors are, on the one hand, relatively weak, since both social solidarity and cultural-linguistic commonality are weaker today, and, on the other hand, those resources are relatively diverse and not easily combinable, since the institutional rules developed within the participating nation-states are often only similar in broad form but not in detail (see Zimmermann et al. 1999). In such a situation, neo-liberalism apparently provides an easy way out with its simple idea of 'flexibility' because it implies an overall reduction of the need to communicate about common rules and to justify them in terms of available registers of action: it carries a much lighter 'onus of argument', to return to Taylor's formula. The imaginary signification of European modernity has an in-built bias towards individual autonomy, as mentioned above, and, while having raised the stakes of politics as an entirely self-determining game without pre-given rules or norms, it risks eroding the interpretative resources for collective deliberation. The example of the building of national institutions roughly a century ago, however, despite all its ambivalence, shows that there is no linear trend in history. The difficulty is not a principled, but a specific, socio-historical one: the issue is how to significantly restructure existing institutions without losing them in a process that may, to some extent, require dismantling prior to rebuilding.

Part III

Interpretations of Epistemic Modernity: Distance and Involvement

Overture: The Quest for Knowledge beyond Experience and Interpretation

The so-called scientific revolution of the seventeenth century is often regarded as historically the first of those liberating revolutions that brought forth a novel institutional arrangement in which 'modern institutions' became the containers for free human action. It is said to have liberated the search for knowledge from imposed constraints and brought about the idea of self-regulation through communication between scholars, later to be known as the 'autonomy of science'. As such, it is regarded to have created an institutional answer to the epistemic *problématique*. The 'record' of this revolution, however, is much more complex than this modernist representation suggests.

The first image that comes to mind with regard to the scientific revolution is the invention of new tools that either make aspects of reality visible that could not be perceived before, such as the discovery of celestial bodies and movements through the telescope, or that intervene in matter so that connections between bodies and movements become explorable in novel ways, such as the possibility of creating a vacuum by means of the air pump. Innovations such as these, and the spirit behind them, mark the origins of modern *experimental* science, and their 'modernity' resides in at least two features, a third one long having been overlooked.

First, by shifting the boundaries of perception beyond the bodily possible, these scholars removed the respect for God's creation that had allegedly long impeded scientific progress, and thus inaugurated *intellectual autonomy*. This view, partly valid as it is, overlooks both that some considerable kind of experimentation had gone on earlier in Europe, not least in ancient Greece, and elsewhere in the world, such as China, and that the 'early-modern' Europeans who embarked on such activity were most often firm believers in the Christian god.

Second, by setting up associations for scholarly communication and evaluation, such as academies and royal societies, *organizational autonomy* of scientific activity was introduced. While there is some truth to this view, too, here it is often overlooked that such associations remained related to, and dependent on, the monarchical authority in the respective institutional contexts. If they were truly characteristic of the changes that occurred in knowledge-seeking, these features could indeed be seen as moves of liberation from intellectual and organizational restraint respectively, and as such they have been construed as establishing science as a novel force in society, neutral with regard to religion, politics and commerce and not least for this reason particularly powerful.

The third feature sits uneasily with this view, and that is why it has long remained neglected. In as far as scholars experiment with natural matter, namely, they intervene in nature and potentially create material novelty. This *power of science to transform and master* – rather than merely explore – the world was emphasized in the context of the alliance of science with industry from the industrial revolution onwards, but it was rarely seen as a feature of science on its own, which was rather portrayed as 'neutral' and 'objective'.

The emphasis on experimental method, which is mostly placed in the centre of accounts of the 'scientific revolution', was accompanied – and to some extent preceded – by another major change in the attitude towards knowledge, the precise connection of which to 'science' remains a disputed matter in the philosophy of science. The seventeenth century, namely, witnessed the arguably hitherto most radical attempt to overcome scepticism, and this attempt – in contrast to experimental investigation – needed to identify other sources of certainty than those arrived at through 'experience', which could always be treacherous. The exemplary text here is René Descartes' *Discourse on Method*, which in many interpretations marks the onset of the philosophy of modernity with its rejection of all epistemic foundations outside of the human capacity to think and its attempt to identify the then remaining sources of certainty as precisely as possible. The *rationalism* that emerges from this perspective is in many respects at odds with the *empiricism* that could be said to guide much of the experimental science that developed during the same period. The difference between a radically modern philosophy, on the one hand, and a radically hands-on experimental practice, on the other, which nevertheless together mark the new attitude towards knowledge of the world, leads us to describe the epistemic changes as a combined philosophical and scientific revolution, rather than as a scientific revolution alone.

In his *Critique of Pure Reason*, roughly one and a half centuries after the beginnings of both the empirically oriented 'scientific revolution' and the rationalistically oriented philosophical revolution, Immanuel Kant tried to synthesize the critiques of both empiricism and rationalism and thus inaugurated a new relation between 'philosophy' and 'science'. His distinction between *noumena* and phenomena can at first sight be interpreted in a Cartesian way, i.e., by considering *noumena*, although they cannot be experienced, as theoretical entities the relations between which are governed by laws. A science developing such laws could arguably be elaborated on such assumption, and it would be truthfully representing the world. Throughout the nineteenth century and into the twentieth century, indeed, such novel sciences developed enormously. They achieved what we still consider major breakthroughs in knowledge, and they specialized and grew, first, into the disciplines of the natural sciences.

Within this broader context of general scientific developments, those approaches that we now know as the social sciences gained more pronounced intellectual contours in the course of the nineteenth century. Steps towards academic institutionalization occurred from the end of that century onwards and, more successfully, in the twentieth century, in many countries only after the Second World War. The early social sciences – in the sense of intellectual endeavours easily recognizable to us as 'social sciences' – emerged in the context of the so-called democratic revolutions and offered a variety of ways of dealing with the new, post-revolutionary political situation which was characterized by the fact that human beings saw themselves increasingly as being both enabled and obliged to create their own rules for social action and political order. The general idea of providing and using social knowledge for government and policy was certainly not new at this point. The post-revolutionary situation, however, had introduced novel elements into the observation of, and reflection upon, the social world. On the one hand, a much more radical uncertainty had been created by the commitment, even if often a reluctant one, to the self-determination of the people, that is, the radically modern opening of the political *problématique*, a step which at first sight appeared to limit the possibility of predictive empirical knowledge. On the other hand, this radical openness had been accompanied by the hope for the self-organization of society and its rational individuals, so that the desire for valid knowledge now turned towards the discovery of the laws of societal self-development and rational action.

The objective of this Part III is to review the development of the sciences (in chapter 8), and the social sciences in particular (in chapter 9) under the angle of the relation, under conditions of modernity, between the epistemic *problématique*, on the one hand, and the economic and political *problématiques*, on the other. Given that it was part of the quest of the sciences to step out of the specificity of single experiences and to establish certainty by constructing concepts under which large varieties of different experiences could be subsumed, the main thrust of the following argument can be summarized in terms of the restoration of the significance of experiences and their interpretations even for the epistemic *problématique*.

The two chapters proceed in slightly different ways. Chapter 8 reviews the quest for epistemic certainty in the sciences by pointing to the historico-political experiences against the background of which this quest was raised as well as by underlining the transformation of the world as a consequence of particular 'scientific' ways to answer this quest. Chapter 9, in turn, starts out from what was often seen as a specificity of the social sciences, namely that they are interpretative sciences that refer to the ways meaning is given to the world by human beings in the light of the experiences they have. It discusses critically one major observation in this context, namely the debate about 'national traditions' of the social sciences, and argues that this – only partly superseded – debate can be read as an indication of the social sciences' contribution to providing plural interpretations of modernity. Some aspects of the debate about the social sciences will be taken up again in chapter 13 (in Part V), in which the relation of social theory to the experience of the democratic revolution, as mentioned above, is discussed in more detail.

8

The Critique of Science and its Prospects

There are periods in human history during which the perennial discussion about knowledge resorts to politico-military metaphors. Thus, from the middle of the twentieth century onwards, the term 'scientific revolution' was increasingly used to refer to those changes in the human view of the world that emerged between the late sixteenth and the eighteenth centuries and brought about what we now tend to call 'modern science'.[1] More recently, we have heard of 'science wars', and although the major battleground seems to be in North America, some hostilities have also been observed in other parts of the world.

There is a deep connection between revolutions and wars. It is a feature of revolutions in the modern sense of the term to aim at spreading their impact beyond their place of origin, and they often do so by military means. Just as often, though, and only partly in response to revolutionary wars, the resistance to revolution also resorts to violent means. Such wars are then wars against revolutions, counter-revolutionary wars. Furthermore, it is also true that revolutions tend to occur at the end of wars, when there often is a desire to build some new order. But I will come back to this question only at the end of my reflections.

Given that these terms, 'scientific revolution' and 'science wars', are creatures of the twentieth century and have somewhat uncertain temporal connotations, it is far from self-evident whether the wars in question are revolutionary wars, aiming at continuing the conquest of the world by scientific knowledge, or counter-revolutionary wars, bringing finally to a halt the devastation of the world under the reign of scientific knowledge. As often happens with wars, even the outbreak of hostilities is subject to a variety of interpretations. Historians of wars and revolutions can often tell us about asymmetries in the socio-political constellations that were in the background of those events and go quite far in helping us understand why they occurred. Mostly, however, they are quite at a loss in explaining when they occurred, why hostilities started at a specific moment and not sooner or later. On the battleground of the recent so-called science wars, there was, in the view of the warriors for science, a provocation that required retaliation, namely combined effects of the radically empirical and 'symmetric' turn in the social studies of science and the 'linguistic turn' in the human sciences, often, but misleadingly, referred to together under the label 'post-modernism'.[2] But on a closer look there was no declaration of war by the 'post-modernists' at all; all that was going on was the breaking up of unfounded and self-serving assumptions about what science is by looking at the actual activities of scientists and at the concepts they use to describe them, by looking at experiences and their interpretations.[3] One contributor to this debate, Boaventura de Sousa Santos, was indeed arguing for nothing but 'common sense'.[4] And we will see in a moment that he even argued quite commonsensically for common sense. It needed quite some rhetorical armoury to reinterpret the close analysis of scientific practices as a declaration of war on the sciences. One is tempted to say that a little bit more common sense could have prevented the outbreak of hostilities. But it is one of the problems with wars that they are difficult to stop and that they tend to spread, involving ever more combatants as well as innocent civilians.

The warriors for the cause of science may object that, while their critics may not have been declaring war, they were declaring revolution, for instance, as Santos did, by diagnosing an 'emergent paradigm' that breaks with common scientific practices and aims at opening up broader perspectives. This claim certainly was provocative. Rather than revolutionary, established scientists may even have seen it as counter-revolutionary, as rolling back namely the accomplishments of the scientific revolution. Ironically, those accomplishments, as scientists tend to see them, can be described in terms that are structurally similar to the critical diagnosis.

Scientists claim to break with 'traditional' knowledge practices and, thus, achieve a superior understanding of the world. An important element of their self-view is the systematic questioning of the world by means of empirical investigations and the subjection of their own findings to criticism by other scientists on grounds of results from further investigation. They reject the suggestion that their investigations should be halted and we should again accept the world as it appears to us, 'traditionally'. They are 'reminded' – in the sense of a long cultural memory – of religious indictments against interrogating worldly phenomena. That is why, in search of more contemporary examples, Stalinism, Nazism and most recently Islamism come to their mind – all regimes, or aspiring regimes, by the way, that hardly ever left an opportunity of applying scientific insights for their purposes unused.

What the warriors on behalf of science persistently fail to understand is that nothing could be further from the contemporary agenda in the discussion about knowledge. If Santos was arguing for a revolution, in terms of an 'emergent paradigm', it was not a counter-revolution against science, but a revolution to add on to the scientific revolution, to carry critical investigation further, and not to halt it. Enlightened scientists should join in this call, on the basis of their own self-understanding, and not fight against it. To understand this call better, at least as I see it, we need three brief forays into adjacent territories: into philosophy, into history and into politics.

Science and the question of representation

Philosophers and scientists have always been concerned about the relation of their knowledge about the world to (the rest of) this world. This concern has sometimes been phrased as the question of the representation of the social world in and through the writing of scholars, or as the *adaequatio intellectus et rei*, the reaching of such adequacy being the objective of scientific inquiry. From Plato and Aristotle, and then Thomas of Aquinas, this epistemic *problématique* stretches into the positivism of the sciences of the nineteenth century, including the social sciences, as well as its critical alternative, scientific Marxism. With important qualifications, it was revived in the neo-positivism of the twentieth century and the unified science programme that tried to (re-)integrate the social sciences with the natural sciences.

Despite this continuity of concern, the very concept of representation of the world has also been heavily criticized. At several points in intellectual history it appeared as if the whole idea needed to be abandoned because there just is no way to verify the relation between the world and thoughts about the world other than again by the use of thought (even though not exclusively by thought). Thus, certain knowledge of *adaequatio* is in principle unattainable. In most recent debate, during the closing decades of the twentieth century, the accumulation of such doubt has often been labelled a 'crisis of representation', implicitly and misleadingly pretending novelty of these doubts. This crisis is in many respects the background to the 'science wars'. Through all of the earlier such crises, however, the epistemic *problématique* keeps reviving, often with new qualifications, and those who revive it often argue that it cannot be entirely abandoned either, since otherwise the status of statements about the world would become entirely unclear. A war over this issue, thus, would be a very peculiar war: it cannot be won, not even by the attempt at annihilation of one of the belligerent parties, since such annihilation is impossible.

Even though this debate about representation has been going on virtually through all of the history of philosophy, the break that came with the radical scepticism characteristic of what can be called the philosophy of modernity is often seen as shifting the terrain. Between the middle of the seventeenth century, Descartes' time of writing, and the end of the eighteenth century, Kant's time, the ground on which representation could be possible was systematically explored. This period, of course, is precisely also the period of the so-called scientific revolution. Furthermore, it is also the period of the immediate aftermath of the religious wars in Europe – an issue to which I will return. The novel sciences that developed on this basis were meant to provide new certainties in an era of uncertainty. Arguably, however, the more significant impulse from these one and a half centuries of debate was an aggravation of the general problem of representation, at least within the philosophical mode of reasoning. This crisis of representation stemmed from the increasing gap between the perceiving and knowing subject and the world.[5]

The combined outcome of the Cartesian and the Kantian moves, namely, was that, on the one hand, philosophical reasoning appeared to have exhausted its possibilities, at least for the time being. At the end-point of this reasoning, on the other hand, a space had been opened for a different form of inquiry. The gap between the subject and the world, or between the *noumena* and the phenomena, permitted, maybe even invited, attempts to fill it by positive, empirical knowledge, elaborated in systematic, conceptually guided ways. A terminological shift accompanied these debates. Natural philosophy was increasingly complemented by – some may want to say: gave way to – 'empirical philosophy'. And the latter inaugurates precisely that mode of investigation that we now know under the name of science. During this period of rapid scientific development, it was largely and easily forgotten that the turn towards empirical investigation had by far not answered the question of representation satisfactorily or, in other words, that the relation between philosophy and the sciences remained an important one, despite all claims on the part of the sciences to have emancipated from philosophy.[6] The explicit reopening of that question should only be a matter of time.

Science and its critics: a recurring debate

'Man who lives in a world of hazards is compelled to seek for security.' Thus starts a book that was published in the United States of America on 11 October 1929. Only a few days later, Wall Street crashed, and security was in short supply. The book was John Dewey's *The Quest for Certainty*, and the precise timing of its publication was only coincidentally related to the Wall Street crash. However, there is a broader context of crisis to which it indeed responds. For decades, concern had again been growing about the relation between the truth claims of philosophers, on the one hand, and, on the other, the kind of knowledge the sciences had been producing with increasing success throughout the nineteenth century. Those sciences, including the social sciences, were seen as overspecialized and fragmented while at the same time highly successful in generating new insights and in transforming the world through science-based technology. Having initially developed under the shelter of philosophy, they seemed to make philosophy – just like religion – both superfluous and unsustainable, since no – ontological or metaphysical – claims about any continuity of the order of things nor any ground for that order could be upheld in the face of rapidly changing scientific concepts and empirical insights.

Through the early decades of the twentieth century, however, novel conceptions of the relation between philosophy and the sciences were proposed that were based not least on a critique of what John Dewey (1984 [1929], p. 195) called the 'spectator theory of knowing'. With this term, he summarized all views, for him characteristic of most philosophy and science, that saw the world as exposed to the human gaze and assumed that it is exactly this distance between the knowing subject and the object to be known that allows for certain knowledge. The spectator theory of knowing thus starts out from a radical scepticism, from the attitude that nothing can be taken for granted. And it is in response to the doubts about the world around us as we experience it that the quest for certainty needs to proceed through a distancing from the world to gain an 'outside' look at it. The distancing from the sensations of the world had been considered a precondition for the identification of those assumptions on which claims for valid knowledge could be erected. By the same move, the question of epistemology itself had emerged as the problem of the relation between the 'reality' of the world and the 'representations' that human beings provide of the world in their philosophy and science. The preference in the philosophy of science was for a long time, as Dewey points out, for an epistemological formalism that presupposes this distance between the knower and that which is to be known. Thus emerges what I would call the modernist conception of the epistemic *problématique* (Wagner 2001a, chapter 1). It went along with the – quasi-sociological – idea of separating out a social realm in which the pursuit of knowledge was possible in independence from other concerns of social life. But, of course, as Dewey insists, human beings cannot step out of the world they inhabit and of which they are a part.

Similar turns were made in European philosophy during the same period. Ludwig Wittgenstein had hoped to clarify the problem of representation in the *Tractatus logicus-philosophicus*, in which he employs a picture theory of knowing, whereas in the *Philosophical Investigations* he sees our languages as being part of our forms of life, and thus not as looking at life from a distance. In *Holzwege*, Martin Heidegger analysed the modernist theory of knowledge as representation comprehensively as the attempt 'to provide oneself a picture' of the world by making a world that is placed in front of oneself. Rather than making 'a picture of the world', however, this move 'grasps the world as picture', relates to the world as if it were an object in front of us. In two intertwined processes, the world becomes a picture and the human being a subject. Richard Rorty tried to summarize this reinterpretation of the history of philosophy and the sciences provided by Dewey, Heidegger and Wittgenstein as the abdication of the attempt at seeing knowledge as 'the mirror of nature' (Rorty 1980).

Rorty's synthesis roughly coincided with Santos' *Discourse*, mentioned above. The 1980s became a new period of reflection about the sciences and the kind of knowledge they were producing. Dewey had already spoken of an emergent paradigm – to use Santos' term – even though Dewey conceptualized the shift somewhat differently. In the concluding lecture of *The Quest for Certainty*, he likened the development of the sciences of his time to a 'Copernican revolution', borrowing the term from Kant, the implications of which for philosophy he aimed to spell out.

> The old centre was mind knowing by means of an equipment of powers complete within itself, and merely exercised upon an antecedent external material equally complete in itself. The new centre is indefinite

interactions taking place within a course of nature which is not fixed and complete, but which is capable of direction to new and different results through the mediation of intentional operations. (Dewey 1984, pp. 231–2)

One of the key events in Dewey's history of the sciences is Heisenberg's work on the 'uncertainty principle', just as it is for Santos. How similar is the earlier debate to the current one?

Most contributors to the debate in the early twentieth century worked with a strong distinction between philosophy and the sciences. In many of the European contributions, the loss of the hegemony of philosophy over the sciences was central to the problem. The initial observation of the fragmentation and compartmentalization of the sciences as a consequence of the loss of the philosophical umbrella led later to diagnoses such as the hegemony of instrumental reason – and thus the 'eclipse' of reason in a more comprehensive sense – in Horkheimer, and the emergence of modern technology as a new metaphysics in Heidegger (see chapters 5 and 6 above). The alternatives these authors offered in their early writings pointed into different directions for rethinking but in both cases they entailed a return to philosophy, even though in highly different guises.

The alternative approach was to reject any return to philosophy, however conceptualized, and to embrace the new sciences. In different, even directly opposed, ways, this was what the (neo-)positivism of the Vienna School and American pragmatism proposed. In Dewey's terms, positivism would transfer the – misguided, in his view – quest for certainty from philosophy to the sciences. Positivism basically works with a model of a mind-independent reality and draws a clear boundary between knowing and acting. As a philosophy of science, positivism tries to establish the claim for the certainty of superior scientific knowledge in a new form, based not least on logic and mathematics which for Dewey are merely one pole of possible knowledge. Dewey himself, in contrast, also embraces the sciences, but only because he sees them undergoing a decisive change in orientation, his 'Copernican revolution', as a consequence of Heisenberg's discovery of the principle of indeterminacy. Science will no longer want to discover laws of motion of antecedent objects, to which human beings have to conform, but will move to 'constructing enjoyable objects directed by knowledge of consequences' (Dewey 1984, p. 217). Was it possibly John Dewey, whom nobody suspected, who declared war on the scientific establishment?

But a declaration of war, or of revolution, that passes unnoticed is no declaration of war at all. Five decades later, Richard Rorty (1980) would claim that Dewey, Heidegger and Wittgenstein were the most important thinkers of the twentieth century, and this not least because of their rethinking of knowledge, science and philosophy, all with a view to overcoming metaphysics and epistemology. But had these thinkers really been influential in this way at their time, then the epistemic *problématique* should long have been put to rest. However, this was far from being the case. Half a century after *The Quest for Certainty*, another 'report on knowledge' underlined the fact that the sciences of the twentieth century had continued to make unwarranted claims to superior knowledge. The author, Jean-François Lyotard (1979, pp. 25–7), resorted to Wittgenstein's notions of language games and their irreducible plurality to explain why such a claim could not be upheld. He thus became one of those who triggered off a new debate on epistemology, often now referred to in the context of discussions about post-modernity. Similarly, Santos' observations form part of a renewed reflection on the time-honoured debate about the ways in which the sciences relate to the world that they investigate, or in other words, how they claim to have resolved the epistemic *problématique*.

The outraged reactions to the so-called post-modernist challenge to epistemology and to the sciences, though, operate as if no such debate had ever happened. Why is it then, we may ask, that such debates recur instead of having the 'revolutionary' impact on our understanding of knowledge that both Dewey and Santos expected and hoped for? To give some answer to this question, we need to review the epistemic *problématique*, with a view to both its conceptualization and its actual practice in the history of modernity.

Science and its applications: science-inspired transformations of the world

Both the authors of the inter-war period and those of the 1970s and 1980s look back at an immediate past during which the large-scale application of science-based technology considerably transformed the world they were experiencing. Dewey, Heidegger and Wittgenstein were writing after what was later called the second industrial revolution, with the development of the electrical and chemical industry as well as a revolution in transportation, and the application of all of this during the First World War, of crucial importance at least for the Europeans. This is the period that gave rise to the economic-epistemic determinism that is a major component of the critical tradition in the analysis of modernity (see chapter 5 above). Santos,

Lyotard and those historians and sociologists of science who have started to seriously study empirically the activities of scientists from the late 1970s onwards, in turn, write after those 'thirty glorious years' of economic growth after the Second World War that transformed the face of the earth in an unprecedented way.

Contextually sensitive historians of ideas will agree that such observation helps us understand the recurrence of topics. Unlike what Dewey thought, no revolution in philosophy and science was taking place during the inter-war years, so that a similar problematic phenomenon could reoccur. Nor was, we may add today, a new paradigm emerging during the 1980s, unlike Santos thought. Science-inspired transformations of the world have remained a topic of some urgency. However, scientists may rather easily reject any responsibility for those developments philosophers and historians of science were observing. Ironically, or maybe significantly, what allows them to deny any such responsibility is precisely the self-understanding of science in relation to the world that is diagnosed by their critics. They will claim that their activity proceeds according to its own rules, at a certain distance from worldly affairs. These rules, as scientists tend to argue, both support their claim to epistemological superiority and the absence of any responsibility for 'application' since this is what happens after they have done their work and is therefore beyond their control.

The claim to superior knowledge, though, can be used to add a further twist to the reasoning. Despite denying responsibility for hazards resulting from application because their approach is neutral, objective, methodical and self-driven, scientists are often ready to accept praise for their useful knowledge (and funding to produce more of it), which is useful precisely because it is superior to other knowledge. There is a saying to describe this attitude: to have one's cake and eat it. The point here is not the denial of the usefulness of some technical innovations that follow upon scientific discovery. The point is to understand what the relation of distancing and intervening is in the scientific-technological enterprise. Bruno Latour (1993) – one of the favourite enemies of the warriors on behalf of science – has aptly described the apparent paradox as part of what he calls the modern constitution: because the scientific attitude claims to take – objectifying – distance from the world, it is not only able to look at the world but also to act upon it, apparently from the outside.

Some observers, especially during the 1930s, have moved from similar insights to the diagnosis of the reign of instrumental reason or of unfettered technology. In Horkheimer and Heidegger, for instance, such a view was the direct outcome of their philosophy of knowledge and technology. From Dewey's standpoint, such an outcome is a mere historical-empirical possibility, and he was even optimistic that the 'Copernican revolution' under way would lead to a new conception of knowledge. In the more recent debate, often known under the label of post-modernism, a strong view on historical direction is avoided (with Lyotard coming closest to having one but remaining peculiarly undecided). In contrast, this debate has been the most explicit expression of generalized epistemological uncertainty.

This range of quite diverse interpretations suggests above all the need for a more sustained historical-comparative analysis of the sciences. Such analysis should not start out from a denunciation of the scientists' claim but should see their practices as the search for alternative ways to certainty. Exactly because – against the scientists' own claims – they entailed action, such as experimentation with nature, not just observation, the sciences could *create certainty* rather than merely *postulating* it. Some observations may indicate the direction in which such historical analysis would have to go.

Descartes has long been accused of promoting the unachievable and ultimately damaging project of grounding certainty beyond the specificity of experience. More recently, Descartes' discourse on method has been read in context, that is as addressing the question of security in human social life at a time when the consequences of the Reformation and the religious wars signalled one major step in the destruction of the foundations of certainty (Toulmin 1990). Similarly, the long neglected controversy between Hobbes and Boyle about the grounding of knowledge in experience – and, thus, scientific experiment – marks another case in which the fervour of the attempts to re-establish certainties can hardly be explained otherwise than through the impact of violent religious strife on the consciousness of the authors (Shapin and Schaffer 1985; Latour 1993; Stengers 1993). The scientific revolution was a revolution that followed a war; and it aimed at providing foundations for a new order. This order was, in the view of the revolutionaries, to be built on a belief that was of a different kind than any religious belief, on versions of which earlier orders had been grounded. What its protagonists failed to recognize was that any belief in a higher order is not only ultimately erected on uncertain ground, it is also bound to create resistance. The scientific revolution may have aimed to end a war to make the world safe for rationality. What it indeed accomplished was to shift the terrain on which wars were fought.

In such a contextual perspective, namely, the specificity of Descartes', Boyle's and Hobbes's attempts is in the first instance a high awareness of an inescapable dilemma. On the one hand, there is a deep intellectual consciousness of contingency, of the lack of stability and certainty in the world. Radical doubt is indeed the starting point of the reasoning. In this sense, these episodes are rightly regarded as high points in the history of modernist thought, indeed inaugurating modernist discourse in philosophy and in political theory. On the other hand, Boyle, Hobbes and Descartes were also driven by the conviction that humankind could not live well without some categories of social and natural life that impose themselves on everybody, and such categories would only impose themselves if and because they were undeniably valid. The uncertainty that was experientially self-evident in a context of devastating religious and political strife had to be overcome by appeal to an instance that in their view could only be outside such experience. The co-existence of these two apparently incompatible convictions gives their work a character which one might label dogmatically modernist: radical in their rejection of unfounded assumptions, but inflexible in their insistence on some definable minimum conditions of cognitive and political order that could, and would have to, be universally established. Scientists up to this day have inherited much of this attitude.

Rather than interpreting the writings of Descartes, Boyle and Hobbes as distanced philosophical-scientific truths, we could, however, also regard them as activities that perform an operation on the world with a view to giving that world a new direction. This is especially clear with experiments on nature, as argued for by Boyle, which of course do not just observe the truth of nature but act upon nature. From such an angle, the authors would be seen as identifying a *problématique* in a given situation, would aim at problem-solving and would be driven by a situation-specific sense of urgency – rather than aiming to provide a timeless truth of philosophy or science (which, of course, was how they themselves described their activities). If the history of philosophy and the sciences is read from such an angle, we become able to address issues that cannot be addressed by either principled defenders of modernist science or similarly principled critics of it.

As Boaventura de Sousa Santos points out in more recent writings (Santos 2001), the insistence on knowing as intelligent problem-solving in a given situation has to allow for different kinds of situations and for different experiences of a situation – not least, situations with greater or lesser degrees of (experienced) security – and for different interpretations of such situations to solve the problems at hand – not least, solutions that work by generalization and solutions that work by specification, or as he calls it: small-scale, coarse-grain resolution versus large-scale, fine-grain resolution knowledge. Modernism would then no longer fall into a separate category of knowledge-seeking, but would merely be that approach that insists on the need for generalization in – and because of – situations characterized by high insecurity.

Varieties of epistemic certainty

As a consequence of such differentiation, this approach would allow for varieties in the search for certainty. More specifically, it would invite us to re-read the debate about 'the crisis of the European sciences' (Husserl 1970 [1935]) as a dispute about various ways of engaging the world. The dispute was certainly marked by the diagnosis that an instrumental concept of knowledge lending itself to the transformation of the world by means of technology was about to become predominant. In the first instance, however, it relied on the possibility of making distinctions between various conceptions of knowledge.

Dewey reserved a strong verdict for a philosophy that sticks to its quest for certainty:

> Any philosophy that in its quest for certainty ignores the reality of the uncertain in the ongoing processes of nature denies the conditions out of which it arises. The attempt to include all that is doubtful within the fixed grasp of that which is theoretically certain is committed to insincerity and evasion, and in consequence will have the stigmata of internal contradiction. (1984, p. 195)

In the light of our earlier considerations this statement may be read as an indictment of the modernist sciences.[7] They rested on assumptions about the certainty of the world, and that is indeed where they failed – proved both contradictory and evasive, sometimes also insincere – when nature proved to be more uncertain than expected. Nevertheless the reference to 'the reality of the uncertain' contains a significant openness. It invites the question about the degree of certainty that is attainable in different states of the real. Rather than attacking critics, scientists may better aim at understanding historically variable degrees of attainable certainty of their knowledge – or what Santos terms 'epistemological confidence'.

From our brief analysis two conclusions can now be drawn. First, this critique of science – both in the 1930s and in the 1970s/1980s – had particular historical contexts of emergence. In the first case, it followed upon the rapid development of the scientific disciplines during the nineteenth century and the increasing application of their findings in what is often called the second industrial revolution at the end of that century and then, in the second case, in the even much more widespread diffusion of these applications. Its interpretation of the epistemic *problématique* is circumscribed by the exigency to develop a critical perspective on the impact of modernism, on the one hand, but the lack of plausibility of any recourse to 'tradition' or 'embeddedness' of social life, which would appear as an impossible return in time, on the other (on the rupture with tradition, see chapter 1 above and, more specifically, chapter 11 below).

Second, though, the strong critique of science as the one-dimensional imposition of instrumental reason is ultimately not entirely persuasive. It relies on strong presuppositions about both the nature of modernist science and its all-pervasiveness, on the one hand, and the society on which such conception can so apparently easily be imposed, on the other. The emphasis on varieties of ways of world-making, paraphrasing Nelson Goodman, and consequently variable degrees of certainty leads towards a more fruitful perspective. In turn, however, one should not forget the history of imposition of modernist science that started the critique of science in the first place. It is at this point that Boaventura de Sousa Santos, if I see it correctly, aims to carry the debate further, in his *Discourse on the Sciences* and in his more recent writings (Santos 2001), on which my concluding discussion will concentrate.

Epistemology and critique: knowledge as regulation and knowledge as emancipation

On a closer look, there are two views of knowledge in Boaventura de Sousa Santos' programme; I will call them the strong view and the weak view. His conceptualization proceeds through the diagnosis of two epistemological breaks. The first break leads from common sense to science as we know it, a modernist science that develops knowledge-as-regulation and that supports colonization and order. The second break, yet to be accomplished, will then lead out of mainstream science to the new common sense, and that is to knowledge-as-emancipation, a knowledge that enhances solidarity. This is the strong view. There is, however, also a softer, weaker version of the programme. In this version, the second break leads here to a variety of perspectives, to a 'plurality of knowledges', to a new situation thus, in which knowledge appears in a multiplicity of forms.

The strong view draws a sharp line between regulation and emancipation and their respective knowledge forms. Thus, it follows many critical philosophies of social science, from Karl Marx to the early Jürgen Habermas. Those critical philosophies insist rightly – against objectivism and positivism, including the claims of what Santos calls 'mainstream science' – on the indissoluble connection between knowledge, on the one hand, and the world that it is meant to be about, on the other. However, many, if not most, of these philosophies abandon their own questioning immediately after having developed it, namely by postulating that they have already found the answer to it. Instead of one form of valid knowledge, there are then two: one that dominates because it supports domination, and another one that struggles to come into being because it undermines domination. This simple solution fundamentally neglects – or even denies – the ambivalence of modernity. If modernity, whether it actually exists or is an emancipatory and always unfinished project, is about freedom and autonomy, that is, self-determination, then it is also about self-regulation. There is no true knowledge of emancipation that would not in some sense also have to be a knowledge of regulation, namely of self-regulation. The history of modernity certainly was a history of barbarisms, and science-based instrumental knowledge was enlisted in support of those. But if there is any way to read it fruitfully for the present, it needs to be read as a history of civilization failing. Otherwise, we would never see, let alone understand, the attempts made. There certainly has been what Santos calls a historical process of the 'cannibalization of social emancipation'. But we would need to know much more – in the form of fine-grain resolution, large-scale analyses, in Santos' terms – about how precisely this came about. An interpretation of the 'first epistemological break' goes wrong if it totally denies the ambition of emancipation even in modernism and its science in the face of an otherwise appropriate critique of the rising asymmetry between 'regulation' and 'emancipation'.[8]

A certain lack of ambivalence with regard to the first break is repeated in the discussion of the second epistemological break. In the strong reading of his proposal, Santos appears to succumb to the time-honoured inclination of rather markedly outlining a not-yet-existing alternative that solves all problems, an alternative in which knowledge and solidarity become one. But a quick historical observation suggests that he may be running into a trap that he himself posed. Is such a conception not precisely reviving the Enlightenment dream of a self-regulating society, a dream about which one can justifiably say that at least in some of its versions it has been converted from being emancipatory to being regulatory, and now in the sense of regulation by some imposed on others, and not as self-regulation? Why should we assume that something similar could not again be the case if we follow that same route?[9] In Santos' own, fruitful terms, the problem here is that one should not move from the absolute reign of experience over expectation, or from total indifference both to experience and expectation, towards a similarly unconstrained reign of expectation over experience. That is a recipe for disillusionment, at best, and was historically a recipe for disaster. The challenge of knowledge rather is to find the situationwise appropriate relation of expectation to experience.[10]

Santos rightly underlines that there is conflict and struggle in the social world. However, even if we could assume that friend and foe could be clearly identified, there is struggle not merely between regulators and emancipators. If this were the case, then the struggle would be over once that fight is won. Under conditions of modernity, there will always be contestation, always struggle between different perspectives. And it is unlikely that there will be a knowledge that unequivocally is associated with emancipation and solidarity. Rather, even among those who support those goals, there will be a variety of perspectives and, thus, a 'constellation of knowledges' will emerge that does not settle a dispute, but provides it with resources for reasoning. Against indifference, one then would not just posit solidarity with friends. Rather, concern for others would show precisely in both solidarity and dispute, and both at the same time (see Karagiannis 2007a for an elaboration of this idea). This is what I see in the second, the weak programme in Boaventura de Sousa Santos' work, and it is the one I fully agree with.

In his strong programme, he continues the tradition of critique pointing to something that is not, but could be, and elevates this to a higher position, seen as immediately reachable, if not even reached, as soon as the obstacles are removed. Something of such a critical perspective will be needed as long as there is a strong asymmetry in the acceptance of knowledge claims in the world, as long as, in other words, modernist science can easily align itself with the powers-that-be on the terms of instrumental reason. But such critique should not overdraw its positive claims. Santos' weak programme instead suggests a different understanding of critique, pointing also to something that is not, but that is always struggling to come into existence, thus is always present but in the form of failing. An epistemology of seeing, as he calls it, would not merely show the way to knowledge, it would also need to make visible the obstacles on that way. Since many of those obstacles will not disappear under any circumstances, the search for knowledge means the search for the different ways to overcome them.

In this light, we will have to conclude that there will be no easily established new order after the revolution. There is no single best solution for the epistemic *problématique*. There is a need for a revolution, but maybe not in the form of a new paradigm that governs all our knowledge-seeking practices, rather in the form of putting the practices of the sciences into a place in this world, relativizing their claims to epistemic certainty by making them communicate with other ways of engaging the world. Because we are far away from such a situation, because of the strong asymmetries in the world of knowledge, there is a need for revolution. But this revolution does not necessitate a war, just a considerable dose of common sense or, maybe, new common sense.

9

Varieties of Socio-political Interpretations of Modernity

The social sciences (as well as the historical sciences) have often been portrayed as being bound by their time and social context. The debate in the philosophy of the social sciences is as old as those sciences themselves. The stress on epistemology in this debate, however, remains rather neutral with regard to the form and structure this knowledge-shaping 'context' takes. A more specific, and much more historically and politically, rather than philosophically, orientated discussion claimed that the social sciences occur in the form of national traditions, that it is the nation, and in particular the nation-state, that provides the particular context for intellectual-academic concern about the social world. It was, thus, suggested that forms of social knowledge corresponded to forms of socio-political organization, and in particular to the form of the state. Most broadly, this reasoning maintains that the social sciences always are interpretations of the experiences to which they refer and in which they arise.

In the following, I will review the background assumptions for this reasoning. At the end, I will argue that the complications of this case arise from a double feature: on the one hand, national traditions are a *historically contingent* expression of a *persistent* feature of the social sciences, their contextuality, or in other words, their – implicit or explicit – reference to experience. And on the other hand, the variety of national traditions – since it would be pointless to speak of one tradition only – gives expression to the plurality of *interpretations of modernity* as the most general contextual condition of this form of social knowledge that we call social sciences. While the national form may be largely superseded at the beginning of the twenty-first century, these two features prevail. Concludingly, therefore, we need to briefly ask the question about the contemporary, post-national expression of social knowledge and its relation to political form.[1]

National identities and sociological *problématiques*

Looking at examples from the heyday of national forms of social knowledge, one may immediately note that there are two main versions in which the claim that there are national traditions in the social sciences has been put forward. In its moderate, rather straightforward empirical guise, it notes the existence of national patterns or styles of intellectual-academic work. A number of socio-historical explanations for their occurrence may be attached to that observation. A more radical version (which may explicitly or implicitly include the moderate one) holds that, at least in the social sciences, these national discourses express main features of the practical social philosophy of the respective society, of its socio-political self-understanding.

In that sense, then, the assumption of 'society' as a basic unit in Durkheimian sociology, which was what defined the 'French school', pointed towards both a social realism and a social determinism that was characteristic of French society after the revolution that hailed equality and fraternity as much as liberty. On those grounds, it appeared natural that this thinking should become hegemonic during the Third Republic. Similarly, the German school of economics, with its emphasis on history and institutions, expressed the rejection of the abstract individualism not only of the mainstream of political economy and neo-classical economics, but also of the Enlightenment. And the American social philosophy of pragmatism was exactly as action-orientated and problem-orientated as was American society at large with its limited sense of tradition and thoughtfulness. Abstract collectivism, cultural collectivism and problem-solving voluntarism were thus turned into indications of national character recognizable in the 'national' social sciences; and often enough it remained unclear whether those social sciences merely expressed such a national character that existed independently of it, or whether they aimed at providing an orientation for a social body that was in search of a direction, a social body that had its institutional form in the nation-state.

After sustained processes of institutionalization and professionalization in the social sciences, not least under American hegemony in the first two post-Second World War decades, the idea of national traditions in the social sciences appeared for some time to be fading into an increasingly distant past (for a rather sophisticated version of this argument, see Shils 1965). An era of 'globalization' may have done away with, for better or worse, such remnants of times when constraints to communication still mattered. In more recent years, however, doubts have re-emerged as to whether such debates can really be consigned to the dustbin of history or, which may amount to the same, be declared of interest purely to historians.

The period when it may have seemed that there was one internationally dominant model of inquiry in the social sciences is over (whether it may return in a new guise will be discussed in chapter 11 below). The modernization-orientated social science of the 1960s combined an emphasis on quantitative methodology and behaviourist ontology with the more substantive functionalist-systemic social theory and the economics of growth and development that resulted from a peculiar synthesis of Keynesian and neo-classical elements (see Wagner 1994, chapters 7 and 9). In this form, it appeared as truly global and truly modern at the same time; and the opposition towards it, though never silent, seemed to argue from either an antiquated or a utopian position. Already from the late 1960s onwards, however, this international social science started to lose its hegemony. And even though the critical approaches originally were not less globally oriented than the mighty opponent, this unity crumbled the more successful the mission came to be.

In the names of both post-colonialism and post-modernism, the interest in local forms of knowledge revived. And if one sees these intellectual movements in conjunction with the so-called linguistic turn in the human sciences, i.e., the inescapability of interpretation and the ambiguity of language, and with the post-Kuhnian sociology of scientific knowledge, i.e., the need for the impartial, 'symmetric', analysis of knowledge claims, then the issue of the rootedness of knowledge in social life is firmly back on the agenda (see chapter 8 above). While these developments appear to remain predominantly critical rather than become constructive, there are also moments in current intellectual debate that claim to contain at least germs of an alternative to any international and hegemonic conception of social science. They proceed in two quite different ways: on the one hand, forms of knowledge are (again) seen as rooted in particular social identities; on the other, the history of knowledge forms is used to uncover and identify a plurality of *problématiques* that need to be dealt with when aiming at making the social world intelligible.

Recent years have witnessed a broad revival of theorizing about cultural identities in the social sciences as well as in political debates. As part of these debates, views of social science have resurfaced that link forms of knowledge directly to existing social configurations. A significant example is provided by the renewed interest in the specificity of 'Europe' in social and political as well as intellectual terms, an interest that was bound to clash with Europe's most significant Other for the past two centuries, the United States of America.[2]

A vivid debate was unleashed when Richard Münch, a German sociologist of quite international orientation, offered a comparison of sociological styles that, at least in the eyes of cosmopolitan American readers such as Jeffrey Alexander, seemed to revive old stereotypes and to smack of a cultural nationalism which the international sociological community had taken to be superseded. Münch describes the British tradition of sociology as emphasizing class and conflict, the French one as focusing on society and structure, and the German one as developing a dialectical view on the social world. The American one, opposed to all European ones, does not seem to have any substantive core at all, but is characterized by standardization and homogenization of scholarly expression (Münch 1991, 1993, 1995; Alexander 1994). In the light of such crudeness, Alexander's strong reaction is understandable, even though the charge of nationalism is most certainly not justified with regard to this particular author.

Another recent analysis that also reasons in terms of national traditions in sociology is Donald Levine's (1995a) history of sociological visions. Levine identifies seven major versions of the sociological project, six of which carry spatial-cultural denominations, the Marxian tradition being the only exception. Of the remaining six, the 'Hellenic' one should certainly also be given a special place, since it could as well be called Aristotelian and since it occupies a distinct historical time compared to all other 'sociologies'. For the rest, however, Levine associates specific ways of thinking sociology with existing national cultures during the history of the West between the late eighteenth and the early twentieth century; he talks about a British (which includes both the English and the Scottish), a French, a German, an Italian and an American tradition of sociology.

Compared to Münch, Levine provides a much more subtle and differentiated perspective which, however, shows many of the same contours. He sees British sociologists as elaborating a Newtonian image of the social world. In the search for a secular ethic, the atomic view of nature is transposed into the human world. Individualism and evolutionism (plus organicism) are the predominant theoretical perspectives, combined with a strong concern for measurability. The French approach, which emerges not least in debate with the British, in contrast, starts out from the postulate of societal realism, in which the social formation predominates over natural individual propensities. Society itself is seen as a source of sentiments, and, consequently, a societal normativity as well as a societal morality prevails. The German tradition of sociology, to confine my background image to these three national cultures, emphasizes a subject which is interpretive and capable of self-determination as well as able to identify and make choices between good and evil. The triple ambition of German sociology then, according to Levine, is to understand the expressive subject, to recognize the cognitive subject and to analyse the voluntaristic subject (Levine 1995a, chapters 7 to 9).

If read as a contribution to the historiography of social thought, Levine's account is limited in many respects. However, this may not have been the author's primary objective. He opposes existing 'narratives' of the development of the discipline of sociology, all of which are 'tunnel histories' in which the past ultimately, and finally inevitably, leads to the achievements of the present, to his 'national' accounts; and this opposition seems to be a heuristic device to unfold an array of intellectual possibilities to conceptualize the social world. It is in this way that the identification of national traditions serves to underpin the observation of a plurality of ways of dealing with *problématiques* that came to be defined as sociological and, in a second step, to understand those *problématiques* better than one could from any single one of those perspectives.

National traditions in the social sciences: analytical possibilities

This reading of Levine may have been overly generous and even in my brief account the question is left open why *problématiques* should come in national guises at all.[3] If we accept for a moment that there are, or at least have been, national traditions in the social sciences, there is a number of quite distinct ways to try to account for this feature.

The historical nature of the objects of social knowledge

The major reason for the national form of social knowledge can be seen to reside in the fact that the objects of the social sciences are themselves historical and cultural and in this sense always unique and particular. On the basis of some realist philosophy of social science, even in reasonably weak versions, one would assume that scholarly knowledge of this social world reflects the particularity and uniqueness of the object. Such a notion would make it understandable that social knowledge will not easily 'internationalize' as long as the forms of social relations do not themselves 'internationalize' (see Manicas 2006 for a recent such argument).

To explain a national form of social knowledge on this basis, one would have to make the additional assumption that a main feature of these objects is their being themselves of a national extension – like the national 'society' of much of the sociology of the nineteenth and twentieth century which corresponded to the political institutions of the nation-state – or at least, being a characteristic part of a bigger object that is national, and carrying some of the features of that bigger object. For much research and debate in the social sciences, this perspective forms a valid part of an overall explanation as to why there may be national forms of knowledge. In earlier work, I have myself come to the conclusion that the historical forms of the social sciences in continental Europe, in particular during the nineteenth and early twentieth century, were related to the forms and self-understandings of statehood (Wagner 1989, 1990). A pronounced national character of the social sciences emerges if and when the socio-political orders and the interpretation of problems they elaborate differ considerably. For the major continental nations or would-be nations – France, Italy, Germany – it could be shown that this was indeed visibly the case.

In general, such a finding should not be too surprising, in particular for some of the older of the social science disciplines which had been rather clearly and unproblematically defined by their relation to social practices and institutions during the nineteenth century. History provided accounts of the development of national states and commonly showed a considerable dose of patriotism and nationalism. Law interpreted and systematized national legal systems; it provided them with justification and trained their practitioners. The state sciences – now often considered to be the forerunner to current political science – aimed at a comprehensive approach to problems of governance and policy-making in and for the existing polities. And geography and demography, whose objects are not national institutions per se, but social phenomena that were conceptualized so as to overlap with nations, provided nation-specific accounts of the state of the territory and its population.

The relation between the form of the object and the form of the knowledge about the object, however, while plausible, is insufficient when trying to account for national traditions in the social sciences. In particular towards the turn of the nineteenth century, scholars in these fields felt the need to define their work more precisely in academic terms, an operation that often implied some distancing from the concrete object under study. Partly following the model of the natural sciences, which had developed so enormously during the nineteenth century, partly responding to broader transformations of the university, which re-emerged as the institutional locus of systematic research, social scientists devoted much energy to developing a scholarly definition and demarcation of their fields, be it through disciplinary treatises, such as for history and geography, or through the choice of theoretical foundations such as legal positivism in law or the theorem of the optimum population in demography (Rothblatt and Wittrock 1993).

In this context, it is noteworthy that, despite similar attempts, state/political scientists did not achieve a recognized degree of disciplinary consolidation in similar form (with the exception of the USA), and the area suffered from a loss of influence to other disciplines (Manicas 1987; Wagner, Wittrock and Whitley 1991). Among the disciplines that profited from the decline of the state sciences, the most notable ones were economics, in its new guise after the marginalist revolution, and sociology, gaining a foothold at academic institutions for the first time. At this point, I just want to suggest that the rise of these two disciplines at this historical moment may have had to do with their being less 'national' and more 'international' than law, history or the state sciences or, in other words, with their trying to gain some distance from the concreteness of the economic and social relations that surrounded them. This hypothesis will need to be explored in more depth at a later point in my argument.

The constitutively national nature of social knowledge

An alternative way to explain the nation-specific variation in forms of social knowledge is to look not at the specificities of the objects but at those of the observers and scholars. In this view, regardless of the nature of the objects, social scientists always look from a specific standpoint, and this standpoint influences, or even determines, what they can see. The resources which they use for concept formation are drawn from their own social world and, thus, are impregnated with it, in the sense of the well-known double hermeneutics of social science knowledge, drawing on 'lay' knowledge in concept formation, on the one hand, and returning concepts for 'lay' appropriation, on the other. This view is clearly compatible with the view on the historical nature of the social world itself, but its focus is different. To put the difference in extreme terms: even if there was some social phenomenon that was identical wherever it occurred, social scientists would perceive and conceptualize it differently according to the cultural resources they had at hand in their own, particular context.

Again, this reasoning needs an additional assumption to explain why the social sciences should come in specifically national, rather than more generally culturally different, forms. This reasoning is provided by cultural-linguistic theories of the social world, which hold that human social life occurs in the form of communities who, most importantly, share a language, but also key norms and values. In its 'modern' form, this reasoning emerged in eighteenth-century Germany, not least as a reaction against the 'French' Enlightenment as well as, slightly later, against the Revolution that was fought in the name of 'abstract' human values rather than culturally grounded ones. It is originally associated with the names of philosophers and theorists of language such as Herder, Schleiermacher and Humboldt and recently revived not least in 'communitarian' positions in political philosophy.[4]

As in the case of the first type of explanation, the general validity of the reasoning cannot be denied. However, further questions remain as to the strength, i.e., the determining nature, of the cultural-linguistic constitution of knowledge as well as to, first, the solidity of the connection between culture and language and, second, the identification of any such cultural-linguistic entity with the historically existing nations and nation-states. If these linkages are tenuous, as some cultural-expressivist theorists would grant, this approach on its own does not go far enough in explaining any national forms of knowledge.

National fields of scholarly practices

In a third way of reasoning, the social sciences acquire a national form because they are produced by agents inhabiting a structured field in which certain rules govern and which, for historically contingent reasons, has national extension. Pierre Bourdieu's sociology of science has featured such a notion of field and its related concepts, like habitus, position in a field, and strategy. It has thus opened the way for an analysis of scholarly practices that allows the study of intellectual strategies without either presupposing or abandoning ideas of valid knowledge and to approach scholarly interactions in fine detail without making it impossible to relate them to institutional or political dimensions (see, among many other writings, Bourdieu 1984; and the early programmatic article Bourdieu 1975).

This approach, while not excluding the earlier two, goes beyond them by introducing agents and institutions – such as socialization in teacher–disciple relations – into the analysis of changing forms and structures of knowledge. It also assumes that there is always a diversity of positions within a national field – as a force field – and, thus, allows for more fine-grained analyses. Importantly, it opens the possibility, indeed discussed by Bourdieu, of a strategy of importing elements of an external discourse into a national field to enhance one's own position therein. Thus, it is open towards an analysis of relations across the boundaries of national fields. In principle, therefore, Bourdieu's field analysis of scholarly practices should allow a study of both the emergence of national fields and their later questioning in calls for 'transnationality'. There are, however, two major deficiencies, or rather lacunae, in this approach.

First, Bourdieu himself has never provided sociological analyses of knowledge forms that cross boundaries (though some historians and sociologists influenced by his perspective have done so). It seems that he took the national extension of the fields largely for granted, thus turning it into an implicit, undiscussed issue, a presupposition for analysis rather than a feature itself to be analysed. When his analyses proceed historically (and only some of them do), the interest is in the emergence of a new field in a process of separation from pre-existing ones, such as in the case of the emergence of an 'autonomous' field of cultural production, or in the changing constellations within an existing field, such as 'the death and resurrection of a philosophy without subject' in French philosophy and sociology (Bourdieu 1992; Bourdieu and Passeron 1968). In Bourdieu's approach, neither the constitution nor the development of fields are in any significant way shaped by what goes on outside the national framework. For our question here, however, any preconceived notion of a nationally confined field is of little use. What is needed, beyond Bourdieu, is an understanding of the historical constellation of fields that implies a notion of the historical moment under analysis and thus is open to a consideration of the restructuring of the boundaries of fields themselves in changing relations of the 'national' to other dimensions of scholarly practices (see Werner and Zimmermann 2002 for the proposal of a *histoire croisée*).

Second, there is a tendency in Bourdieu's work – though admittedly rather subtly at times – to fully explain the development of academic discourses or other cultural products through the location of the agents in intellectual, political and institutional fields rather than treating such factors as elements in a broader configuration that is not exhausted by them. In a sense, this is precisely Bourdieu's contribution to the sociology of science and an important achievement without doubt. No returns to either a 'great men' theory of the author or a theory of smooth intellectual progress supported by functionally designed institutions should be possible from there. However, this perspective tends to systematically under-explore those aspects of (what I would call) intellectual projects that cannot be explained by the parameters of the field itself. It appears to me to be in the nature of 'cultural production' that, while drawing on the institutional, political and intellectual resources at hand and employing them with reference to the structures of the field, it has the potential to create something not yet available and propose this creation for further use in and beyond the given moment.[5]

The case against national traditions in sociology

After this exploration of conceptual possibilities, I will return to the question of national traditions in sociology and the other social sciences and try to reassess the case. In sum, my proposal to complement, rather than contradict, the existing approaches to the question of national traditions in sociology proceeds by understanding the sociological discourses as intellectual projects in their historical moments or as interpretations in response to experiences. In the following, I shall provide some observations, each further one building on the preceding one, on this kind of argument, which will finally lead to the full elaboration of the alternative point of view. I will start out discussing the social sciences in general, but will later focus on the specific position of sociology.

Spaces of tensions

Any assertion of national intellectual commonalities runs into difficulties when it has to note that a scholarly viewpoint found its fiercest opponents in the same country rather than elsewhere. This is the case, for instance, for Immanuel Kant, with whom in Levine's view the German sociological tradition originates but whose conception of freedom and of the subject were most strongly rejected by Georg Wilhelm Friedrich Hegel rather than by non-German social philosophers. Similarly, but across a larger time-span, Kant's views on morality were combated by Friedrich Nietzsche possibly more strongly than by anybody else. And Emile Durkheim saw his major opponents not in any British sociologist or German 'cultural scientist', but in the individualistically orientated economists and psychologists in his own country.[6]

These observations, casual as they are, can indeed be taken to confirm the idea of a national field in Bourdieu's sense, a structured space in which a variety of positions are possible. But this very notion entails that the field is heterogeneous, is united by conflictual relations rather than by cultural commonality – though these two features are certainly not mutually exclusive.

The same point is underlined by the observation of historical oscillations in an intellectual field, i.e., characteristic movements from one pole to another one in a rather clearly structured field. Bourdieu and Passeron's analysis of the 'death and resurrection of a philosophy without subject', already cited above, proceeds in such a way. The authors may certainly be seen to describe a characteristic of French social philosophy, namely its subjectlessness since structuralism and Durkheimian sociology. Such an observation would overlap with both Levine's and Münch's characterization of the French sociological tradition. At least similarly important in their analysis, however, is the move back and forth between such subjectlessness and highly subject-centred philosophical positions such as existentialism. Thus, they identify less any common substance or perspective than rather a common theme or concern around which different positions are developed whose relative strength varies over time.

The field of the social sciences and its sub-fields

Should, one may want to ask, existentialism be considered as part of any sociological tradition at all, rather than of philosophy? Certainly, this question may justifiably be answered in the negative. However, such an answer would not only prevent us from fully locating that major French post-Second World War sociologist who was deeply inspired by Jean-Paul Sartre's works, namely Alain Touraine, in the intellectual field. It would also beg further questions concerning the location of the social sciences (as well as their subdivisions in the form of disciplines) in the overall field of scholarly practices or, in terms of different dividing lines, in the broader intellectual field.

If we pose this question with particular regard to sociology, then we shall immediately see that the early history of this field was marked by pronounced differences between national institutional situations. We shall first have to note that sociology, the term being coined by Auguste Comte in 1838, was not institutionalized anywhere before the late nineteenth century. To integrate earlier writers into a 'sociological tradition' is not totally unjustifiable, indeed may reveal important intellectual linkages and transitions, but it will also always be marked by some inevitable arbitrariness or by implicit presuppositions as to what sociology is about.

At the end of the nineteenth century then, more particularly, the Durkheimian project in France was formulated, in intellectual terms, as a counter-project to economics and psychology with their individualistic and rationalistic assumptions. The alleged society-centred and 'subjectless' character of French sociology has its origins in this intellectual motivation which proved to be shaping the field. In institutional terms, however, sociology grew under the shelter of philosophy and the *Faculté des lettres*, which helps to explain its persistent proximity to philosophical debates and even to literature. This is what allows the writing, as Bourdieu and Passeron do, of an overlapping history of both sociology and philosophy in France.

In Germany, in contrast, the term 'sociology' – or even *Gesellschafts-Wissenschaft*, the German term initially coined after 'sociology' – was almost unanimously rejected during the nineteenth century and only reluctantly adopted afterwards. Max Weber, though founding member of the German Society for Sociology in 1909, preferred the term 'cultural sciences'. The social science approach that was dominant in Imperial Germany, as practised in the *Verein für Socialpolitik*, had closer ties to economics, history and law than to philosophy, and it grew mostly in the *Staatswissenschaftliche Fakultät* (Faculty for State Sciences) rather than in the one for Philosophy. When chairs for sociology started being created in the Weimar Republic after the First World War, this was hardly any separate institutionalization at all, since most such chairs carried a double denomination, in law, economics or social policy and in sociology.

In England, Spencer notwithstanding, sociology emerged as an institution-based discipline only after the Second World War, whereas social research and concerns of 'social administration' were widely accepted from the late nineteenth century onwards. The emphasis on measurability that Levine detected may thus not necessarily be a characteristic of sociology as an academic discipline, but rather of an older tradition of institutionalized social research on policy-related issues, not least on poverty.

These observations may lead to the conclusion that the variation across national sociologies can largely be explained by the institutional position sociology gained in academia, its overall status in universities and its relation to other, more established disciplines. This suggestion considerably modifies, or even refutes, the more common idea of seeing prevailing perspectives in the social sciences as some expression of a national culture or of forms of the state.[7]

At the same time, however, there are some cross-national similarities in the institutional trajectories of 'sociology', all differences notwithstanding, whatever goes under that name in any given country.

When, at the beginning of the twentieth century, most of the other social science disciplines were already relatively well established, sociology was still struggling to come into existence. The particular institutional place of sociology among what we now call the social sciences is characterized by the fact that it emerged relatively late and that there is no specific realm or aspect of social life for the study of which sociologists could claim to have a particular competence.

When it was proposed as a discipline, sociology was meant to study contemporary Western society. It did not claim special expertise for the past, as history did, or for societies elsewhere, as anthropology did. Nor could any field of analysis directly comparable to the relations of production and exchange, as for economics, or to the modes of setting and implementing common rules, as for political science, or to the workings of the soul, as for psychology, be identified for sociology. As a consequence, sociologists sometimes made the claim to provide the most comprehensive study of all social relations, as Emile Durkheim did in France, subordinating all other fields, or, much more modestly, they aimed at providing a necessary complement to the substantive fields of inquiry by studying the mere form of social relations, as Leopold von Wiese argued in Germany. However, the former kind of claim had to arouse the opposition of scholars from other, mostly more established, fields; the latter, while more acceptable, could hardly be considered very appealing.

It is a common institutional characteristic of the various sociologies that they were proposed in an institutionally already well-occupied and demarcated field at the turn of the nineteenth century. This leads to two further suggestions regarding the particular nature of sociology. First, rather than expressing any hegemonic national culture, it may be an approach to the contemporary social world that runs counter to the 'official' national view as expressed by the existing set of disciplines. And second, if those existing disciplines, owing to their formation in the national educational institutions during the nationalist nineteenth century, are indeed national forms of knowledge, the newcomer, intent to mark a difference, may turn out to be rather more international in orientation. These suggestions will be discussed in the following two sections.

'Sociology' versus 'national culture'?

If we compare them to history, law and the state sciences, both economics and sociology appeared considerably less 'national' and more 'international' in outlook at the end of the nineteenth century.

Certainly, the marginalist revolution in economics had created a truly international discourse with a strong degree of formalization. Though it did not become dominant everywhere as the accepted core of the discipline, certainly not in Germany, and did not penetrate economics as a more broadly defined field of scholarly practice, even where it was intellectually dominant, such as in England (Tribe 1991), 'neo-classical' economics had at least a virtual presence as the international approach to economics throughout the world. A similar argument is more difficult to sustain for 'classical' sociology. After all, we are talking here about the period during which, among others, the 'French school' of sociology emerged. Nevertheless, as I shall argue later, a version of such an 'internationalist' view of sociology is tenable.

Let us note first of all that sociology is a discipline for which an international association, the *Institut International de Sociologie* (IIS), was founded, in Paris in 1893, before national associations were set up – such as the American Society for Sociology in 1905, the German Society for Sociology in 1909, the Society of Japanese Sociology in 1912 and its more liberal counterpart, the Japan Sociological Society in 1923, or the first Russian Sociological Society, with its base in Petrograd, in 1916. Admittedly, the IIS never gained an important role, was eclipsed even in its founding location, Paris, by the rise of Durkheimism, and only recently re-emerged from the secondary role it played since the founding of a competitor organization, the International Sociological Association (ISA), with the support of UNESCO after the Second World War.

But secondly, and more importantly, sociologists offered an analysis of the contemporary social world that situated it in its own time, in the historically developed societal configuration, rather than in an essentially unchangeable place. Despite its many variations, most sociologies tended to adopt analytical perspectives which they considered specific to industrial society, or by whatever other name they called the social configurations of their time, and preferred those to ideas of cultural-linguistic determination of the social world, sometimes relegated to a pre-industrial, pre-bureaucratic past.[8] This is one justifiable way of calling 'classical' sociology truly modern, namely, as in Baudelaire's sense, trying to catch the eternal moment together with and through the fleeting present.

In educational institutions that were not least designed to cultivate and transmit the national heritage, such a viewpoint could not be expected to be easily accepted. Lacking the depth of time-honoured wisdom and of historical experience, sociology was often seen as flat and shallow. As a consequence, the newcomer was regarded as a parvenu in academic institutions; and its arrival was often obstructed, certainly not much welcomed. In Italy, for instance, the influential Benedetto Croce, often considered the spokesperson for Italian culture during the first half of the twentieth century, spoke for many philosophers when in 1906 he called sociology a 'chaotic mixture of natural and moral sciences;... another "new science", which as a philosophical science is unjustifiable and as an empirical science anything else but new. It is new only as "sociology", that is as a barbaric positivistic incursion into the domains of philosophy and history' (for more detail and full reference, see Wagner 1990, chapter 7).

As a consequence, as briefly observed earlier, any characterization of a national sociological tradition, including those by Münch and Levine, is often at odds with general characterizations of a culture. Orientations towards the individual and to measurement in English sociology contrast with the emphasis on habits and traditions in English culture, in as far as such a statement can be made at all.[9] If Weber had any strong methodological point to make, it was the one against any rushed use of 'collective concepts', in strong tension to accounts of 'the German ideology' of collectivism and hierarchy such as provided later by Louis Dumont (1991). And, as mentioned earlier, while Durkheim's concept of society may resonate with the French revolutionary tradition of solidarity, it runs against the individualism which is supposed to be typical of French culture.

One may conclude from these observations that, to a certain extent, classical sociologies did not exactly express the national cultures from which they emerged, but aimed at gaining some distance from them. It is this feature of sociological discourse that I shall finally explore before summarizing my argument.

Sociological distancing

The activity of 'thinking' can generally be described as an attempt to gain distance from the present moment, to liberate oneself from the seemingly continuous flow of time, to create 'a gap between past and future' (Arendt 1978). Obviously, however, thinking does not happen all the time, and its aims are not always fulfilled.

Up to this point, we have identified three elements of the late nineteenth-century intellectual, political and institutional configuration which can be seen as broadly conducive to a distancing exercise. First, a conception of science had developed, in particular in the natural sciences, that made forms of distancing through experiments and conceptualization constitutive for knowledge-seeking. On the one hand, this conception had been enormously successful during the nineteenth century; on the other hand, its inclination towards specialization and fragmentation of knowledge was increasingly criticized (see chapter 8 above). In different ways, both evaluations lent themselves to a further distancing scrutiny of the scientific enterprise itself, especially in the social sciences which underwent a formative moment.

Second, to some observers who then turned sociologists it appeared as if a major social transformation was under way that happened in several of the European nations in largely similar form and that could not sufficiently be understood by the established intellectual means. Clearly, these assessments were not shared by many of the university mandarins in France, Germany, Italy or the Austro-Hungarian Empire. But it was exactly their combination, a society-transcending change towards a novel configuration, that called for a new science of the social world, for an approach that gained distance from the traditions of thought established in national institutions.

Third, at the time when this new science was proposed, that part of the intellectual field that is devoted to the interpretation of the contemporary world was already well occupied by a variety of positions from several disciplines (contemporary history, philosophy, state sciences, but also from medicine and other less obvious disciplines). For the proponents of the emerging sociology this meant, on the one hand, that they had to gain distance from those established positions, and, on the other hand, that competition as a form of intellectual exchange was already introduced in this area.

All elements taken together, the ground was certainly prepared for an interpretation of the contemporary social world that distanced itself from the prevailing national culture. This interpretation nevertheless needed to be substantively developed. The question of where the would-be sociologists found the resources to develop their views can in many cases receive a straightforward answer: they found them abroad.

It is well known, but little discussed, that Emile Durkheim spent some time in Germany at the beginning of his career and wrote a series of articles on *La science positive de la morale en Allemagne* for the *Revue philosophique* after his return. His basic concern was clearly present in these essays: he looked for a renewal of moral philosophy in the light of the social situation of his time, and he surmised that such a philosophy would have to be 'positive', that is, would study the specific condition of human social life empirically and historically. He was impressed by the German scholars' sense of historic specificity, unlike the speculative and abstract philosophy prevailing in France. Though his own 'rules of sociological method' would take a different shape later on, the visit to Germany gave him the angle from which to gradually define the novelty of his own project in France.

Max Weber was one of those historically minded German scholars, though he was himself too young to catch Durkheim's attention. He, however, saw a need to get beyond the unquestioned truths of the historical school of economics in Germany. His methodological writings are interventions in the 'historians' dispute', the main protagonists of which were the German Gustav Schmoller and the Austrian Carl Menger, himself also one of the inventors of marginalism in economics. Weber tended to side with Menger, but the nationality is here less important than the fact that Menger's position can be described as the 'internationalist' one against the emphasis in Schmoller on historical and cultural rootedness, with regard to both the object and the observer.

The examples could be continued but this is not the place for a detailed analysis of 'transfers' in the social sciences.[10] These observations leave us with two new possibilities. As a consequence of these borrowings, sociology could either develop as a counter-discourse to the prevailing one in each national culture; and such counter-discourses could each also be nationally specific. Or these borrowings could have proliferated to such an extent that a truly international discourse of sociology emerged.

Sociology as an international discourse?

The question, then, is whether the multiple reactions to established national self-understandings showed any commonalities. Often quite consciously, though again in a variety of forms, the emerging social sciences of the nineteenth century defined themselves as responses to the economic and political revolutions of the late eighteenth and early nineteenth centuries (Therborn 1976; Hawthorn 1978; see also chapter 13 below). To this extent, the debates had strong international features.

A particular example of an approach whose sources were supranational and which was conceptualized as truly international in more than one respect was Marx's synthesis, as Lenin put it, of historical materialism from three intellectual sources: German idealism, English political economy and French socialism (Lenin 1966). The Marxian sociological tradition, to use Levine's term, is significant also in institutional terms. While it barely gained a foothold in established academic institutions during the nineteenth century, Italian ones being one major exception, its alliance with the workers' movement, which it had itself contributed to form, enabled it to organize a 'scientific field' of its own. As the intellectual wing of this movement, the Marxian tradition developed – and reproduced itself – through journals, schools and meetings much like academic social science, but without strong national boundaries in the field (see Wuthnow 1989).

The internationality of the Marxian tradition is, however, exceptional. Although, as we keep arguing, it is a distortion to portray the social sciences as national traditions, no fully international discourse emerged either. Instead we see intellectual struggles over the interpretation of the contemporary social situation. And national strengths remained very visible in these power struggles. Let us just note as one example Robert von Mohl's mid-century failure to get the 'sciences of society' accepted as a counterpart to the state sciences in the German lands. His attempt, drawing heavily on French inspiration, gives testimony to an existing internationality and to the strength of national boundaries at the same time.[11]

In general, the opposition to sociology that arose in many countries can be read along similar lines. When historical and cultural scholars in Germany protested against this alleged Western aberration, they were simultaneously making a case for a national tradition, their own, and against an opponent whose nation-transcending potential they well recognized – and feared. While those Germans tended to reject even the name of sociology, intellectual opposition to 'Western' sociology elsewhere, and later also in Germany, adopted the label while proposing organicist or other holistic views of society. This was notably the case in the Southern US and in Japan, where authentic responses to 'Western' modernity were searched for (Ross 1990; Kawamura 1994). Indeed, on a closer look, 'Western' sociology appears less monolithic than its opponents thought, and the alternative proposals less incompatible with it. An overall transformation of thinking about 'society' occurred in which the recourse to the 'national' and the 'international' was part of an intellectual struggle rather than any unequivocal description of a cognitive position.

What emerged as 'sociology' was an intellectual space which, while recognizably distinct from other ways of thinking about the social world, included a variety of specific *problématiques* for which different solutions were possible. The inability to solve these *problématiques* permanently leaves room for particularity. Such particularity has often taken national form but it need not do so. In a final step, a description of this space shall be attempted, together with some observations on the current forms of particularity within this space.

Persistent variation in the interpretation of modernity

The emergence of sociology dates to the period following the American and French Revolutions. It is a study of social life that is decisively marked by liberal thinking in the sense that it does not take social order for granted, does not see this order as given by some superior, or even extra-human, authority. At the same time, however, it breaks with the liberal political philosophy of the seventeenth and eighteenth centuries by insisting that there is a social reality between the individuals and the polity. From a sociological point of view, political order is not necessarily to be understood as the result of some agreement between atomistic individuals; its form and substance rather is related to a structure of social relations; to identify and analyse that structure is the task of sociology (see chapter 13 below).

Thus, sociology marked its difference from economics and psychology, on the one hand, and political science and law, on the other, less by carving out a specific realm of social life, but rather by developing a particular perspective. It focused on sociality as a characteristic of human beings and, as a consequence of such sociality, on the emergence of a structured set of social relations between human beings, also called society, a phenomenon which was neither the inadvertent result of multiple independent preferences of individuals nor identical to the formal set of common rules known as law and institutionalized in the state.

To put the issue in such terms meant that sociology was 'modern' in the sense that it accepted the assumptions and outcomes of the revolutions: there was an autonomy of human action that could not be subjected to imposed laws. As a consequence, human social life developed along novel paths; there was a break with earlier human societies. But this did not entail either that the new situation was basically well grasped by individualist liberalism or that it was in principle unknowable because of the unpredictable nature of autonomous action. In contrast to both these views, sociology proposed to make the new set of social relations intelligible through the study of social relations and the emergent social order. In this sense, sociology posed as the science of 'modern society' per se, with its own very distinctive programme.

The outlines of this programme were identifiable early in the nineteenth century, most clearly – though not under the name of sociology – probably in Georg Friedrich Wilhelm Hegel's *Elements of a Philosophy of Right*. This text refers to the abstractions of liberal theorizing critically and negatively but as an inescapable condition that needed to be overcome. While this insight proved valid to the present day, Hegel erred when he thought he could outline the contours of the thinking that overcomes individualist liberalism as a 'philosophy of right'. This is the intellectual space which a variety of sociologies were to struggle about.

And it is a space that transcended national boundaries. Its emergence can be traced to rather particular origins: early modern political theory around Hobbes, Locke and Rousseau; the American Revolution; the French Enlightenment and Revolution, in particular. But the challenge that issued from these events did not escape observers elsewhere. As a response, a number of different discourses were proposed from the late eighteenth century onwards. Between the late eighteenth and the middle of the nineteenth century, a pool of forms of theorizing social configurations of modernity was created on the diversity of which we basically still draw. During the nineteenth century, there probably were nationally specific patterns in drawing on this pool, and probably even more so attempts to stereotype national responses to the *problématiques* of modernity.

If some of these discourses had territorial inscriptions, however, it is very dubitable whether these inscriptions should be treated otherwise than as historically contingent. It is much more important to take the diversity of approaches as an indication for the inability of the 'originally modern' discourse to deal satisfactorily with some of the issues it had itself raised. As a consequence, the emerging variety proved persistent, as a variety of interpretations of modernity.

Among those issues, with which the reader is by now familiar, are the quest for valid knowledge, the search for a good and viable polity, and the quest to satisfy human needs, or in other words, the epistemic, political and economic *problématiques*. Under conditions of modernity, human beings have recognized that there are no solid, fixed solutions to these issues, but that they will need some feasible, workable solutions for their own individual or collective lives nevertheless.

Sociology has claimed to be able to deal with such issues using a new combination of empirical and conceptual work. For classical sociology, to return to our key example, it can easily be shown that the search for such new solutions by new, sociological means was a key concern. Later, twentieth-century social science took those issues to be basically solved and moved any remaining concerns to other realms of discourse, notably epistemology, political philosophy and economics. There were no such solutions, however, and mere neglect was no way out since sociology had historically been constituted by taking this specific stand on these issues. The confinement of those issues to sub-fields such as the sociology of knowledge, political sociology and economic sociology hides this fundamental, constitutive importance.

As a consequence, these issues return in the form of fundamental disputes in social philosophy and in the philosophy of the social sciences. Recent debates about liberalism and communitarianism or about modernity and post-modernity are the latest instances of such disputes. Whoever attempted to reconstruct national contexts for those debates would encounter the same problems that our preceding analysis identified: one would locate the emergence of communitarianism in the allegedly most liberal-individualist culture of the West, the USA; one would find the strongest commitment to reason, personified by Jürgen Habermas and his followers, in the land of the dialectics where any such claim had been dismantled many times; and, in contrast, the farewell to reason would appear to be voiced in the country of the Enlightenment.

The counter-arguments to any such construction are too evident to belabour here. The important insight is the one in the inevitably persistent variety of interpretations of modernity, wherever any particular variety may find a temporary home. And, as our historical sketch was meant to have demonstrated, none of the modes of answering these questions can lay a specific claim to being modern. It is rather the impossibility to give any one superior answer, together with the inevitable persistence of the questions, that modernity is about.

Forms of social knowledge and the contemporary condition of modernity

Such conclusion, though, may be far too inconclusive to be satisfactory. While it can be convincingly ascertained that the national forms of social knowledge were the result of historically contingent circumstances, it remains striking that such form could assert itself so strongly over a major, indeed also a constitutive, period of the social sciences. At the same time, there are reasons to assume that the social sciences acquired during their national period a rather limited – and constraining – conception of the relation between their own knowledge and the political forms within which they were developing. During the post-classical period, that is, from the 1930s, but in particular from the 1950s onwards, social knowledge was increasingly conceptualized as the systematic gathering of empirical information on the state of a society that was considered to be moulded and shaped by enlightened intervention by policy-makers. The national traditions of social knowledge waned and gave way to forms of social knowledge about a national society that was the passive object of external intervention. In the light of such observations, the debates in the recent two or three decades can be seen as entailing a double shift – a renewed understanding of the 'local' character of all knowledge, and a reorientation with regard to the political form to which social knowledge addresses itself.

Like all knowledge claims, first, the social sciences move constantly between particularity and universality. As a knowledge about the social world, any social-science knowledge will always have a strong local component. At the same time, the social sciences as a historical project that constituted itself in the context of the American and French Revolutions also have a particular agenda that may be broadened and altered but hardly abandoned. In other words, modernity is the key theme and condition of the social sciences, if modernity is understood as a situation in which human beings see themselves facing the freedom and predicament to give themselves their own laws. This situation has now become global; even those who may want to reject or modify this predicament cannot but see themselves confronted with the modernist claim.

Given its European and American roots, there is always the risk that this concern with modernity will be cast in parochial terms. The classical era witnessed international and intranational strife about this issue. During much of the twentieth century, in particular after the end of the Second World War, the social sciences promoted a particular image of Western modernity. At the beginning of the twenty-first century, however, it should be possible to conceptualize interlocking socio-cultural and intellectual varieties of modernity instead of either a set of mutually incompatible national projects of modernity or one-dimensional globalization.

If this is the case, though, secondly, should we then assume that the debate over the most appropriate interpretation of modernity will in our post-national era occur without any territorial inscriptions? Should one think about the politico-intellectual competition in this field rather in analogy to the rise of Marxism as an internationally operating alternative interpretation of the modern project? While it is certainly true that strong territorial inscriptions in analogy to the 'national schools' of the era around 1900 are unlikely to recur in a period of enhanced global communication flows, interpretations of modernity will always only flourish if they relate to existing experiences and institutional forms, in particular forms of the polity, and those forms in turn will have a territorial base, even in the era of alleged 'empire'. More particularly, it is indeed observable in our period that two major interpretations of modernity crystallize and compete with one another, a North American and a European one, if one wants to attach territorial labels to them (see chapter 11 below for further discussion). At the same time, a return to an opposition between mutually incompatible such interpretations is neither likely nor desirable. Rather, the insight that work in the social sciences is not about claims to certainty in abstraction from experience but always involves a contribution to the interpretation of modernity that is itself based on experience could provide a useful frame for constructive intellectual exchange between the varieties of such interpretations.

Part IV

The European Experience and Interpretation of Modernity

Overture: European Integration as an Interpretation of Modernity

Up to this point, I have tried to propose a general analysis of modernity in terms of the experiences with the rules for life in common, with the satisfaction of needs and with the search for valid knowledge, and have regarded the interpretations derived from those experiences as those which provide the dynamics of modernity and lead to major transformations of the institutions of modernity. Looking at experiences and their interpretations, this analysis had to be both conceptual and historical, since purely theoretical responses to the political, economic and epistemic *problématiques*, 'abstracting' from experience, will always be found wanting. My historical examples were drawn from 'Western' modernity – without, though, suggesting that modernity is a Western phenomenon alone – and at times I have introduced elements of a comparison between Europe and North America. At this point, I shift emphasis and focus on one example, Europe, to 'apply' the approach to a long historical sequence of experiences, the interpretations of which have given rise, arguably, to a rather specific interpretation of modernity within the 'spatio-temporal envelope' of Europe.

There are three main reasons for choosing Europe as such a case. First, as discussed in chapter 1, Europe has often been seen as the birthplace of modernity, the place from which the programme and project of modernity unfolds in a rather linear way. An analysis of modernity as experience and interpretation can accept, as I would, that there were significant occurrences early in European history suggesting those interpretative moves that we regard as epitomes of modernity. However, those interpretations were specifically related to certain experiences and they did not provide a blueprint for modernity to be applied in other settings without regard for context. Thus, they need to be re-read in the light of this specificity and their long-term sequence needs to be reconstructed as a specific trajectory on which one response given to the modern *problématiques* creates particular novel situations and problems in need of further specific interpretation. Such reconstruction is the task of chapter 10, first elaborating the long-term perspective and later focusing on the gradual emergence of a somewhat common European space of experience and interpretation in the more recent past.

The second reason is the recent process of European integration. The institutional development of the European Union has been subject to numerous analyses, but those have mostly regarded this process as a rather mechanical response to the *problématiques* of the governance of the common and the satisfaction of needs. The technocratically inclined theories of the European polity, as briefly discussed in chapter 3, are an example for the former, and the theories of 'market-making', be they of a neo-liberal or critical orientation, demonstrate the latter. Rather few analyses have suggested that something more is at stake, in terms namely of a normative reorientation of the West European polities or of the explicitation of a specific normative self-understanding of European modernity (see Balibar 2001; Bellamy and Castiglione 2003; Habermas 2001, for examples).

This reluctance is surprising in one sense; in another it is not. Academic discourse is inherently conservative. It tends to explain occurrences by subordinating them under existing concepts and applying existing theories. If there are laws of social life and if social science has discovered them, then any new occurrence must be covered by those laws that we already know. Radical novelty is not foreseen in that perspective. Thus, on the one hand, it is only consistent with such a view that novelty is denied to the process of creating a European polity. On the other hand, however, this process is so striking that, from an 'ordinary', non-scientific perspective, it is hard to understand how its innovativeness can fail to be perceived. It is not only the case that European states were at cruel warfare with each other barely more than half a century ago. The West European states had even embarked on an economic and political reorganization during the post-war decades that was often analysed as a 'miracle' and sometimes praised as a 'model'. Why should such societies, which were successful to the extent of becoming overly self-satisfied and complacent, embark on a risky adventure of restructuring their political and economic institutions without any master-plan and without any even moderately clearly visible final objective?

The answer to this question that will be explored here is the following: the construction of a European polity should be seen as the Europeans' contemporary response to the persistent problem of interpreting and institutionalizing modernity; that is, their way of being autonomous. Even when their institutional arrangements were still working remarkably well in the West, Europeans had started to experience the limits of the order they had constructed during the post-Second World War years (see chapters 4 and 7 above for examples). There was – and still is – no general agreement over the ways in which those limits can be overcome but three (related) insights are widespread: that the challenges are of such a nature that any solution would be insufficient if it just tinkered with existing arrangements; that there is sufficient commonality within Europe to aim at a Europe-wide response; and that such a response is desirable in the light of many contemporary issues related to 'globalization' in the broadest sense. The upshot of these insights is that a new interpretation of European modernity requires a new political form. That is why the analysis should start out from the question of political form, basically as I had left it at the end of chapter 3.

In the light of the experience of extended internal and external warfare, the post-Second World War period had brought with it the construction of a temporarily stable compromise between liberal-democratic, cultural-linguistic and socio-economic foundations of the polity, institutionally expressed in the form of democratic-capitalist welfare states in Western Europe. One additional part of that compromise had been, already in the 1950s, the association of West European nation-states in what is now called the European Union. Although being created as a direct conclusion from the experience of intra-European warfare, this association was long not understood as a political form proper, the cultural-linguistic understanding of the national polity remaining predominant. Another – so to say, external – dimension of that post-war compromise was the political division of Europe, a division that, among many other things, was also part of a – divided – answer to the question of organized social solidarity, divided namely between the socialist and Christian responses on the one side, and the communist one on the other. If the last three decades effectively challenged that arrangement, with the fall of Soviet socialism finally bringing it down, it is significant to observe that the construction of a truly European polity experienced an upsurge at the very moment of the final collapse of the Cold War order.

The current institutional and intellectual restructurings, thus, entail the reopening of the question of the form of political modernity in

Europe, which was temporarily closed as an effect of the stability of the post-war – and Cold War – institutional compromise over justifications.[1] A novel answer to the political *problématique* could still just aim at restabilizing a version of the old compromise over justifications, as Eurosceptics maintain. Despite all obstacles, though, it seems more likely that the forthcoming answer will introduce an unprecedented balance of justifications. The following two chapters are a contribution to the interpretation of European modernity in terms of a reconstruction of the latter's specific trajectory. Furthermore, they can also be read as a modest intervention into the work at reinterpretation, as they suggest some contours of the normative demands that such reinterpretation needs to live up to. And this is the third reason for focusing here on Europe as a 'case' on which my approach can be brought to work, and it can be described in two ways. As a European committed to modernity, first, I am held to contribute to elaborate an interpretation of a modernity that would be 'our own', to use Isaiah Berlin's language, and that would address the contemporary political and economic situation with the appropriate interpretative resources. Second, I am also willing to suggest that the European interpretation of contemporary modernity has something significant, and critical, to contribute to a better understanding of the current global situation and to indicate ways for its improvement. Readers may want to argue that this second description is only a consequence of the first: that my being European makes me inclined to prefer European interpretations of modernity over others. This is possible. But the analysis of the epistemic *problématique* in the preceding part should have made clear that I embrace a contextual approach to knowledge, though not any determinist standpoint theory. In other words, I would like to consider the suggestion that my standpoint may determine my outlook as an invitation for discussion – a discussion over the substantive reasoning provided in the following two chapters.

Chapter 10 returns first to the question of changing political forms, as explored in chapter 3, but does so now with a view to taking up the question of the unity of a European interpretation of the political *problématique*. The argument is that such European political self-understanding never existed in the form of any 'identity' but was elaborated in the course of the historical experience of tension-rich struggles over the considerations that need to enter into a viable answer to the political *problématique*. By the end of the nineteenth century, these struggles had not produced any European answer but a political Europe that was divided into nation-states sustained by nationalisms that tended to turn aggressive. The First World War, even though many factors were involved in its origins, was at the time often understood as a kind of 'clash of civilizations'. A European space of interpretation was only gradually created during the twentieth century, and this not least in the light of the disastrous experience of that war. The other major experience Europeans were facing was the rise of the USA as 'another modernity'. Chapter 11, then, moves to the current situation and analyses contemporary European modernity in a global context – a context that is not least defined by the difficulty of avoiding or overcoming interpretations of modernity that focus on the individual and on instrumental rationality, a general danger that emerged from the discussion of the three *problématiques* in the preceding parts of this book.

Both chapter titles paraphrase the recent work of scholars whose approaches are very close to the one I am proposing here, even though from somewhat different angles and with different substantive emphases. William H. Sewell's *Logics of History* (2005) emphasizes the ways in which historical events transform the structures of socio-political life, not least because the experience of those events is the background for novel interpretations of socio-political life. Dipesh Chakrabarty's *Provincializing Europe* (2000) goes far beyond post-colonial critiques of colonial domination towards work at retrieval of interpretative tools that have become means of connecting experiences and need to be put to work for such end, rather than being merely denounced. Both these scholars elaborate understandings of historicity that link experiences to interpretations and build analyses of entire socio-political configurations and their transformations on such approaches. The following reflections on Europe in past and present try to do something very similar with the tools for the analysis of modernity that I hope to have developed in the preceding sections.

10

Logics of European History

A self-defining slogan of the European Union is 'united in diversity'. This statement is normatively sufficiently innocent, and at the same time historically not refutable, so that everyone should be satisfied with it. However, this is not the case. The construction of European political institutions has been accompanied by a discussion about a 'European identity', suggesting a much stronger understanding of commonality and constancy than the official slogan. The term was first officially mentioned in 1973 (see Stråth 2000) and found strong expression in the Charter of Fundamental Rights in 2000 as well as in the debate about a constitution of the European Union which came to an end with the rejection of an already agreed-upon proposal in referenda in France and the Netherlands in 2005. The degree of unity or diversity of Europe, thus, is a matter of some topical concern; and the position taken on this issue can have a considerable impact on the shape Europe will take in the future.

Sceptical observers may nevertheless be tempted to see these debates as attempts at squaring the circle, in theoretical terms or, in political terms, at arriving at rhetorical, 'superstructural' formulae needed to hold together an instrumental institutional construction for everybody's benefit. Such interpretations, though, would already look at the process of European integration from a distant outside, through some kind of hermeneutics of suspicion. In turn, what seems at stake is precisely the description of a hermeneutic relation, of a form of engagement with others and with the world, that is possibly a common European value, and that as such a value goes beyond an instrumental relation to others and the world, as it is promoted globally from other positions today.

Thus, those debates should be taken seriously, and one can start by disentangling their components. The normative connotations are rather clear. Those who, on the one hand, hold that strong common-alities are a requirement for building and sustaining a polity – that is, latter-day communitarians – demand an effort to find and spell out the identity of Europe and use it as an underpinning for the further development of the polity. This position is contrasted by those who associate any strong commitment to a common cultural heritage with a high risk of exclusion and restrictive cultural determinism. The radical alternative is a purely procedural liberalism that would demand of the citizens of a polity nothing more than acceptance of common procedural rules and leave all questions of beliefs and value commitments to the private sphere that should be interfered with as little as ever possible by public intervention.

Whatever one thinks of those views, each one of them needs to face a kind of reality test. The positioning of an actual polity, like the European Union, within the spectrum of available normative politi-cal philosophies is not a matter of mere choice in the present. There is facticity, too, as Jürgen Habermas would say. Europeans do hold values and beliefs, and to some extent the question of whether they hold common or diverse beliefs is open to empirical investigation. Thus, it seems right – within limits in turn to be defined – to argue that, say, the constitution of a polity should not merely express some abstract political philosophy in legal and institutional terms but should rather reflect the existing 'morality of custom' (G. W. F. Hegel) of the society to which it refers. Some participants in the European debates use – or in some cases rather consciously abuse – such a valid observation to make a historical-empirical claim on the unity of actu-ally held values in Europe and argue that any European constitution should reflect those factual commitments and express them in a binding way for all citizens of the polity. The most common such argument, to which we shall return, is the claim that Europe is histori-cally Christian and that Christian values should guide constitutional design, from the preamble onwards.

Such an argument succumbs to a historical determinism that is difficult to sustain. This is less a matter of evidence, because no his-torical evidence over such a large 'spatio-temporal envelope' as the history of Europe from Konstantinos to the present would be entirely conclusive – although evidence certainly counts. Rather, this view faces two other, more principled obstacles. First, even the best-known, most straightforward historical occurrence or trajectory does not speak on its own in the present. It is in need of interpretation, and interpretation can always occur in plural forms. Second, despite common usage (see Hirschman 1991), it is no compelling normative argument to suggest that things need to continue as they are because they are good as they are. Political action has always also made use of the argument for rupture, for breaking with the past, and there is no general normative reason that gives priority to conservatism over progressivism – nor the other way round, for that matter. It is true, though, that an argument for rupture would need to be made in strong terms if there were indeed a relatively straight historical trajectory of unity and constancy.

In the light of the above considerations, this chapter aims at reviewing the historical argument about European unity with a normative twist. European history, in all due brevity, will be read in the light of the questions that normative political philosophy poses but is unable to answer by its own means. Thus, the politico-philosophical means of abstracting from a context, of taking distance from experiences, is abandoned, in a first step, in favour of a contextual reading of history aiming to stay close to the problems human beings were identifying in the situations they faced. In a second step, then, the interpretations they gave to their experiences can be reconnected and, thus, the problems of political philosophy will re-emerge, but in a new guise. The question of the unity of Europe will be rephrased in the course of the argument. Rather than trying to identify cross-historical constancy and commonality, one needs to ask if and how far Europeans had experiences in common and arrived at shared interpretations of those experiences.

European unity – the standard view

I shall start with the standard view, which implies some considerable degree of unity across European history. As a geographical term, the name Europe came into currency after the split of the Roman Empire to denote the area of the empire's Western part, then closely associated with Catholicism. Over time, the reach of the meaning was extended northwestwards, and the religiously defined boundary between Orthodox Christianity and Islam remained debated. Through the Middle Ages, Europe was considered a religious-politico-territorial unit, however loosely understood.

This is indeed the period in history to which the argument for a Christian Europe refers as evidence (for a thorough recent analysis of 'Europe after Rome', see Smith 2005). In this form, it is today being employed against the accession of Turkey to the European Union, even though its proponents had been silent with regard to the accession of Greece – a name with too high a symbolic connotation for Europe – and lenient with regard to the accession of, say, Bulgaria.[1] European history after this period, in turn, poses considerable problems for the view that there is unitary Christian continuity but defenders of this position have found ways to overcome the obstacles. They argue that Christianity uniquely introduces individualism and universalism into political thought and that this heritage remains alive even after its adoption and transformation by secular world-views. In this view, concepts such as human dignity and human rights have their origins in Christian thought. While not entirely without validity in terms of conceptual-historical reconstruction, this argument hardly carries any weight for defining Europe today as united by Christian values and beliefs.

According to the standard view, the division into two major Western Christian religious denominations and into sovereign states at the onset of what is often referred to as early modern times had relatively little impact on the similarity of intellectual orientations from the Renaissance to the Enlightenment. Thus, there is supposed to be intellectual continuity in political theory from Thomas Hobbes to John Locke and Jean-Jacques Rousseau in terms of the gradual elaboration of concepts such as sovereignty and citizenship. With the building of nation-states from the late eighteenth century onwards, furthermore, a common notion of popular sovereignty is being elaborated and employed, though in somewhat different ways for different nations. At this moment, the Christian commitment to the individual is joined by the commitment to collective self-determination, or democracy. Thus, Europe stands for the harmonious articulation of human rights and democracy, as exemplified by the French Declaration of Human and Citizen Rights. Critical observers, including such committed liberals as Isaiah Berlin, have often observed that the relation between individual liberty and democracy is rather 'tenuous', as we have seen (chapter 2 above), but such objections have not prevented a dominant ideology from emerging that holds these commitments not only to be easily compatible but also realized in 'the West'.

From the eighteenth century onwards, furthermore, the view emerged that Europe had a specific role and position in world history, a view that transformed from Enlightenment universalism into nine-teenth-century evolutionism in which Europe was seen as the spear-head of historical progress. Historico-sociological research connected with what is now known as classical social theory aimed at investigating and substantiating this view, most prominently in Max Weber's exploration of the specificity of Western rationalism. With varying emphasis, a cumulation of historical events was seen as the background to the specificity of Europe, starting with the rise of the universities, the extension of trade relations and the increasing autonomy of commercial cities in the late Middle Ages. The sequence of so-called revolutions reaching from the Reformation to the scientific-philosophical, the market-industrial and the liberal-democratic revolutions was later interpreted as steps on a basically linear trajectory of modernization culminating in full-fledged modern society based on the principle of functional differentiation and leading to a higher rationality of societal arrangements (see chapter 1 above). In this view, Europe was not only unified in its outlook on the world but had also provided a model of 'universal significance', to refer to Weber's words. The fact that the centre of elaboration of this model, and thus of gravity of world history, had shifted to North America by the time of Weber's writing, was for this interpretation mostly of little concern.

European unity – two dissident views

Even though few historical sociologists and social theorists today would entirely discard the relevance of the question of Europe's specificity, the Weberian *problématique*, few would any longer agree with such a linear, progressive interpretation either. Europe can only with difficulty be seen as the avant-garde of history, regardless of which criterion is applied. Before aiming at proposing a full-scale alternative view, two relatively recent reinterpretations that partially remedy the problem of plausibility in the standard view shall be mentioned.

On the one hand, the European trajectory has been reinterpreted by extending the period of historical reference and by pluralizing the perspective on world history. The most consistent such approach uses the so-called axial age, the period between roughly the seventh and the fourth century BCE, as a period of major social transformations in Eurasia that sets world history on a new course by introducing in a variety of ways distinctions between the existing (ordinary, profane) world and another (transcendental) world and suggesting that these ways are at the origins of a multiplicity of world civilizations (see briefly above chapter 3 and, for a comprehensive recent reassessment of the debate, Arnason, Eisenstadt and Wittrock 2005).

For the view of Europe, this approach has several implications. As the reference period predates Christianity, it makes it impossible to straightforwardly conclude on a Christian identity for Europe. In turn, though, it may be seen to suggest some European unity, as the European 'civilization' can be regarded as one of the offspring of the axial-age transformations. Thirdly, it places such European history within the context of a world history in which several civilizations exist, none of which demonstrates any principled superiority over any other. In the latter regard, the debate has enabled the emergence of the idea of multiple modernities in the present and has thus considerably widened the sociological diagnosis of the present modern condition. Despite this pluralization, however, the approach works with a considerable component of cultural determinism. Even though the idea of contestation over the relation between the profane and the sacred is introduced, the approach does suggest that some 'cultural programme' (Eisenstadt) unfolds in the various civilizations so that, for instance, we should aim to understand Chinese civilization still today predominantly from its formative origins.

On the other hand, the idea of internal diversity has been made much stronger in a second 'dissident' recent view of European history. Mixing the axial-age hypothesis with the standard view, the observation that the existence of an identifiable Europe dates back to the Western Roman Empire has been considerably reinterpreted by the rejection of seeing in this historical background anything like an origin that gives rise to an identity in the form of stably shared values and beliefs. Rather, the Western Roman heritage is itself seen as resting on divided orientations, or more precisely, being secondary to something else, in two major respects. In terms of religion, the Christian orientation is secondary to the Jewish one; and in terms of political philosophy, the Roman republican tradition is secondary to the Greek invention of democracy in the form of the *polis*. This 'secondarity' leads to what has been called an 'eccentric identity' that as such may be a more plausible background to what then appears as the specifically European restlessness – rather than rationality (Brague 1999).

The concept of an 'eccentric identity' is not very convincing, though. Whereas the term 'identity' suggests not only commonality at a given moment but also constancy over time, Brague maintains that Europe's eccentric identity precisely entails that Europe is ever-changing. This allows him to work, on the one hand, with the reference to Western Christianity, his 'Roman way', while, on the other hand, reconciling the Catholic tradition with the present by means of the dynamism that for him is characteristic of Europe.

The following analysis will build on the pluralization of world history, as suggested in the 'axial age' approach, and it will build on the introduction of a basic dynamics into European history, as suggested in the 'eccentric identity' approach. However, it will go beyond those by arguing, first, that the contemporary European outlook on the world – if there is any such common outlook – was shaped by later occurrences in European history, from the so-called early modern period to at least the middle of the twentieth century. Second, it will suggest that many of these later occurrences cannot easily be inscribed into a history of European unity but that they should be seen as constituting deep divisions within Europe.

European divisions – a brief history of European diversity

Political power in Europe had already been divided from the moment the emperor of the Holy Roman Empire moved into conflict with the papacy. As there was pronounced dispute about the allocation of power, it is problematic to describe this relation as a precursor to the modern division of power in institutionalized democracies. However, it seems certain that this contestation created interstices of power in which other actors with claims to control over resources, economic or epistemic, could emerge, such as the trading cities and the universities. The late European Middle Ages thus witnessed an unorganized plurality of sites of action and power, loosely held together by the universalist claims of both empire and papacy. This plurality may have been a precondition for later divisions, but it was not as such a deep divide within Europe.

The first major divide within this area emerged with the Reformation, thus a novel division within Christianity, and the religious wars that followed upon it and devastated major parts of Europe for many decades. The exit from this era was found in the idea of state sovereignty and largely implemented with the Peace of Westphalia in 1648. It was effective in the sense that religiously motivated violence became rare among Christians in Western Europe, a major exception being Northern Ireland. (It needs to be added, though, that violence towards non-Christians remained unconcerned by the settlement, most importantly towards Jews, a religion without a region, paraphrasing the famous slogan.) The price that was paid for this solution was the division of Europe into a system of territorially defined, sovereign states. Even if one were ready to consider that these states knew a high degree of internal peace, through the sovereign exercise of power of the ruler over the subjects, the relations between them remained without agreed rules. Still today the demand for an international legal order, voiced maybe most strongly by Europeans, refers to the problem that was created in the seventeenth century.

The second major divide in Europe was inaugurated with the democratic revolutions, the French Revolution being the event that transformed European politico-historical consciousness. In terms of political theory, it is usually interpreted as the practical transformation of the concept of state sovereignty into the one of popular sovereignty, thus transforming the absolutist state into a – potentially – democratic one. In this line of thinking, it is often overlooked that the Revolution identified the 'people' as the 'nation'. This conception of the subject of collective self-determination suggested to many of those Europeans who looked at the French Revolution from outside, or even as affected by Napoleonic imperial attempts, that they might define such a subject in their own way, which often meant that they defined it in cultural-linguistic terms.

This reaction is in some sense an effect of the French Revolution. The fact that it was not intended, that is, that it was not as such contained in the revolutionary agenda, does not mean that it was not implied in the transformation of political self-understandings that the Revolution brought about. Once a collectivity aims at self-determining its life in common, the question of membership in that collectivity becomes important, and commonality of culture suggested itself as a plausible criterion. As a consequence, though, a novel kind of divide emerged in Europe, only partly overlapping with the boundaries of the post-Westphalian states, the one between nations in which some form of nationalism became an important part of the self-understanding in the course of the nineteenth century.

There were many reasons for the outbreak of the First World War, among them imperial political and economic competition as well as the crisis of empires in the face of calls for self-determination of member groups. However, the increasingly aggressive nationalism among the established nations was certainly an important element in its own right, as not least the contemporary, battle-driven interpretation of the war as a struggle between the French 'ideas of 1789' and the German 'ideas of 1914' showed. Referred to as a fight between 'culture' and 'civilization', it was turned into a 'clash of civilizations' much before the arrival of the ill-conceived term. Significantly, the war was also the first war with mass mobilization in the sense that entire populations got involved in direct military, economic or ideological ways. Even though universal-suffrage democracy – or at least universal male suffrage – was introduced in many countries only at the end of the war, it was thus also the first war of the democratic era in Europe.

Religious reformation and political revolution were dramatic events that visibly transformed Europe within a short time-span. A third division emerged less dramatically but was not for that reason less significant. The 'culture of individual autonomy' (to which I referred in chapter 1 above) opened for human beings the perspective of self-realization also in tension to the community and to the societal whole. A distinction between the private and the public sphere emerged in the course of the eighteenth century – as an important precedent of the democratic revolution, as it turned out – that should remain important for European political thinking to the present. As a consequence, we today tend to see private life as the realm of the formation of the self and in turn the public sphere as the basis for well-informed political decision-making, with which this citizen-self then would be concerned. The exact delimitation of those realms, however, remains contested, as for instance the so-called headscarf disputes in France and Germany show.

The right to individual autonomy included the 'freedom of commerce'; as such the rise of the private sphere is related to the industrial and market revolution and the rise of capitalism. This event produced a fourth deep division in Europe, namely the one between social classes that were often opposed to each other in an irreconcilable way. One of the self-declared spokesmen of the working class spoke of 'class antagonism', but it was a leading British politician, Benjamin Disraeli, who referred to nineteenth-century England as being inhabited by 'two nations' between which there was neither social intercourse nor any sympathy. This diagnosis, thus, did not only refer to the rising social inequality that was widely observable. It also touched upon a certain incompatibility of forms of life, thus to what would now be called cultural distance.

While the formation of nations was based on the idea of cultural-linguistic identity, the formation of classes led to some kind of socio-cultural identity that emerged everywhere, more or less pronouncedly, in the industrial regions of Europe. The divide between social democracy and communism over the appropriate political interpretation of class-formation should later, with Soviet socialism, lead to a novel political division of Europe with highly rigid boundaries.

These four major divides are historically not as neatly separate as I describe them here. The formation of territorial states in the first divide should become a basis for some of the nation-states that were created after the second divide. And, as briefly mentioned, the rise of individual autonomy is in some way connected to the rise of a commercial society. More connections could be mentioned. However, my representation serves not only, and not even predominantly, to underline the divisions of Europe in contrast to any – standard or dissident – representation of European unity. Rather, it is only a first step in the elaboration of a narrative of European history that takes the interplay between the experience of historical events and their interpretation seriously.

Processes of problem-creation

Thus, the point here was not to suggest that there is no European unity at all. Rather, the point is to say that if there is any unity, it cannot but be the result of the interpretations drawn from the experiences of those major transformations and of the divisions they produced.

In such light, a first conclusion from the account up to this point would be to say that Europe is united by some kind of *negative* identity, based on the mistakes and errors of the past. If we take a second look at those grand historical processes in which religion, nation, class and the relation between the private and the public spheres take centre stage, though, then we can recognize the persistent *problématiques* that human beings have to master in their common lives, even though in a somewhat different, we may say more concrete or substantive, light. In other words, in the course of their history, Europeans gradually posed those questions explicitly and radically to which they then gradually tried to find answers.

Michael Walzer, as mentioned above (chapter 2), once referred to liberalism as the 'art of separation'. Liberal thought creates spaces of freedom by separating issues – and sometimes people – from each other, the holding together of which would limit freedom. This is an important observation. In historical reality, however, such separations often occur violently and they are by far not always inspired by liberal thought. Thus, I will continue my reasoning by demonstrating which questions were opened up by the above-mentioned separations. In a final step, then, I want to ask if and how contemporary Europe has been shaped by these experiences and their interpretations.

True, Reformation and religious wars destroyed the unity of (Western) Europe. But they also posed the question of *plurality* of human ways of life in an inescapable manner. From this moment onwards, it was no longer possible to press the variety of human strivings into a single model of the good life. Political thought of the seventeenth and eighteenth century was certainly working at the elaboration of new models of order after the chaos of warfare. The big step that was then taken, though, was to accept that variety of strivings as the starting point of the search for order instead of trying to identify a sole commanding external source for such order.

From the eighteenth century onwards, the hope became more widely diffused that a new, self-determined and peaceful order was indeed possible. This, too, was a meaning of the democratic revolutions: they were the attempt to lay the foundations for a better world through action in common. The concepts of revolution and *progress*, which entered into our political language at that moment, expressed the expectation of an open horizon of the future, to use Reinhart Koselleck's term.

The democratic revolution signalled collective self-determination and the creation of a better political order. In turn, the separation of the private from the public was a precondition for a viable connection between the *personal freedom* of the singular human being and the political freedom towards collective self-determination. This connection remained problematic ever since, as I had occasion to point out (above and in chapters 2 and 3). Some authors even draw a direct line from the French to the Russian Revolution and further to National Socialism, and thus from the promise of collective self-determination towards totalitarianism. This line is not as straight as suggested, but the history of democracy is also the history of the dangers towards which democracy exposes itself (see now Karagiannis 2007b).

The expansion of markets and the formation of classes, finally, opens up the question of well-being and *solidarity*. The industrial division of labour and the idea of self-regulation of free commercial exchange had given rise to the promise of the 'wealth of nations' (Adam Smith) as well as of the pacification of human social life. One who relates to other human beings by *doux commerce* will not want to fight those others with whom one has become interdependent, so the argument goes. Both well-being of the population and peace in society remained a long time in waiting. But the struggle against impoverishment and rising inequality led to the creation of the concept of solidarity which gradually was transformed from a battle concept in class struggle towards a means of organizing society within a welfare state that was based on a considerable degree of redistribution of resources among its members (Karagiannis 2007c).

Reversal of a developmental trajectory

This second brief representation of European history was meant to show that the violent divisions of Europe can also – with some effort – be read in a *positive* light. Key issues of human life in common were raised in a radical and inescapable way. To elaborate on them in such a way was maybe only possible against the background of the experience of deep divisions.

As we have seen, at times the hope was raised that those questions could be answered once and for all in a good and stable way. This was in particular the case during the Enlightenment and its expectation of the realization of reason. When Max Weber translated reason as rationality more than a century later, then this hope had long given way to rising scepticism. Maybe Weber can be interpreted as regarding European history as a history of rationalization. Certainly, though, his own view of this history was not unambivalently optimistic. In the early twentieth century, in general, scepticism prevailed in Europe to such an extent that the whole developmental trajectory of this world region was sometimes seen as a fatal error. But such negative response is merely the full-scale inversion of Enlightenment optimism. Rather, one should accept that eternally valid answers to these questions cannot be given, and that the answers we may find need to be revised in the face of new experiences. This is what happened in Europe, I want to argue and briefly demonstrate, in the course of the twentieth century. Towards that end, I propose a third parcours through European history, focusing on the last century and discussing some of its occurrences in a slightly more detailed manner than before.

Thus, Europe will here not be identified with the origin of modernity but will be regarded as a region of the world – as one among many, but with specificities which would need to be analysed in terms of spaces of experience and interpretation.[2] Five aspects of the European experience that are significant when aiming to grasp any contemporary specificity of European modernity will be singled out for this purpose.

One aspect of nineteenth-century Europe that was a constitutive component of the identification of Europe with modernity was rarely given central place in accounts of this modernity: *Europe as colonial power*. The history of colonialism sees Europe certainly as its subject and as the master of the world; it thus emphasizes the modernity of Europe. European history as colonial history establishes precisely the relation between Europe and other parts of the world as relations between 'modernity' and 'tradition', of rupture in temporality and the 'denial of coevalness' (Johannes Fabian). At the same time, it invited the conceptual distinctions between the 'rational' and the 'cultural', and between the universal and the particular.

However, in terms of an account of modernity as interpretation and experience, one important qualification needs to be made: it was not Europe, but it was the European nation-states that were colonial powers. There is a remark in Edward Said's *Orientalism* about the figure of Mr Casaubon in George Eliot's *Middlemarch*, which is more significant than the author may initially have thought: 'One reason Casaubon cannot finish his Key to All Mythologies is [...] that he is unacquainted with German scholarship' (Said 1978, p. 19). After this unnecessary remark – he did not need to excuse himself – Said embarked on a more complex and hardly sustainable reasoning. On the one hand, he claimed that German scholarship on the East was not in partnership with 'a protracted, sustained *national* interest in the Orient'; thus, it was secondary and not very significant. On the other hand, though, he saw it as sharing with 'Anglo-French and later American Orientalism [...] a kind of intellectual *authority* over the Orient within Western culture'. This statement suggests not only a somewhat off-the-cuff sociology of knowledge; it also compresses intellectual history over quite some space and time into a straitjacket. It underestimates the variety of 'European' relations with other parts of the world during the nineteenth century and the variety of forms of knowledge that were produced about these other parts, and it suggests too smooth a move, in both respects, to US dominance in the twentieth century which then just looks like 'more of the same'.

No comment on the contemporary relation between the 'West' and the 'Orient' shall be added here, tempting as it may be. At this point, it should just be underlined that the history of the construction of Europe as a region of the world – under its proper name – is a process of, by and large, the last half century only. In particular during the nineteenth and the first half of the twentieth century, Europe as a space of common experience hardly existed, if not as one of the experience of power rivalry, and as a space of common interpretation neither. The attempts at creating a space of common interpretation after Nazism and the Second World War were at least in part a response to, and a consequence of, the 'decentring of Europe' in the course of the disastrous first half of the twentieth century. Such decentring was prepared by what has been called a 'break of tradition' in Europe.

Studies of the 'colonial encounter' (to use Talal Asad's term) often stress the destruction or dissolution of forms of knowledge, of means of interpretation, of situating oneself in the world, as the result of an occurrence. In post-colonial studies, such an encounter is seen as a confrontation with something that comes from the outside. When modernity was thought of in terms of a break with tradition, as it mostly was, that break was seen as an accomplishment, not without frictions certainly, but achieved from within European society and leading to a superior way of engaging with others and the world.

There is, thus, in theorizing modernity, at least a dual meaning of the idea of a 'break with tradition', an enabling one if the break comes from within, and a disabling one if the break is imposed, to speak loosely. In this light, I now want to suggest that Europe has undergone, in addition to that break that allegedly set it on to the route of modernity, a second 'break with tradition' that resembles more the breaks that result from a sudden, shock-like encounter with the unknown.

This latter break was in Europe most strongly marked by the experience of the First World War but in a broader sense its experience stretched from the late nineteenth century to the end of the Second World War. This experience led first of all to the questioning of the concept of the 'rupture' itself as it was constitutive for thinking the advent of modernity. Rather than using such a notion as an explanatory tool to conceptualize the difference between 'modernity' and 'tradition', it will be taken now as opening the space for a variety of ways to conceive of that relation.

Arguably, this mode of thinking was inaugurated with Friedrich Nietzsche's (1990 [1874]) 'untimely meditation' on the 'use and disadvantage of history for life'. By distinguishing a multiplicity of ways of relating to the past, Nietzsche opened up this relation to indeterminacy. This step was recognized as well as considerably sharpened and accentuated between the two world wars by thinkers such as Martin Heidegger, Walter Benjamin and later Hannah Arendt. In early writings, already during the First World War, both Heidegger and Benjamin radically questioned the accessibility of the past. Heidegger (1978 [1916], p. 427) emphasized the 'qualitative otherness of past times', which entailed that the past was never available to the present as such, but only through a relation of present valuation. Drawing on Heidegger, Benjamin developed then the ideas about the course of history that he would last express in the theses 'on the concept of history'. In the essay on the work of art in the age of its technical reproducibility, he spoke about 'the shattering of tradition' (1978 [1934], p. 439). Reading Kafka and reflecting about the politico-philosophical choices during the inter-war period, Hannah Arendt later described the present as a 'gap between the past and the future'.

Those interpretations can be related to the experiences of the first half of the twentieth century, especially since the end of the First World War. Already as it was waging, the war meant to many observers the abandonment of any hope that 'modernity' was on an essentially peaceful and progressive path and, with this, it conveyed the undeniable insight that 'modernity' included the possibility of unprecedented horrors. The inter-war years – with hindsight nothing more than an extended cease-fire – witnessed the increasing confrontation between opposed proposals to organize a modernity that had proven more shaky and crisis-prone than its proponents had expected. Then, the Nazi government reopened the war and led it recklessly against the populations of Europe, including a major part of its own and the entire European Jewry. When this war was over at mid-century, Continental Europe was emptied of any possibility to resort to tradition. The accumulated experiences of this whole period provide the historical background to the emergence of the philosophical debate about the shattering of tradition.

In the light of these observations, a step towards a reassessment of European societal developments during the second half of the twentieth century can be taken. The predominant view sees the social world gradually take its modern organized form during the second half of the nineteenth century up to the First World War in parallel processes of industrialization, urbanization, rationalization (through the modern sciences, but also through bureaucracy) and democratization. While some of these processes advance faster than others and in some societies more than in others, everything accelerates after the end of the Second World War and by the 1960s socio-political modernity is firmly established in northwest Europe and North America. Western modernity seemed to have re-embarked on its successful historical trajectory, if we are willing to believe the standard view. In contrast to this view, I propose to see the struggles over modernity during the first half of the twentieth century and, to speak again loosely, the damage it has inflicted as the major reason for the shaping of European societies after the Second World War. Thus, there was no continuation on a path of modernization but conclusions drawn collectively, although in their specific results unintendedly, from a historical experience.

This view underlines an overlooked feature of post-war European societies, namely the perceived loss of origins that has now moved far from the philosophical or religious-cosmological issue towards the general impossibility of making actual reference to any 'morality of custom' in everyday social life. The break with all established ways of judging the good, the true and the beautiful was imposed twice – first by the political and military mass mobilizations of the early century and then by the destruction through totalitarianism, war and genocide. And this break was imposed in such a way that large segments of society could not escape the reach of that destruction. The massive material need for reconstruction after the war as well as the re-education programmes in the defeated societies, and the silencing of the rift between resisters and collaborators in the liberated societies, assured the presence of that experience until far into the post-war period.[3]

These observations lead directly to the third aspect of European modernity: during the same period, the early twentieth century, Europeans did not only witness the crisis of their own self-understanding but at the same time the *rise of another modernity*, the one of the USA, an occurrence that made it impossible for them to see themselves any longer as the vanguard of modernity but rather, at best, as one among several modernities. In their relation to the USA as a different socio-political configuration, Europeans saw their own modernity as in many respects inferior, especially with regard to technology, economy, organization, social life, including importantly gender relations, and politics. In significant respects, however, they also saw themselves as still superior, namely with regard to morality and philosophy, thus giving a strong normative tone to many of the writings about America during the inter-war period.

Overall, an image of America as 'the other' of Europe emerged. In brief: 'America' in this view is what we may call *presentist*, that is, without history and tradition. As Ferdinand Tönnies (1922, p. 356) wrote in 1922 about public opinion in America: 'Its knowledge of the old world, thus of the foundations of its own culture, is rather deficient; it thus lives much more in the present and in representations of the future which are exclusively determined by the present'. America is also *individualist*, that is, there are no ties between the human beings except for those that they themselves create. And it is *rationalist*, that is, it knows no norms and values except the increase of instrumental mastery, the striving to efficiently use whatever is at hand to reach one's purposes. Again Tönnies (1922, p. 357), here using Weber's concept of rationality, expresses succinctly his view on American public opinion as 'the essential expression of the spirit of a nation': it is '"rationalistic" [...] in the sense of a reason which prefers to be occupied with the means for external purposes'. And, finally, America is what we may call *immanentist*, that is, it rejects the notion of any common higher purpose, anything that transcends individual lives and may give them orientation and direction.

Rather than an enumeration of distinct features, this is a cascade of characteristics where each single one refers to all the other ones. Individualism is directly related to the absence of history, which namely could have been a source of commonalities; and instrumental rationalism may be seen to follow from the absence of any common higher orientation. Trying to condense the imagery even further, we can say that the 'America' the Europeans perceived was the uncontaminated realization of the modernist principles of *autonomy* and *rationality*. America was *pure modernity*. The significance of this view does not lie in the degree of correspondence to any American reality, and no such claim is intended here, but in the possibility of thinking about modernity in terms of a variety of different socio-political instantiations (see chapter 11 below for a continuation of this argument).

The European experience of a different American modernity, thus, opens the space for an understanding of 'varieties of modernity'. But any such conceptualization advanced but little at this time, because this thinking takes place under the threat of losing all that is important. A highly asymmetrical relation between these two modernities is assumed; and European modernity is no longer the spearhead of progressive history, but becomes a 'tradition of modernity' (Derrida 1989). If we consider the earlier observation of a 'break with tradition' in European modernity together with the one about the rise of 'other modernities', we see how Europe moves closer to the colonized world. A 'decentring of Europe' takes place in the self-awareness of Europeans. It opens a way for, within certain limits, pursuing European studies as subaltern studies.

The final two observations about European specificities refer to the post-Second World War period, and these orientations are in many respects consequences from the insights into the former experiences, i.e., a reinterpretation of the experiences from the first half of the twentieth century. The first of these concern the 'internal' self-understanding of modernity in Europe, the second one its relation to the world, its position in it.

Between 1800 and 1950, as pointed out earlier, European history is predominantly a history of nation-states. Collective memory during this period acquires ever more the form of national memory – across a historical trajectory that reaches from cultural-linguistic theories of the polity in romanticism to national-liberal movements to the so-called national unifications, e.g. of Italy and Germany, to the increasingly aggressive nationalism of the early twentieth century. In this light, the current process of European integration is a quite extraordinary occurrence. If conflicts between West European nations are today utterly inconceivable, this is so because of an effective overcoming of the idea of an absolute tie to the national form in the wake of the preceding historical experience.

In terms of political theory, Jean-Marc Ferry (2000) has recently claimed that a '*self-critical attitude towards national historical memory*' has become part of the 'ethical substance' of the European polity. There is likely to be too much of an evolutionary understanding in this view, leading straight from Hegel's 'ethical substance' to Habermas's hope for 'expanding normative-political horizons', but nevertheless Ferry captures an important aspect of recent European developments. There is one addition that needs to be made to this observation; and this addition changes the picture rather radically. It needs emphasizing, namely, that this evolution, if it is one, has occurred not in any process of societal rationalization, as modernists including Habermas would always prefer, but through the experience of failure, and through the insight into such failure. It takes place against the background of the experience of a break with tradition and of the rise of other modernities.[4] As far as I can see, and obviously without ruling out the possibility of similar developments elsewhere in the world, this pronounced self-critical attitude to collective memory is indeed a specificity of contemporary European modernity. It supports the repositioning of the nations within European history in terms of what one may call an internal decentring of Europe.

The final question, then, is whether there is a similar, or at least related, repositioning of Europe within the world, or in other words, whether the combined effect of decolonization and the rise of a post-colonial intellectual perspective has made a difference for the self-understanding of European modernity. A recent analysis of the transformations of the European development policy discourse towards the African, Caribbean and Pacific countries reveals significant shifts in the self-understanding of European development policy over the past three decades (for details concerning this and the paragraph below, see Karagiannis 2004). In particular, shifts in the use of the term 'responsibility' signal changes in the European attitude to the presence of the colonial past. Responsibility, which was once understood hierarchically, as a responsibility of the Europeans for their colonial past and its consequences, is increasingly understood in an egalitarian way, as a mutual responsibility of European and ACP countries for sustainable development. Parallel shifts in the use of 'efficiency', both in terms of a generally increased importance and in terms of a reinterpretation, appear to reflect experiences in the post-colonial interaction. Efficiency, which was once understood in an 'industrial' sense, that is as using scarce means rationally towards a preconceived purpose, namely development, is increasingly used rather in a 'market' sense, that is, in terms of removing obstacles to free exchange, which as such will guarantee a rational outcome.[5]

The analysis in question remains far from any mere denunciation of those shifts – e.g., in terms of an attempt at liberation from historical guilt or of full subordination to a *pensée unique* of market efficiency – but insists instead on the plurality of possibilities of justification and their ambivalence in any complex constellation such as the one between the EU and the ACP countries. Conversely, such analysis is obviously also far from suggesting that European development policy stands on normatively sound foundations or that it is in any way to be considered adequate to the situation. But it does underline that there has been an ongoing debate about *the meaning of European modernity in relation to Europe's former colonies*, a debate with a certain degree of sophistication and, more importantly, one that explicitly employs repertoires of moral-political evaluation with a variety of possible outcomes and, indeed, undergoes change over time.

European unity – again

Is there any conclusion to be drawn from this representation of European history, in particular any conclusion about the unity and diversity of Europe? Clearly, Europe is not rooted in its history in such a way that its destiny could be derived from it. However, Europeans have had significant experiences in their history, and they have time and again attempted to elaborate common interpretations of these experiences. From such interpretations, an 'identity' may emerge that can guide action in the present and, possibly, make a difference in the contemporary world. If the so-called globalization can also be understood as a cultural dispute over the shape of the world of tomorrow, then Europe may possibly be a space from which a proposal for world-making emerges that links critically to one's own experiences and their interpretations and builds on them. This possibility will be discussed in the following chapter.

11

Regionalizing European Modernity

The preceding chapter suggested in conclusion that European modernity, in the specific engagement with the world that had been elaborated in the course of European history, could make a significant contribution to the transformations that the contemporary world is undergoing, captured by terms such as 'globalization' or emerging 'empire'. This idea is not widely accepted in the social and political sciences or in public debate, but rather meets pronounced scepticism. Most of the sceptics hold their view on what they think are 'realist' grounds (see Davis 2007; Kratochwil 2007, for further discussion). In this view, politics is about power and interest, and states are the containers of power and interest in the global arena. One can, however, also be sceptical about the possibility and desirability of any specifically European self-understanding of political modernity for normative reasons. To those who try to identify normative underpinnings for European political integration, it has been objected that such European self-understanding is *either* entirely indistinct from the general self-understanding of the West, i.e., a commitment to human rights and liberal democracy, *or* highly problematic because it is based on 'thick' presuppositions that are untenable against the background of European cultural diversity and risk reviving non-liberal European political traditions.

If a general, universalist commitment to liberal democracy were indeed sufficient to understand Western polities, any discussion about varieties of world-making would have a very limited scope.[1] One world only could be normatively defended, a West based on this universalist understanding, and all other varieties would need to be rejected. The argument is familiar in our times but frequency of evocation does not make it any more valid. What its defenders fail to understand is the possibility that a basic commitment to personal liberty and collective self-determination can be interpreted in a variety of ways, none of which has any evident claim to superiority. This commitment can be called 'modern' but there is more than one way of being so.

In particular, as I argued at various points above (most specifically in Part III), modernity is marked by a tension between the decontextualizing move that is necessary to generate a normative argument of some reach, on the one hand, and the requirement to link any justification to a situation for which it is adequate, on the other. In the current global contest over ways of world-making, one of the sites in which this tension becomes visible is the European attempt at creating a self-understanding that forms itself in its particularity, on the one side, and an approach that claims validity and applicability without regard for context, on the other, an approach that will here be referred to as imperial modernism.[2]

Unavoidably falling far short of a comprehensive analysis, this contest over world-making will here be discussed by taking two rather illustrative steps. First, a slightly schematic comparison of social and political thought in Europe and the US will be provided (the ground for which was prepared in chapters 9 and 10 above), showing the basic features of imperial modernism and indicating some – historical and contingent – reasons for its dominance in the USA, even though its sources are to be found in Europe. This relation of current dominance to historical sources will be illustrated with the help of the well-known theme of conflict between two brothers, thus demonstrating a relation of both similarity and difference, and one marked by a struggle over its interpretation as either equal and symmetrical or hierarchical and asymmetrical. Since this first step will show that individualism and instrumentalism are the key features of imperial modernism (see also chapter 6 above for an elaboration of this view), the second step will discuss the consequences of any future hegemony of such thinking, by exploring namely how the question of the common has become problematic in political philosophy in the light of the rise of individualist and instrumentalist liberalism. In conclusion, I will briefly come back to the question of whether any elements of an alternative to such hegemony can be identified in European political integration.

Plural interpretations of modernity and the meaning of empire

When the late Pope John Paul II visited Israel several years ago, a process of rapprochement of the Catholic Church towards the Jewish religious community, which had started with the visit of the Pope to the synagogue in Rome in 1986, reached a high point. John Paul II, contributing to the general movement of reconciliation and pardoning that marked the 1990s, addressed his audience in Rome as 'Dear Jewish and Christian friends and brothers', and when turning explicitly to the Jewish listeners he uttered a phrase that has often been quoted since: 'You are our favourite brothers and, in a certain sense we may say, our elder brothers.' On this occasion, as on many others, the speech was interrupted by sustained applause, as observers report.

Some years later, there was a little uproar in Italian political-intellectual circles when historian Carlo Ginzburg (1998, pp. 210–15) dared to pour some water into the wine. He recalled the fact that the term 'the elder brother' had a long history in Christian thought, even a constitutive semantic role in that history. It was used by Paul – the first Paul – in the letter to the Romans, and Paul in turn referred to the Lord telling Rebecca, who was pregnant with twins, that 'the elder shall serve the younger' (Romans 9: 12). And this was as it turned out to be: Jacob, the younger son, bought the rights of the first-born, Esau, for a lentil dish, after having cheated him about the legitimacy of that transaction.

This is not the place to comment on the interpretations of John Paul's speech or to intervene in any way in the discussions about the relations between Christianity and Judaism in general. Rather, I want to suggest that we can think fruitfully about the relations between Americans and Europeans, and in particular about their intellectual – or spiritual-intellectual (*geistige*) – relations in analogy to this time-honoured story of the two siblings. Not aiming at an – impossible – overall comparison of American and European social and political thought in our time, I want to point to a structural feature in our ways of analysing the social world: a structural feature that exists on both sides of the Atlantic, but that finds observably different expressions on each side. And with the rise of the younger brother to dominance, the story of the two siblings provides a way of describing that structure as a potentially imperial one.

The story suggests a relation in which the elder brother – 'the European' – can say that he is the rightful inheritor of great intellectual traditions, but that over time the younger brother – 'the American' – appropriated this heritage, indeed developed but also changed it, and partly turned it against the elder – with success, since he had grown much more powerful. The younger brother would admit that he has a debt towards the elder one because the latter gave him the main ideas and practices. But he would insist that he improved on those ideas and practices and put them right where the elder brother still tended to get them wrong. In the younger brother's view, it needed him to lift these ideas out of their context of origin to develop them into the powerful intellectual tools that they now are.

Such discourse, it may be remembered, especially from the elder brother's end, was quite common in broader intellectual circles during the inter-war period – that is, the first moment when Europeans strongly experienced the presence of the USA in terms of superiority. That situation gave rise to a critical, self-reflexive discourse on the modernity of Europe (see chapter 10 above). For current purposes, though, I want to demonstrate – by means of four examples – how such a structure in intellectual relations can be detected in the social and political sciences.

First, *individualist liberalism as a political philosophy* gradually emerged in the European seventeenth and eighteenth centuries. It became inescapable with the American and French Revolutions, the onset of political modernity, as one might say, although it did not yet become widely accepted on those grounds. Rather, it started to flourish in political theory at US – and partly UK – universities after the Second World War with, again somewhat later, John Rawls's *Theory of Justice* (1971) becoming the landmark publication. Since then, individualist liberalism has become the pivotal approach to political theory. The current situation can be described by an anecdote: an English philosopher, specializing in so-called Continental Philosophy, went to Frankfurt on a Humboldt Foundation scholarship some years ago hoping to live and work for a while in the Frankfurt School milieu. All he found, as he said, were discussions about Rawls and Michael Walzer and the dispute between liberals and communitarians.

Second, *rational choice* theorists normally do not endow their approach with a long history. In their view, it started only in the middle of the twentieth century. However, a lineage can easily be traced that goes back to Hobbes and then leads to Condorcet and some other Enlightenment thinkers. Through political economy, the approach receives a clear place in moral philosophy, as well as an objective, the increase in the wealth of nations. Thus, it addresses issues of a theory of social order and of distributive justice at the same time. Modified and formalized in the neo-classical mode of economics which emerges from the marginalist revolution in the late nineteenth century, it acquires the potential to become a *general theory of action* – a potential that is realized after the Second World War. This thinking is now widespread across the globe and across the disciplines of the social sciences, but nowhere as strongly as in the USA.

Third, explicit moves towards *quantification as a methodology* in philosophy and the social sciences are normally dated to the seventeenth century and to political arithmetic in England and France, which worked with state-provided data. Statistics became a more refined and reflected tool in the late nineteenth and early twentieth century. But the key social scientist to mention in this context is a young Austrian socialist and mathematician, who tried to put his skills to good use in the socialist-led city administration of 'Red Vienna' after the First World War. Paul Felix Lazarsfeld later went into exile in the USA and founded the Bureau for Applied Social Research at Columbia University. After the Second World War, he was probably the leading methodologist in American social science.

Social scientists today, fourth, naturally think about their fields of inquiry in terms of *disciplinary organization and professionalization*. There are, however, many ways of dividing up the modes to study the social world. The major social-science perspectives such as the economic, sociological, cultural or statistical ones were all well developed at the end of the nineteenth century. But in Europe, they mostly did not give rise at that time to separate disciplines and professions with well-demarcated fields and boundaries. Current thinking about the disciplines of the social sciences is indeed often based on a view that takes their American history as the model. In the USA, a non-disciplinary, quite amateurish and politically oriented American Social Science Association (ASSA), which was founded in 1865, came under increasing pressure towards the end of the nineteenth century to develop a proper scientific and professional statute. Since it proved unable to reform itself, disciplinary associations were formed one after the other by breaking away from ASSA, following the example set by the American Historical Association (AHA) in 1884. Thus, the American Economic Association (AEA), founded in 1885, the American Political Science Association, founded in 1903, and the American Society for Sociology (ASS, now ASA), splitting off from AEA, were formed, providing by the beginning of this century the ideal picture of social science disciplines that is still familiar today (Manicas 1987). Under the guidance of UNESCO, this model was globalized after the Second World War, not least by founding the international associations such as the International Sociological Association (ISA) and the International Political Science Association (IPSA).

Even in the absence of a comprehensive comparative study, few would contradict the statement that these four approaches and orientations are more widespread in the American than in the European social and political sciences. Rather than the comparative observation as such, though, another question is of significance here: how could the recent versions of these approaches make a claim to intellectual superiority with regard to the broader traditions from which they have emerged – that is, superiority of the younger brother over the elder one? There is an asymmetry in the current intellectual constellation that is worth exploring because it provides the ground for the thinking of empire.

It is not difficult to find explicit claims to such superiority in the approaches just described. One example from political philosophy may suffice to illustrate the nature of the claim. Speaking about some version of liberalism, namely in terms of 'the growth of freedom' and 'the rise of liberal institutions and customs', an American philosopher recently claimed that 'Western social and political thought may have had the last conceptual revolution it needs.' One should think that such a phrase contains far too much vulgar philosophy of history to be seriously sustained at the end of the twentieth century. But the author was not Francis Fukuyama; it was, as we had seen before, Richard Rorty (1989, p. 63; for a reflection on this phrase, see Gander 1999). Despite the fact that this statement, just like any other claim to superiority, did not go uncontested, I do not want to move to a refutation now (steps towards it will be taken in the next section). A particular vision of modernity is embedded in those approaches; and it is first necessary to understand how this vision has come to be seen as unsurpassable.

The four approaches to the social and political sciences as described above radicalize the modern orientation, the dual commitment of human beings to autonomy and to mastery. As far as the organizational and methodological models – institutionalization of social sciences and quantitative research – are concerned, their ambition to order and master the world is rather straightforward. For the two theoretical approaches – the political philosophy and the theory of action – the relation between autonomy and mastery is more complex. Both individualist liberalism and individualist rationalism are theories of freedom but they conceptualize freedom in a very particular way. Their specificity is to start out from the singular human being, defined as an individual, devoid of any specificity, rather than from social relations or from any form of collectivity of humans. From this starting point, they devise a relation of such individual to the world in terms of instrumental or procedural rationality. They can hardly do otherwise, since all substantive features of social life were eliminated in their conceptualization of the individual.

This is a very specific interpretation of autonomy and mastery – autonomy as individual, and mastery as instrumental. It is a somewhat dogmatic rendering of what modernity is about. That is why I prefer to call those approaches 'modernist' rather than just 'modern'. What this approach claims to accomplish is this: it removes all contaminations of history and sociality from analysis and, thus, creates a distance from context and situation that is, so the argument goes, required for social and political theorizing.[3] In other words, modernism claims to create a purity that underpins universality (or, at least, universalizability). By virtue of this move, it pushes everything else – the approaches of its critics – into the realm of the specific, the particular, or even – when a direction of history is implied – of a remnant of tradition. In this regard, thus, it is different from all other approaches to understanding the social world. Even though the superiority of this 'younger brother' on account of such striving for purity may be questioned on good grounds (as I will aim to do below), it is true that this move created an asymmetric relation between the 'brothers', the fact of which provided the ground for an imperial claim.

Clearly, such claim to hegemony cannot be accepted; its forceful existence, however, brings about a need to interpret its basis, even though in other terms. To at least indicate the direction in which such an interpretation needs to go, I will use again briefly Rémi Brague's *Europe, la voie romaine* (1999), not least because it discusses the specificity of Europe by means of a related image of twinness (see above chapter 10). To recall, Brague suggests that a tension between two sources for each major component of its self-understanding, the religious and the political one, provides for the specificity of Europe. This 'secondarity' gave Europe its historical dynamism, the searching and self-questioning nature of its philosophical and political life. For the present purpose, I shall just suggest that European modernity may have created anew some such tension, namely the one between 'modernism' and its critics in political philosophy and in social theory; and that this tension can to some extent – with all due caution – be mapped onto the actually existing social world: as 'America' and as 'Europe' (in the form of a geo-philosophy of 'the West', to employ and modify Massimo Cacciari's (1994) term).

In this sense, the approaches briefly discussed above are expressions of the search for an identity of modernity, for the specifically modern solutions to the socio-political *problématiques*. The quest for purity, as just discussed, can be understood as the search for the specificity of modernity, which, in the view of modernism, would generally – and, thus, universally – be found wherever the socio-political world turns modern. Such striving for purity, however, it seems, is both necessary and futile.

It is necessary because its 'method' (using the term broadly) of distancing from the context provided intellectual means to deal with problematic historical situations. Thus, liberalism, in its origins, was developed to deal with religious wars and revolutions and with the diversity of human strivings that thus became politically visible. Individualist rationalism provided ways of dealing with the emergence of an industrial-capitalist mode of production and with 'the social question'. Quantification was developed as a means for dealing with the novel issues emerging with mass-democratic societies and welfare states. Clear-cut and coherent institutionalization of social-science disciplines reflects the quest for a well-ordered society, matched by a well-ordered set of knowledge forms.

But such striving is also futile because these approaches (to political philosophy, social theory, methodology and institutionalization) do not provide self-sufficient modes of analysing the social world – self-sufficient in the sense of proceeding without regard for context or situation. Such striving means the attempt to overcome secondarity, and the tensions and ambiguities that come with it. But, if it could succeed, the elimination of those tensions would precisely do away with that which generates creativity and plurality in the interpretive struggles over what modernity is about. By implication, such a move would distance the others who do not follow it, treat them as 'less advanced' (as the elder, European brother already did during his age of colonization with those who were colonized). It would mean the attempt to dominate the elder brother.[4]

In contrast, precisely the space of reasoning that opens up between the purity of imperial modernism and its critics is of interest. This space provides the interpretive possibility to think of varieties of modernity as varieties of conceptualizing autonomy and mastery and their relation to one another. Then, the relation between America and Europe – and their respective social and political sciences – would not be the one of a younger, more energetic modernity that has outperformed the older one, but the relation of one interpretation of modernity to others – and yet others outside of the so-called West. Since the individual, seen as an atom linked to other human beings only through instrumental rationality, is at the centre of imperial modernism, I shall in a second step explore the consequences of the rise of this mode of thinking for political philosophy, and in particular for the question of the common that is at the core of all things political.

Freedom and the common: rethinking modernity beyond imperial modernism

Under the impact of contemporary imperial modernism, the history of political philosophy is sometimes read in terms of a gradual but irresistible rise of individualist liberalism. Individualism, and increasingly individualist liberalism, experienced renewed break-throughs after major socio-political transformations, such as the end of the religious wars, the French Revolution and the rise of capitalism, and the end of totalitarianism. Such historical experiences seemed to strongly suggest that rights-based individualism was the only viable basis for political theory. In the aftermath of totalitarianism, as we have seen (chapter 2 above), versions of individualism have dominated the scene, reaching from Isaiah Berlin's famous defence of 'negative liberty' to John Rawls's individualist reasoning for limited policies of redistribution. To speak loosely, one could suggest that wars and revolutions were so destructive – or, at least, transformative – of the social bond that in their aftermath doubts were raised about the possibility of strong substantive ties between human beings that could sustain a sense of the common (see chapters 6 and 8 above).

When, some two decades ago, communitarianism was proposed in the US as a response to this dominance, it provided the historically weakest argument ever in defence of holist and/or collectivist views of the social and political world – 'weak' in the sense of having most of all accepted the rise of individualism as, at least, a historical fact and context, or even as theoretically unavoidable. The European intellectual traditions of political Catholicism, nationalism, socialism and communism had all given stronger grounds for a thick political life, or, we may say, they have upheld a strong conception of the common. With the partial exception of Catholicism, however, they all appeared rather discredited after the end of the Second World War and, more so, after the demise of Soviet socialism.

There are reasons to argue, though, that individualist liberalism is insufficient in *theoretical* terms because it lacks criteria for determining that which members of the polity have in common – while necessarily remaining interested in the question. In the face of that absence it tends to resort to a concept of reason, which in turn – far too much a term meant to close an aporia rather than accepting it – tends to be interpreted as instrumental rationality. In terms of *political* experience, furthermore, individualist liberalism tends to combine two potentially dangerous effects. Given that, in this view, the protection of negative liberty is all the polity is about, it tends to withdraw political energy from the effort of determining what members of a polity have in common – thus mirroring the theoretical insufficiency in political life. The dedication to private affairs, which it in turn encourages, is not problematic in itself, but under conditions of extended market relations it may be steadily transforming the world, thus increasing the worldlessness that further undermines action in common.

Persistent criticism along both of these lines has made the debate between individualist liberalism and its critics continue, even though the former seems to become ever more dominant. At the same time, little advance can be noticed in this debate: the individualist-liberal tradition, defined most clearly by Locke and Kant, found its strongest contemporary representation in John Rawls's *A Theory of Justice* in 1971. The first strong response that emerged historically towards this tradition, while accepting the idea of individual freedom, is Hegel's; and it has been taken up in our time, among others, by Charles Taylor in his *Hegel* and in *Hegel and Modern Society* during the 1970s. Across this period of more than two centuries, the basic constellation seems to have remained the same: individualist liberalism is unable to develop a sufficient concept of the common, but its alternatives, as shall be shown in a brief reconstruction below, either entertain overly strong, and thus normatively problematic, conceptions of the common, with a risk of violating the commitment to personal freedom, or their concept of the common is too weak to sustain the self-understanding of a polity.

The question, then, is to retrieve a concept of *the common* that goes beyond individualist liberalism but fully sustains the normative ideas of *personal as well as of political freedom*. Such retrieval is possible, in principle, by virtue of the fact that European political thinking, from its Greek origins to republicanism and romanticism to critical theory and phenomenology, has often worked with rich conceptual registers that escaped the theoretical choice between either the abstract freedom of individualism or the pre-definition of the range of permissible freedom by a strong community. However, as political philosophy is itself a historical activity, the reworking of such intellectual traditions needs to live up to the demands of its time and needs to develop its perspectives for the current moment of political restructuring under conditions of so-called globalization and, intellectually speaking, imperial modernism.

Historically, one can observe two major ways of criticizing the individualist-liberal position: on the one hand, the claim was made that human beings entertain strong links to one another before they enter into interaction as individuals in polity and society. Such attempts to theorize, as we may say, *pre-political* bonds all start out from the critical observation that the human being who enters into political relations is not such a kind of individual as liberal political theory described her, and that the hypothesis of any original position would lead to serious flaws in the conclusions. This thinking emphasizes the rootedness of the singular human beings in *contexts* from which their ways of giving *meaning* to the world stem. The broadest intellectual movement of this kind has been the *cultural-linguistic theory* of the boundaries of the polity, with Herder as its most significant representative, which inaugurated culturalist thinking in the social sciences and also became one source of later nationalism. However, the contexts need not necessarily be defined in strong collectivistic terms. They can also be conceptualized as modes of *intersubjectivity* emerging from an idea of *primary sociality* and of *interaction*, such as in the early works by Hegel (for recent appropriations see the work of Axel Honneth and Charles Taylor, for instance), or they can start out from an original condition of *being-in-the-world* and of *being-with*, as developed by Martin Heidegger and his followers (recently, for instance, see the work of Jean-Luc Nancy; and Mouzakitis 2007). In both cases, though, such alternative assumptions do not lead as directly to ideas about the form of the polity as collectivistic theories do.

The other main line of socio-political thought started out from the insights, first, that the basic individualist-liberal assumptions, once they were cast into effective rules, would have durable and important *effects* on what social scientists would soon call the 'structure' of social bonds. In this sense we can refer to those bonds as being conceived as *post-political*. And second, the question of such bonds was forced on to the agenda of social and political thought by virtue of the fact that the liberal assumptions on their own did not suffice to create and justify a political order. The observation of structures of representation was used to enhance stability and certainty in political procedures that otherwise could appear to be opened to all contingencies precisely by the commitment to freedom and by the abolition of any legitimacy of preordained orders. There are then two main strategies for rediscovering certainties: systematic observation and reflective conceptualization. These two intellectual responses to the political *problématique* inaugurate three well-known modes of social theorizing: the *behaviouralist* one based on observation, and, both based on a social-interest theory of representation, the *critical* one and the *structural-functional* one. The latter two do not make individualistic assumptions but aim at grounding socio-political life in purely social forms.

Often, the critique of liberalism that focuses on pre-political human bonds has been seen as politically right-wing because it appears to conceptually rely on some notion of tradition and to politically want to uphold such tradition, a position that appears literally as conservative (but see Mouzakitis 2007 on Gadamer). In turn, the alternative critique, the one that focuses on post-political social structures, has tended to be seen as left-wing because it often diagnoses problematic social results of the application of liberalism, not least in the version of market liberalism, and aims at remedying those problems by resorting to some form of collective intervention. With regard to the latter, the intellectual distinction between mainstream social science and critical theories appeared to resonate with the political distinction between reformist and revolutionary approaches.

Situating political modernity: Europe in context

We have arrived here at a distinction between an individualist way of thinking about the social world, often academically known as political theory, and an alternative view that insists on commonalities between human beings in a variety of ways, mostly referred to as social science or social philosophy. These two approaches are in historical communication, as we have seen in the brief considerations about their emergence, but their validity cannot be adjudicated by theoretical means because they are based on incompatible metaphysics (for a detailed discussion about the relation between the social and the political, see chapter 12 below). At this point, we leap over the 'abstract' argument and keep suggesting that adequacy needs to be related to the experience of problematic situations and their interpretation.

Historically existing polities can then be interpreted as institutionalized compromises of a variety of basic modes of justification. Individualist liberalism can be recognized as providing and sustaining the assumption of common humanity and, as a consequence, of equal liberty. It provides, thus, the background, and also creates the basic *problématique*, against which the other modes of justification are being deployed – but nothing more than that. It allows the issue of the constitution of a polity to be seen as indeed a political one, as the foundation of basic agreement under conditions of liberty. The conceptual separation of the political bond from other bonds between human beings is the consequence of the rise of individualist liberalism as the pivotal philosophy of political modernity: the call for freedom from unlegitimized intervention into personal lives, first, and the call for collective self-determination against the reign of autocratic rulers, second, were grounded on an abstract conception of the individual as well as of the collectivity with a view to elaborating a general, universalist claim beyond the specificity of the given situation.

While such a normative-conceptual move can be understood against the background of the European historical experience of resistance to illegitimate domination, for the same reason of abstraction from context, individualist liberalism proved to be insufficient and unsatisfactory as the guiding political philosophy of modernity whenever polities were to be founded. Political deliberation does not occur under a 'veil of ignorance', and a political theory that aims to address constitutional matters in the process of founding and re-founding polities needs to provide tools to understand and conceptualize the positions from which political actors reason (see Chakrabarty 2007 for a discussion of meanings of the political under different conditions).

Assumptions about the social bond, such as the cultural-linguistic one and the structural-functional one, then stepped in to deal with the *problématique* thus created. They are not just social theories; they support repertoires of justification of immediate political relevance. They may be used to determine, as a matter of principle, whether a human being is a member of a given polity rather than a different one, and what her/his place within that polity is. However, observations on cultural, economic and social relations should not be seen as providing an answer to the political *problématique* of human life but rather as raising questions. Political theory should not, in turn, fall into cultural, economic and/or social determinism, as much of political thinking indeed did during the nineteenth and twentieth century in response to the abstraction from any cultural, economic and social bonds that characterizes individualist liberalism. Conceptually speaking, the response to this double challenge – individualist abstraction versus social determination – lies in seeing observations on such bonds, or on cleavages and boundaries, as resources in political reasoning that can and should be brought in as arguments in favour of some institution or policy over another. They do not have compelling power on their own but are in need of justification under condition of a possible plurality of modes of justification.

The question, then, is how political dispute can be adjudicated under such condition of plurality. The answer cannot but be twofold. First, there is no solution to political dispute offered by political theory alone because the universalist theoretical claims that can be made are insufficiently concrete to guide institutional design or policy-making. They are in need of specific interpretation. Saying this, though, second, does not amount to arguing that those claims are invalid. They have to be confronted with the situation in which policy deliberation takes place. And this situation is defined by two basic components: the problem of the moment that gives rise to deliberation in the first place, and the resources that political actors bring into this moment, based on their observation of the cultural, economic and social bonds and cleavages. The struggles over European political modernity across history, thus, need to be interpreted with a view to grasping how the self-understanding of a modern polity evolved and changed through all of these features: by means of developing core universalist elements of a political philosophy of modernity; by experiencing changing problematic constellations that needed to be dealt with in common; and by elaborating a rich range of resources to guide the situation-specific interpretation of such philosophy with a view to solving those political issues.

Imperial modernism denies these questions any relevance, claiming that there is a singular – individualist-instrumentalist – interpretation of political modernity that, once identified and developed, can be applied and exported in any conceivable situation. That this is not only wrong in terms of political thinking, but also in political history, is evident at the current moment, with disastrous consequences in Iraq.[5] Political developments in Europe, as slow and as hesitant about their proper direction as they may be, exemplify the counterclaim, aiming at creating and instituting an alternative interpretation of political modernity based on a more elaborate balance of the exigencies for personal and collective freedom and at the same time making the broader case – of global significance – that more than one interpretation of modernity can be sustained.

This is where the core of the question about a European political modernity seems to lie today. One could have chosen to write the narrative of political Europe in terms of the European experience with liberty. Had I done so, a story of persistent but also rather slow struggle would have emerged. There would have been no lack of commitment to liberty, but also disastrous, and sometimes widespread and long-lasting, violations of the claim to freedom. The European experience would often have looked rather deficient, in terms of insights arrived at in Europe itself early in its modern history, and also in terms of political experiences elsewhere, in the US, and at the fringes of Europe, in England.

Today, the extent of the European commitment to liberty is – comparatively speaking at least – beyond question and it is accompanied by a pronouncedly self-critical relation to her own history.

Under these circumstances, a different story of European political modernity could be told to balance that narrative of deficient liberty. It is a story of a persistent problematization of liberty (as in chapter 2), of an oscillation between several partial accounts of the meaning of political form (as in chapter 3), and of a process of problem-creation and problem-redefinition (as in the preceding chapter). In this story, European political modernity is marked by an often only half-conscious, often also ill-directed, but nevertheless viable and necessary resistance to accepting individualist liberalism as the bottom-line and only firm ground of a politics of freedom.

There has long been a sense in Europe that an exclusive focus on individual liberty as the basic commitment of a polity is insufficient. Undeniably, many of the discourses and the political activities that were inspired by this insight were problematic if not even profoundly flawed. But once the legitimate questions that motivated them have been retrieved, the history of European political modernity can be re-read in terms of the political projects that were formulated and embarked on at various points in time, the dead ends that some of these projects ended in, and the transformation of political possibilities that the sequence of these projects resulted in. It is to such a retrieval and re-reading that the reasoning of the preceding chapter means to contribute.

The hope – dim as it may be – that political possibilities may be better grasped in the future can ground itself on two observations: first, that political construction today is a European project with wider horizons than the earlier national ones with their particular restrictions and exclusions; and second, that this construction is already broadly inspired by a critical reassessment of the European experience of liberty and of its violations. In this sense, most optimistically, the current steps towards a political Europe could be both an explication of the European resistance to individualist liberalism and the creation of an institutional setting for the realization of a fuller understanding of freedom. While there is, thus, some hope for success in the elaboration and construction of such an alternative in Europe, the struggle still suffers from the claim to superiority the younger brother keeps making. The hesitations in the European developments could possibly be diminished if sustained intellectual efforts were made to oppose this claim to superiority. The two steps of the above reasoning in this chapter are intended as contributions to such an effort.

Part V

The Analysis of Modernity and the Need for a New Sociology

Overture: When the Light of the Cultural Problems has Moved On

Alexis de Tocqueville's analysis of the rise of democracy called for a 'new political science' to understand this new phenomenon (see chapter 2). Three-quarters of a century later, Max Weber suggested that 'objectivity' in the social sciences is possible in as far as there is a relatively stable social world and, importantly, some degree of a common interpretation of that world. Whenever 'the light of the cultural problems moves on', however, new concepts would need to be elaborated for that changing world (see chapters 1 and 10).

Throughout this volume, I have similarly argued that novel experiences call for novel interpretations, and that the concepts elaborated in such interpretations will often be found both viable and useful in as far as they can connect different experiences towards a common interpretation. More specifically, I have suggested that modernity has been undergoing a major transformation in recent decades so that a new interpretation may be required – or at least the question may be raised whether a new interpretation is required (I have offered elements of such a novel interpretation in chapters 10 and 11).

Among the major *problématiques* of modernity, the epistemic *problématique* asks for the creation of valid knowledge by means of human intellectual self-determination. I have argued that the social sciences, and sociology in particular, have been proposed as one means to answer this *problématique*. If the history of sociology is a history of varieties of interpretations of modernity (as argued in chapter 9), then we need to conclude this reasoning by asking which kind of sociology is needed for the analysis of the current transformation of modernity. The contours of such sociology should have become visible in the preceding reflections. The task of this concluding section is to spell out some theoretical and methodological requirements for continuing on the path outlined before.

As any novel interpretation will suggest revisions of earlier interpretations, the following reflections will partly proceed by means of intellectual and disciplinary reconstruction. At various points above (see in particular chapter 5), I have suggested that the relative consolidation of 'organized modernity' between, roughly, the 1890s and the 1960s had led to a separation of sociology as an academic discipline from philosophical and historical concerns. Such concerns remained constitutive of the discipline but they were no longer visible as such (see also Wagner 2001a). To live up to the demands of the current experience of transformation, this separation needs to be overcome and links re-established.

Two main lines of reasoning will be pursued in what follows. First, in chapter 12, I will argue that social theorizing had, by the 1960s, taken over much of the task of understanding political modernity that was earlier addressed by political philosophy, and it had done so by pointing out obvious insufficiencies of the latter. However, social theory turned out to be marked by different insufficiencies that have more recently come clearly to the fore. A reconnection between the two fields of inquiry will not be fruitfully possible by some theoretical synthesis but by recognizing the indeterminacy in their relation, to be addressed only by recourse to situation-adequate interpretations.

The subsequent chapter 13, secondly, addresses the new centrality of interpretation in the social and human sciences, known under the label 'linguistic turn'. It asks in particular how the tradition of historical sociology is used to address the key themes of modernity, democracy and capitalism and how a language-conscious renewal of this field can arrive at a better understanding of the history of modernity as sequences of reinterpretations of basic commitments in the light of new experiences and the problems that emerge with them.

12

The Social Theory and Political Philosophy of Modernity

The social sciences inherited from political philosophy their most basic questions. This observation is the starting point for Luc Boltanski and Laurent Thévenot in *De la justification* (1991, p. 39) to then show that the most clear-cut theoretical approaches in the social sciences – such as the ontological holism in much of sociology and the individualism in economics – should be read as opposed social metaphysics that are unable to understand the superior principle that they share. Trying to find theoretical reason for assuming that agreement between human beings is possible, both of these approaches presuppose one ground for such agreement – 'collective identity or the market value' (p. 44) – at the expense, though, of losing the understanding of how one form of agreement rather than another emerges. Boltanski and Thévenot call this operation a 'reduction of political metaphysics in the social sciences' (p. 43) and their book is devoted to the 'unconcealing of the underlying political metaphysics'. This operation, however, 'is made very difficult because of the rupture with philosophy through which both economics and sociology constituted themselves as scientific disciplines. [...] Both have been born from political philosophies that have served as their matrices and in which the metaphysics are visible' (p. 44).

The reconstruction of those metaphysics that lie behind social-science reasoning, as performed in *De la justification*, has enabled the shift of perspective that has generated the research programme of the group around Boltanski and Thévenot that I have discussed elsewhere (Wagner 1999b, 2004). The repertoires of moral-political evaluation that human beings employ in situations in need of justification are practical political philosophies that are derived from the canonized approaches to political theory. Thus, normative political philosophy is indeed empirically found in social life and this form of reasoning emerges, as is appropriate for the political, whenever there is a search for 'the ground of an agreement', i.e., when a consensus about the interpretation of a situation is to be reached.

While this programme is one of the most important intellectual events in the social and political sciences over the past three decades, it does not answer all the questions that it raises. Among the criticism it faced, one major accusation held that the approach ultimately favours a return of the political, even though in a particular way, and the neglect of, or the emptying out of, the social. While not doing justice to the work of the group, such reproach nevertheless points to the persistence of the divide between the political and the social which opened with the rise of the social sciences and cannot easily be undone. In the light of this observation, it remains important to ask what precisely was the nature of that 'rupture with philosophy' that gave birth to the social sciences, what brought it about, and what are its consequences.[1]

To fully grasp the issues at stake in contemporary social theory, this chapter will proceed through a brief historical reconstruction of the way in which the social was separated from the political, and gradually took over its role. The separation of social theory from political philosophy, as diagnosed by Boltanski and Thévenot, namely is often seen as coinciding with the decline of political philosophy. If this were so, though, then it would be more appropriate to say that the social sciences are a way of solving political issues by other means than philosophy – since political issues will not go away. On a closer look, indeed what happened was not the disappearance of political philosophy but the alignment of a certain form of political theory, with individualist liberalism at its core, with a rather technocratic understanding of social science. Such a combination of genres reigned over the socio-political world during much of the second post-war period. If there are signs today that the end of that reign is reached, it is high time to understand its mode of governance.

The emergence of the social from within the political

From its origins in ancient Greece, the term 'political' refers to that which (any collectivity of) human beings deal with in common, or to their activity of dealing with certain matters in common. The term 'social' – and its correlates in other European languages – refers, in turn, to the connectedness of a human being to others. We could say that it enables us to talk about situations in which human beings create relations to one another. Logically, it seems, the social should include the political. Not always when human beings relate to one another do they do so with a view to dealing with common matters. Whenever they deal with common matters, though, they need to relate to one another.[2] Rather than merely marking a difference between forms of human relations, though, the rise of social theory from the late eighteenth century onwards offered a particular interpretation of that difference. A very specific way of talking about connections between human beings, namely, was introduced with the term 'society'; and as a result the term 'social sciences' emerged in the eighteenth century ever more strongly to gradually replace, or at least diminish the centrality of, terms such as 'moral and political sciences' or 'state sciences'.

The career of the term 'society' went through several phases. Initially, it had no direct political meaning. A 'society' was a voluntary association of human beings that came together for a purpose (Heilbron 1995, p. 87). Gradually, however, it came to be used in the moral and political sciences, in particular within French and Scottish debates, and it acquired the place of the denomination for the key object of socio-political life there. In combinations such as 'political society' and 'civil society', it referred to nothing else but the state, but from a point of view of contract theory, namely as the aggregation of human beings that have come together for a purpose, implying now that all human beings on a given territory agreed on the purpose, unlike in the earlier 'private' meaning of 'society'. Thus, it retained its original meaning, but was now employed, by way of analogy or counterfactual hypothesis, to explain the emergence of a polity of human beings under conditions of equal liberty. Clearly, a 'social' term was here used for 'political' matters: the bond between those beings was political; they only linked up to each other because of a common need or purpose. However, it was also a specific way of thinking the political. In the hypothetical state of nature, i.e., 'before' the formation of the contract, politics does not exist, in this view. Such thinking was alien to ancient political thought, in which the human being was a *zoon politikon*, or in other words, in which the question of handling things in common was a constitutive *problématique* of human life. In contract theory, in contrast, based on modernist individualism, the human being was first thought as a being without political bond. It is only the unpredictable or even outright conflict-prone nature of their social relations that made humans create a political bond.[3]

From such a derivation of the political from the social in individualist theorizing, the next step in conceptual development was a novel form of separating the social from the political, from the late eighteenth century onwards. 'Society' came now to be seen as a phenomenon that was different from the polity, even though it remained articulated with the polity. The idea of 'society' as a *sui generis* reality between the polity and the individuals (or households) continued to suggest, along the lines of the earlier conceptual innovation, that there were social bonds between human beings that were different from their political bonds. In most versions of nineteenth-century social theory, however, the character and extension of the social bond was conceptualized in such a way that it could sustain the political bond (Wagner 2001b, chapter 8). Thus, the social was used to solve the problem of the political, a problem that had become intractable, as I will argue below, under conditions of individual liberty. This kind of thinking continues its grip on our ways of conceptualizing the political. The idea of a 'social substrate' necessarily underlying any viable polity, for instance, is used to analyse the relation between the European democratic nation-states and the emerging European polity (e.g., Offe 1998). True, in some versions, most prominently the Marxian one, it was precisely the tension between the structure of the social bond and the structure of the political bond that provided the moving force for social change. Such thinking, though, rather than providing an alternative, merely inverts the idea that a certain structure of social bonds is required to sustain a polity.

The social bond was conceptually separated from the political one only to be reconnected to it in the next conceptual step.[4] The *separation* was necessary, in the first instance, to underpin an individualist conception of freedom; the *reconnection* was necessary to link freedom to predictability. Even given complete autonomy, so the reasoning of the social sciences goes, human beings would reveal themselves driven by a limited number of well-intelligible inclinations. And this linkage of freedom and predictability became particularly important at the historical moment when the externally imposed barriers to free deliberation threatened to be removed, the moment of the American and French Revolutions.

The moment of the revolution

These revolutions gave institutional expression to the political aspect of a broader culture of individual autonomy that is a key element of modernity. In this sense, much of this era can be seen as a liberation of human beings from imposed ties, but this liberation was far from unproblematic. As Claude Lefort once described this feature of modernity:

> When he is defined as independent, the individual does not exchange [...] one certainty against another one. [...] The new mode of existence of the individual within the horizons of democracy does not merely emerge as the promise to control one's own destiny, but also and not less as the dispossession of the assurance as to one's identity – of the assurance which once appeared to be provided by one's place, by one's social condition, or by the possibility of attaching oneself to a legitimate authority. (1986a, pp. 214–15)

Liberation is here interpreted as an increase of contingency and uncertainty in the lives of human beings.

If this view were unequivocally valid, one should expect a philosophy of contingency – in Richard Rorty's style (1989), for instance – linked to a liberal-individualist political theory to dominate the intellectual scene for ever after the successful revolutions. However, historically this was not at all the case. In contrast, 'the historical moment, about which we speak, emerges in such a way that the real rising of the political instance entails its theoretical abatement' (Manent 1994, p. 123). Instead, the historical moment of liberty coincided with the rise of social theory. 'Society' as the object of the social sciences has been a 'post-revolutionary discovery'; or, to put it even more succinctly, 'the sociological point of view constitutes itself in the moment when the notion of liberty becomes the principal articulation of the human world'.[5] Such apparent paradox reveals the aporia of political thought after liberation. Very generally speaking, social theory was exactly a part of the response human beings gave to their new condition of – self-incurred, one might say – contingency and principled uncertainty. Being unable to rely any longer on externally defined certainties, socio-political thinkers started searching for regularities and continuities which exist without being commanded, or even at all created. Social theory has been a means to decrease contingency.

The problem of post-revolutionary liberty

One can understand such intellectual shift by means of a look at the deep shock the revolutions represented for social and political thought. In a first step, somewhat schematically described, the experience demanded the substitution of the republican concept of liberty for a liberal one. In the Hobbes–Lockean lineage, liberals define liberty as non-interference. The state, founded by free contract, dominates the individuals, but it interferes with their liberties only to the degree required for the maintenance of order. The liberal tradition needs to draw a strong boundary between the public and the private; whatever social bonds exist in the latter, they will not impact on the former, the form of which is determined by reason. Since non-interference of the public with the private is the supreme principle, this thinking can only have a 'thin', asocial concept of membership in a polity. In contrast, republicans define liberty as non-domination. Drawing via Machiavelli on Roman (and Greek) political thought, non-domination is conceptualized in stronger terms than non-interference; it requires security against interference. Such security stems at least in part from the ways in which citizens relate to each other, in other words, from their social bonds, so that there is a less sharp divide between the private and the public and a 'thicker' concept of membership than in liberalism.[6]

Among historians of political thought today, there is broad – maybe too broad – agreement that republicanism was by and large abandoned around the turn of the eighteenth century and liberalism, though it neither appeared particularly powerful nor coherent before, very soon emerged as the pivotal political theory in post-revolutionary polities. Despite being inspired by republican thinking, the revolutions aimed at combining two objectives that proved to be practically impossible to hold together. On the one hand, they aimed at transforming state sovereignty in the hands of the monarch into popular sovereignty, i.e., they worked with extended notions of citizenship and liberty. On the other hand, they held such a transformation of the polity to be conceivable only in the form of the existing territorial state and within its dimensions.

Such double transformation entailed, first, that the existing social bonds between the people, tainted with the suspicion of domination and privilege characteristic of feudal society, had to be weakened or abolished. Thus, however, a major available resource for a substantive, 'thick' grounding of a modern republic was rejected. Second, the idea of extending political rights widely cast doubts on the viability of a demanding, socially rich concept of liberty such as the one upheld in the republican tradition. Caution seemed to demand, not least for some more conservative observers, that the substance of the concept of liberty be limited at the moment at which its reach was extended. As a consequence, the public realm, the polity, was robbed of most of its 'social' substance and the formal process through which common deliberations were reached was emphasized instead. The adoption of some kind of such a proceduralist, individualist liberalism is the main reason why the tradition of political philosophy declined. With the renunciation of any substantive, social foundation of the polity and 'a total grounding of government in self-interest and consent' (Wood 1998 [1969], pp. 614 and 612, about the founding of the USA), the conclusion seemed undeniable that, once the reasonable will of human beings had been cast in institutions, the political order must be seen as intrinsically satisfactory (Manent 1994, pp. 228–9).

The rise of social theory

Not everybody, though, was convinced that such a solution was viable, in particular in Europe where the revolution towards self-determination seemed to be intrinsically connected to the possibility of terror. 'The effect of liberty to individuals is, that they may do what they please: We ought to see what it will please them to do, before we risque congratulations', as Edmund Burke (1993 [1790], pp. 8–9) famously put it in his reflections on the French Revolution. While individualist liberalism may be seen as providing the ('negative') concept of liberty as non-interference that may live up to Burke's requirements under the proviso that the state is capable of maintaining order for and above the individuals (see chapter 2 above), there is another way out of the aporia of liberty, namely the attempt to arrive at knowing 'what it will please them to do' by other means. The American and French Revolutions, thus, strongly suggested the study of what held human beings together, how they would actually organize their lives – individually, in 'associations' (Alexis de Tocqueville) or 'social movements' (Lorenz von Stein), and in the polity and the 'nation' – and what kinds of regularities and orders could be expected, if people were permitted to do so on their own without imposed restrictions. This is a new search for social bonds, which is simultaneously one major root of social theory and a politically motivated search.

It soon emerged that there was a variety of ways to conceptually determine 'what it will please them to do', and this variety forms precisely the social metaphysics that Boltanski and Thévenot chose as the starting point for their reconstruction of practical political philosophy. Some strategies start out directly from the assumptions of individualist liberalism. The rights-endowed individual became in such views the only conceivable ontological as well as the methodological foundation of a science of political matters after the revolutions. Once the rights of man had been generally accepted as self-evident and unalienable, it seemed obvious, to Turgot and

Condorcet for instance, that they were also 'the logical foundation of the science of society' (Baker 1975, p. 218). In rights-based liberalism, the individual is the only category that need not, often in fact cannot, be debated.

Once this assumption was accepted, basically two avenues of constructing a science of the political had opened. Both these forms of theorizing connect modernist political philosophy, i.e., individualist liberalism, to a science of the political.[7] One possibility was to try to identify by theoretical reasoning the basic features of this unit of analysis, the individual human being, and its actions. Since this unit was conceived as an ontological starting point, devoid of all specific, historical and social, ties to the world, its characterization was to proceed from some inherent features. From earlier debates, those features had often been conceived as twofold, as passions and as interests. In the late Enlightenment context, the rational side of this dichotomy was regarded as the one amenable to systematic reasoning. It thus allowed the building of a scientific approach to the study of at least one aspect of human activity, namely the production and distribution of material wealth.[8] This approach inaugurated the tradition of *political economy*, later to be transformed into *neo-classical economics* and, still later, into *rational choice theory*. The moral and political philosophy of the early modern period split into a political theory based on the idea of the social contract and a rationalized moral theory based on the idea of exchange. In both cases, the individual is the starting point and unit of the analysis.

While political economy was based on a highly abstract, but for the same reasons extremely powerful, assumption of human rationality, the other conclusion from the individualist foundational principle was much more cautious. Avoiding any substantive assumptions on the driving forces in human beings at all, the statistical approach, often under the label of *political arithmetic*, resorted to the collection of numerically treatable information about human behaviour. The space of substantive presuppositions was radically emptied in this thinking, but the methodological confidence in mathematics increased in inverse proportion (Desrosières 1993).

Thus, two strands of political thought that had been proposed and elaborated for some time rose to new and greater prominence: political economy and political arithmetic. The denominations these approaches were known by in the late eighteenth century referred explicitly to political matters. Both were to lose these attributes in the nineteenth century when they had consolidated their ways of proceeding and when the application of these cognitive forms had established predominance over political deliberation in decisions on common matters, at least in the view of many economists and statisticians. Mostly, this terminological change has been interpreted as an autonomization of cognitive approaches and as a differentiation of the sciences into disciplines. However, it is not exactly appropriate to say that *economics* and *statistics* separated from politics. Once the approaches of the former two are accepted as comprehensively valid, there is nothing political left to study. The common just emerges from assumptions about rationality or from aggregation.

The acceptance of the economic and the statistical ways of conceiving of the social world did not go without criticism; and they were never accepted as the only possible ways anywhere. However, the critiques and alternatives that were proposed most often accepted the fundamental change in political reasoning after the construction of a polity based on the assumption of free individuals.[9] After such a polity had begun to come into existence, new problems were identified. These were now essentially liberal problems; they resulted, one might say, from the observation that not everything that was needed for organizing a liberal polity could indeed be derived from an 'original position' (John Rawls). Two main types of problems may be distinguished by reference to the hypothetical original position in which individuals meet under a veil of ignorance.

On the one hand, the range of conclusions that could be drawn from the assumption of free and equal individuals was too limited. These individuals' relations were structured by the existence of politically important 'pre-political' social facts, of orientations and links between human beings that were seen to already exist before individuals entered into political communication and deliberation. On the other hand, the working of the liberal rules would produce new kinds of social relations, 'post-political' relations, which would have a structuring impact on the polity in turn (these have been discussed in some detail in chapter 11 above). These were now all approaches that should come to be known as 'social' theories which were dealing with what used to be 'political' matter.

In this light, all basic approaches to social theory are ways of dealing with the problem of contingency after the assertion of human freedom. *Theories* of the *social* are proposed to make intelligible the possibilities and probabilities of actions and their consequences in the space of the political that was widely opened at the moment at which it was exclusively the free will of its members that should determine the polity. *Philosophies* of the *political* had long already known what is at stake and from Greek political thought to Renaissance humanism they had tried to give reasons and means for both accepting the openness of the political and limiting its impact.

Working generally with the view that politics is seen as a human activity that by its nature is open, plural and diverse (Arendt 1958), any strong cognitive linkage of free action and predictable outcome was inconceivable. But political philosophy had never before been required to develop its reasoning under the assumption of equal liberty of all members of the polity and it was under these circumstances that, apparently paradoxically, 'the sociological point of view constitutes itself in the moment when the notion of liberty becomes the principal articulation of the human world', to paraphrase Manent again.

More recently, such social theorizing has come under strong attack, mostly because of its inherent determinism. Orderly outcomes can only result from planned or routine activities, work and labour in Hannah Arendt's terminology, over which certainty can be established before they are started. In contrast, political action in a context of liberty must go along with contingency of outcomes. From an Arendtian viewpoint, thus, social theory establishes an impossible connection. Trying to identify laws and regularities of human action and societal development, social theory necessarily abandoned the heritage of political philosophy, the emphasis on creative agency, irreducible diversity and the permanent possibility of unpredictable beginnings. It is in the light of such considerations that the closing decades of the twentieth century have witnessed a revival of political philosophies of freedom, often going beyond concepts of liberty as held in liberal political theory. These works, by authors such as Claude Lefort, Pierre Manent or, more historically oriented, Quentin Skinner, are not merely contributions to political philosophy or its history. Rather, they challenge the very separation of social theory from political philosophy.

As much as the critique of social theory from such a perspective is highly valid, however, the mere return to political philosophy is no solution to the issues that are raised. Many of the contributions to the current debate fail to address the reasons for the historical decline of political philosophy and the concomitant rise of social theory. And those that do most often conclude on a normative rejection of 'the invention of the social' (Donzelot 1984) because of the implied move towards the 'administration of the social' (Arendt 1958) without, though, fully appreciating the ways in which politics was transformed in response to actually problematic situations rather than merely because of misconceptions of the political. It is on those grounds that this chapter needs to reconstruct, even if in all due brevity, the historical shift from the political to the social with a view to the specific conceptions of the political and of the social bond.

In this brief intellectual history, one key observation concerned the centrality of a notion of equal liberty in European (and North American) history of the past two centuries. This notion is closely related to the assumption of 'common humanity' made by Boltanski and Thévenot to identify the common principles of the social metaphysics. We may say that Boltanski and Thévenot only look at 'modern' modes of justification, or that they only draw on the resources of political modernity in their reconstruction. While they do thematize the boundary they thus create, for instance in their discussion of eugenics, they do not reflect on the conceptual relation of that assumption to the modes of justification that are ruled by it. In the reconstruction above, this assumption is seen as being at the core of individualist liberalism, the pivotal theory of political modernity. If it is accepted as in some way inescapable, there are then three ways to deal with this approach.

First, one can take individualist liberalism as self-sufficient for the normative underpinning of 'modern societies'. All one needs to posit is the equal freedom of rights-endowed human beings and everything else can be left to those human beings' use of the liberties. This is the position to which Burke objected. In the terminology chosen here, it conceives of only a thin political bond between human beings and of no social bond of any interest at all. Secondly, one can argue that equal liberty is only the starting point for reasoning about a political modernity that is furthermore characterized by the communicative interaction between human beings with a view to determining what they need to regulate in common and how they should do so. This is the republican position that has largely been found, even while attractive, implausible and unsustainable under conditions of large societies with complex forms of interaction. It works with a strong assumption about political bonds being woven and constantly re-woven in social interaction, but it says little to nothing about the nature of those bonds. Thirdly, one can respond to the desire of knowing more about the bases on which humans interact by observing and conceptualizing their modes of interaction with various auxiliary means. This is the way social theory and the social sciences went, and it has been accused of socially overdetermining human life. This approach works with a strong conception of the social bond, or rather with a variety of such conceptions, and it has largely forgotten about the political question that stood at its origins.

A comprehensive political sociology that reopens the connection between social theory and political philosophy, and that can draw some inspiration from Boltanski and Thévenot's theory of justification, stands between the second and the third position, while accepting elements of the first as a background. It allows for substantive assumptions, the application of which determines the outcome of interactions and the positions of human beings in society; in this sense it operates in the mode of social theory. But it also holds that the application of such assumptions is itself a possible concern of dispute and interpretation, thus requiring the kind of communicative deliberation that is at the centre of republican political philosophy. There is, thus, a possible theoretical position that integrates again what was separated in the intellectual history of the past two centuries: the conceptualization of the political and of the social.

It still needed to be shown, in part contra Boltanski and Thévenot's own claims, that from this position a sociology of entire social configurations can be developed that sustains the concern for political forms. Such historical-comparative study of modern social configurations and polities from the perspective of such a conjoined social theory and political philosophy needs to focus on three issues: the analysis of the variety of forms of political modernity as institutionalized combinations of individualist liberalism with the socially richer interpretations of the human engagement with the world provided by cultural and social modes of reasoning (see Lamont and Thévenot 2000); the study of the 'cultural' variety of modernity in terms of existing combinations of these latter modes of reasoning as basic modes of societal self-understanding or, in Cornelius Castoriadis's terms, 'imaginary significations of society'; and the study of the use of modes of justification, with a view to overcoming the antinomy between (political) voluntarism and (social) determinism, as actualizations of the commitment to liberty in situational contexts or, as Charles Taylor (1975) would put it, as 'situated freedom'. This book cannot claim to have demonstrated all of this but hopefully it has made some contribution towards it.

13

The Conceptual History and Historical Sociology of Modernity

The past two decades have witnessed many claims that the social sciences were undergoing an interpretive, a cultural, or a linguistic turn (e.g., Toews 1987; Hiley et al. 1991; Bonnell and Hunt 1999). There is certainly no consensus as to what such turns entailed or even what the precise nature of them were, the variety of terms used being indicative of at least a similar variety of views. It seems nevertheless possible, however, to identify here one broad shift – rather than a range of disconnected phenomena – that emphasizes the significance of language and interpretation for human social life, and thus for the study of human social life as well. Beyond its original and much more specific meaning, thus, the description of this shift as a linguistic turn appropriately captures this feature of recent debates.

At the same time, however, the expression 'linguistic turn' has also been used, or interpreted, as a battle-cry introducing a cleavage in the social and human sciences which, in the view of critics, risks undermining the whole intellectual endeavour of those sciences. Not least on grounds of such controversy, the impact of this turn is difficult to assess. For historical sociology, we may legitimately ask whether the linguistic turn has taken place at all or whether it has not been rejected outright. If we look at recent works that ambitiously aim at both continuing and modifying the long tradition of historical sociology, such as Christophe Charle's *La crise des sociétés impériales* (2001), it is sometimes difficult to find any traces of the concern for language that has shaped meta-historiographical debate over the past quarter of a century. Other observers, however, may use the same example to arrive at the opposite conclusion. The striking phenomenon of our time is then rather the fact that works such as Charle's that analyse entire societies over considerable stretches of time, and even in a comparative perspective, are so scarce. In as far as the linguistic turn raised the awareness of the difficulties inherent in analysing historical documents, in drawing conclusions from those documents about the past world, and in writing up those conclusions, its effects – intended or not – may, in this view, have been the destruction of the tradition of historical sociology.

Any further exploration of whether the former or the latter assertion tells us more about the relation between the linguistic turn and the social and human sciences will require both a prior delimitation of those areas of inquiry that are of interest here and an approximate definition of the range of possible impacts of the linguistic turn on them. For the purposes of this chapter, a rather narrow approach to both questions will be taken. In the next section, I will try to define a core area of historical sociology within an otherwise enormously large area of historical social inquiry. Subsequently, I will propose to understand the linguistic turn for my purposes as the emergence of a reflexive consciousness about the structure and uses of language in intellectual history, broadly understood. The main purpose of this chapter is then to demonstrate what happens when historical sociology encounters such language-conscious intellectual history. Rather than being destructive of scholarly possibilities, such an encounter could revive historical sociology by opening new perspectives on old, but insufficiently answered, questions.[1]

Democracy and capitalism in comparative perspective: the legacy of historical sociology

The understanding of historical sociology that will be used in this chapter is a rather limited but at the same time a quite specific one. A facile first approximation is by authors and works. The tradition of historical sociology under consideration here finds its start in works such as Alexis de Tocqueville's *La Démocratie en Amérique* and *L'Ancien régime et la révolution* and Karl Marx's *Capital* and the associated political writings as well as, somewhat later but in evident discussion with the earlier authors, Max Weber's *Protestant Ethic and the 'Spirit' of Capitalism* and his writings on the sociology of world religions. Overshadowed by world-political dispute as well as by intellectual doubts about its very possibility, the tradition is weakened between the two great wars of the twentieth century. Norbert Elias's *Civilizing Process* and Karl Polanyi's *Great Transformation* found the attention they merited only after the second war. After that war, though, the tradition revived with a focus on totalitarianism, Hannah

Arendt's *Origins of Totalitarianism* and Barrington Moore's *Social Origins of Dictatorship and Democracy* being landmark works. Drawing critical inspiration from the latter, in particular, historical sociologists such as Charles Tilly and Theda Skocpol aimed at consolidating the approach and securing it a legitimate place within the discipline of sociology which by then had undergone intense methodological debate with often rather stifling outcomes, especially in the US context.

Trying to go beyond a list of names in delimiting an area of interest, Theda Skocpol's attempt from the early 1980s is indeed useful. She defined historical sociology as 'research devoted to understanding the nature and effects of large-scale structures and fundamental processes of change' (Skocpol 1984a, p. 4).[2] In as far as the focus had long been – although never exclusively so – on the history of European and North American societies, 'large-scale structures' easily translates as states and capitalism and 'fundamental processes of change' as democratization, commodification and bureaucratization as well as revolution as a crucial form of change. In other words, historical sociology focuses on democracy and capitalism as answers to the political and economic *problématiques* and is reflective of the possibilities of knowing these phenomena, thus having an awareness of the epistemic *problématique*. The authors mentioned above, taken together, certainly still provide the key reference to the study of these phenomena. In rough historical sequence, we can see them as, first, being interested in the emergence and breakthrough of novel forms of political and economic organization; second, in the cultural underpinnings of those forms and in their historical transformations; and third, in the fragility of those forms, or more appropriately, in the experience that their assertion cannot be taken for granted as the outcome of any linear process in history.

In this characterization, several aspects need to be underlined because of their relation to intellectual developments during the final quarter of the twentieth century. Methodological debate in the social sciences from the 1950s onwards had raised the stakes in terms of the evidence required for making assertions in historical sociology. A first response was a quantitative turn, a second and related one an emphasis on material-structural features apparently easier to discern than ideational-cultural features. By 1960, Weber appeared to have lost his debate with Marx against the 'economic explanation' of history (Weber 1930, p. 91), although the latter was now much more broadly conceived than by Marx himself. Furthermore, the raising of the methodological stakes also had an impact on the very notion of 'historical explanation' itself. Historical sociology had always tried to keep some distance from the older tradition of philosophy of history; this distance may indeed precisely constitute it as a genre of its own. Being interested in 'fundamental processes of change', however, it proved impossible to throw off the issue of a direction of history entirely. Finally, the historical sociology in question here certainly always was a political sociology, and this in a double sense. First, it was interested in political forms, such as democracy and totalitarianism, their conditions of emergence, their impact on the conduct of life and their fragility and viability. Second, there was a normative interest behind these questions, as an interest in avoiding some of those forms, or some of their consequences on the conduct of life, and in promoting others.

More recent intellectual developments radicalized the debate on all these issues. As much of an outsider to the field as he was, Jean-François Lyotard's (1979) observation on the end of the meta-narratives in connection with his idea about a change in the social bond brought together the otherwise quite varied dimensions of epistemological and methodological criticism of historical sociology. By implication, what he and others were saying suggested that all preceding analyses of long-term processes of change were deeply flawed. They had worked with some version of a material concept of the social bond, whereas the latter should be seen as constituted linguistically and – by possible, though not necessary, implication – as existing in much more varied and open forms than hitherto assumed. As a consequence, that which had been conceived as 'large-scale structures' did not extend and persist in stable form across space and time but always remained dependent upon interpretation by present actors. Any political project or analysis, finally, that derived its conclusions from a structural analysis of those large-scale forms had become impossible.

This brief and almost caricature-like synthesis provides a radical – but not entirely unsubstantiated – view of the possible consequences of the linguistic turn for historical sociology. In this form, it is used almost exclusively by critics of that turn and hardly ever by its proponents. To do justice to the linguistic challenge to conventional historical sociology, a closer look at what it can be seen to entail is required.

Language and history

Put bluntly, the linguistic turn for the social and historical sciences means nothing else than that sociologists and historians should take language – the fact that human beings relate to one another and constitute their world by language – seriously. This seems a strange thing to say since it certainly implies that they have not done so before. And arguably, such neglect of language prevailed during the 1950s and 1960s, being closely related to the philosophical assumption that there is always only ever one adequate relation between reality and its representation in language, i.e., that truth means correspondence between a linguistic statement and the piece of reality to which it refers. Within philosophical debate, from where it emerged (Rorty 1967), the expression 'linguistic turn' describes the shift of attention towards philosophy of language that occurred in the middle of the twentieth century, partly with a view to grounding a correspondence theory of truth in an exploration of its linguistic prerequisites, but increasingly recognizing that philosophy cannot mirror nature, to use Richard Rorty's (1980) celebrated phrase, that the world for human beings is always open to change by redescription (Rorty 1989).

Debate in the social and historical sciences has accompanied, though often only gradually and reluctantly, this shift in philosophical debate. The dispute on positivism in German sociology, for instance, marked the end of the old controversy in the philosophy of the social sciences, in which the claim to positive knowledge was countered by a critique of ideology that itself relied on an alternative social theory and philosophy, i.e., a theory of capitalism grounded in the tradition of German idealism (see chapter 5 above). On either side of the dispute, expression in language was a rather unproblematic issue once the adequate philosophical stand had been taken. And while the dispute went on, research in the social sciences more and more proceeded on the positivist model, even though mostly in a quite unreflected way. The linguistic turn, which was gradually under way at that time, then opened (or reopened) a number of quite different issues.

First, and this may be a case of reopening rather than opening, it brought back the question of ideology, albeit in a new form. As mentioned above, historical sociology had increasingly come to focus on 'material' structures in a broad sense and had forgotten about the Marx–Weber dispute over 'economic' and 'cultural' historical explanation. The emphasis on economic and social factors shaping historical developments was so pronounced that even the call for emphasizing politico-institutional structures had to be made by means of the battle-cry 'Bringing the state back in' (Evans et al. 1985). Cultural-ideational factors, if one wants to use such a term, remained a rather neglected 'third level' of analysis (Ernest Labrousse, with reference to the *Annales* distinction between economy, society and – the third level – civilization). Within a Marxist frame of analysis, recourse to Gramsci opened the way for emphasis on the indeterminacy of this level, i.e., its relative independence from socio-economic structures, unlike in earlier critique of ideology. In historiography, the *histoire des mentalités* claimed the existence and persistence of collective representations, to use Durkheim's term, similarly without any necessary link to other social structures. Once the possibility of both the independent existence of such a 'third level' and its impact on the other two levels had been more broadly accepted, the time-honoured field of intellectual history, or history of ideas, moved more into the centre of the discipline of history. The emergence of cultural history as a new sub-field and the rise in prominence of cultural sociology, or more broadly and ambitiously cultural studies (or *Kulturwissenschaften*, a comprehensive term already used by Max Weber), is also related to the revived interest in ideas. Disregarding for the moment the variety of approaches within these fields, their common denominator is the insistence that social life cannot be studied comprehensively if the ways in which human beings express their lives and condition through language and ideas is not taken into account beyond the apparently 'harder' socio-economic and politico-institutional structures of the social world.

Put like this, though, the concern for language and ideas would have but little impact on the ways in which historical sociology proceeds. A 'third level' could merely be added to the other two, without any other change in the epistemology or philosophy of the social sciences. The picture changes, however, once one asserts that all relations between human beings and the world are constituted by language. Such a claim, second, asserts some epistemic superiority of the so-called third level over the other two. Philosophically, it goes back to the romanticist reaction to the Enlightenment, or more appropriately, to the romanticist enlargement of the Enlightenment philosophical revolution. Once the Enlightenment claim that human beings gain knowledge about the world by distancing themselves from the world had been made, the question of what stands between, or mediates between, those distanced human beings and the world became inescapable. The answer to this question is: language. The relation of human beings to one another and to other aspects of the world is one of interpretation.

From romanticism onwards, this insight stands in the background of the hermeneutic approach to the social sciences, an approach that has been as persistent as it has been marginal in the history of the social sciences. At the time of the linguistic turn, it has been revived in the works of Hans-Georg Gadamer, Paul Ricoeur and, somewhat differently, Jacques Derrida. Gadamer, for instance, has insisted on 'the comprehensive pre-interpretedness of the world' when encountered by the human being (Gadamer 1970, p. 139). The experience of the world is thus linked to the interpretation of the world; 'language as experience of the world' (Gadamer 1979 [1960], p. 397). Or, to anticipate bluntly the argument below about the transfer of this approach into historical sociology: there is no 'class' without a concept of class.

Thirdly, the linguistic turn can also be seen as relating to the writing about history. In this sense, for instance, and quite in line with Gadamer's perspective, Karl Marx's writing about class can no longer be regarded as directly presenting social reality but rather as interpreting that reality. Any textual 'evidence' about historical occurrences is not evidence in a positivist sense but a contemporary interpretation of occurrences. The question about the relation of those interpretations to any 'reality' that remains unknown 'as such' is thus inevitably posed and much of the meta-historical debate after the linguistic turn has been devoted to identifying means to close that 'gap' between text and reality (for an overview, see Ankersmit 1994, drawing on Roland Barthes' notion of 'reality effect', among others). At the same time, any present writing about history necessarily stands in a similarly interpretive relation to that which it is about, to its object. Thus, the raising of this issue could not but lead into a discussion about relativism, dramatized not least by focusing on recent 'revisionisms' in historical interpretation, from the French Revolution to Nazism.

These three implications of the concern for language are each on their own of considerable significance for historical sociology. In their combination, they amount to a forceful questioning of most established practices within that area of research. In what follows, however, I will concentrate on the second aspect, the emphasis on the interpretedness of the world for human experience and will include only the most immediate linkages of this aspect to the other two in the account. In other words, I will not discuss the mere adding of a third, ideational level of reality to what otherwise remains a structural analysis of history. Read purely this way, the linguistic turn could relatively easily be handled within historical sociology but, wherever this issue has opened, it has indeed tended to broaden quickly to include at least the second, sometimes also the third, aspect.[3] And I will not discuss either the more strictly epistemological issues of the third aspect. That discussion has tended to move quickly into a rather barren, dogmatic controversy over the very representability, or intelligibility, of the past social world. My choice of focus is not meant to suggest that the excluded aspects are of little relevance. Rather, it is motivated by a double concern. On the one hand, and as I hope will become clear at the end of my reasoning, I take the linguistic turn to entail the need for a quite radical rethinking of the practices of historical sociology. A look at the first aspect alone would not lead very far in addressing that need. On the other hand, though, this need would not be well responded to if the historical-empirical look at expressions of the human condition were to be replaced, in the face of its undeniable difficulties, by philosophers' claims to reach deeper insight without any historical-empirical look at all.

Discourse formations, speech acts, conceptual history: the revolution in intellectual history

At this point, the focus of the remainder of my argument may be relatively well defined. It is the space where intellectual history, broadly understood, has begun to meet historical sociology in recent years. Such a rapprochement has taken place from three different angles in roughly parallel movements.

Across his early works, such as *Surveiller et punir* (1975) and *L'histoire de la folie* (1976) up to the archaeology of the human sciences as presented in *Les mots et les choses* (1974), Michel Foucault developed an approach to the analysis of discursive formations as well as to the linkage between discourses and practices that has emphasized the weight of such linguistic structures upon human beings, indeed structuring their relation to the world, in contrast to human beings actively structuring their relation to the world via linguistic practices. Even though Foucault and Quentin Skinner's works developed largely in benign mutual neglect, the latter (Skinner 1988) may be seen as taking the opposite stand in his emphasis on speech acts in the history of political thought, regarding authors of texts as intending a meaningful change in political thought via the performative capacity of language. Like Foucault, though, Skinner insists on the significance of the linguistic context in which the speech act primarily takes place, in contrast to an extra-linguistic, social and economic context that was given direct relevance in much of earlier intellectual history, but also in contrast to any view that sees the variety of linguistic expressions in political thought as merely variations around 'perennial problems' that never change. Reinhart Koselleck (1979), thirdly, proposed a historiography of concepts somehow in between Foucault's and Skinner's approaches. Without constructing all-powerful discursive formations, he insists on the embedding of individual concepts in broader linguistic structures and aims at identifying major periods of conceptual change.

All three scholars, thus, share the emphasis on language in historical analysis and they underline this feature of their work as distinct from the approaches to which they critically relate. For Foucault, these are the subject-centred human sciences as well as a structuralism that is incapable of theorizing its own linguistic practice. For Skinner, it is the conventional history of political ideas as well as its *marxisant* counterpart. And for Koselleck, it is a 'social history' that takes the existence of the social phenomena that concepts refer to immediately for granted. Despite all differences, there is therefore a clearly recognizable common methodological and conceptual concern.[4] The commonalities, however, reach even further, namely into the area of the substantive reinterpretation of European history over the past quarter of a millennium.

Foucault (1974) identifies the closing years of the eighteenth century as the period during which the classical episteme is superseded by the discursive formation formed by the disciplines of biology, economics and philology. For Skinner (1998), similarly, the late eighteenth and early nineteenth centuries emerge ever more clearly as a period of a major intellectual transformation in the course of his studies. Focusing explicitly on political thought, he describes this transformation as the decline of republican (or, more recently, neo-Roman) thinking, which experiences its last era of dominance during the American Revolution, and the rise of individualist liberalism, which becomes the pivotal political theory over the course of the nineteenth century. And for Koselleck, the period between 1770 and 1830 forms a transitional period (*Sattelzeit*) as well, a period after which the use of concepts is unproblematically recognizable to us. Defined more precisely as an opening of the horizon of time so that expectations can far exceed experiences, this conceptual revolution thus spells the transition to the contemporary period, the period in which we still live, and which already on those grounds can be referred to as modernity.

All three authors thus identify a similar historical period as a period of discursive transformation during which the discourses that dominate current intellectual and political life emerge.[5] The relation of the present to the era before that transformation is conceptualized differently, though. Foucault rather neutrally observes grand tectonic shifts beyond any human capacity or will. Skinner's account underlies a vague notion of decline, of a loss of something that was important and should be regained, at least as an intellectual resource, if not a political practice. Koselleck, although he writes in the distanced voice of the professional historian, is the only one among the three who may be seen to embrace the modernity the linguistic advent of which he describes.

In all three cases, though, the nature of that modernity that follows up on the discursive transformation is underspecified and/or widely open to dispute. Can one really argue, as Foucault implicitly does, that classical sociology, for instance, placed the human subject indubitably at its centre? Does the accusation of having provided an oversocialized conception of the human being not lead towards emphasizing a quite different feature of the sociological tradition (Wrong 1961)? Is it really the case, as Skinner maintains, that individualist liberalism has governed the self-understanding of political modernity increasingly since the so-called democratic revolutions? What is the relation of republicanism and individualism to nationalism and socialism/communism in the European nineteenth and twentieth centuries (questions that were addressed in the preceding chapter)? And, to continue on that train of thought, has it not been the ambition of social and political philosophy during that period, unlike Koselleck's reasoning implies, to close, or at least stabilize, the horizon of time again, to channel expectations into well-governable directions?

At this point of the argument, one could move to a detailed consideration of the approaches and findings with a view to identifying the reasons for the emergence of such problematic assertions. Rather than doing so, however, I will claim that the basic problem of an intellectual history, broadly understood, that takes language seriously has hitherto been the unwillingness of its promoters to relate it back to a comprehensive study of societal transformations. Intellectual history has effectively challenged a language-unconscious historical sociology but it has not yet demonstrated what a language-conscious historical sociology could or should look like. Such demonstration cannot be substituted for by a mere insistence on taking linguistic change into account (that would be a broadening in the sense of the first aspect mentioned above). Rather, it is likely to entail a recasting of historical sociology's basic *problématiques*.

By pointing, in what follows, to some examples of studies that have gone in such a direction (even though their reach is quite limited in terms of the individual studies), I try to sketch what such a demonstration is likely to entail. This discussion cannot be exhaustive, not only for reasons of space, but also because a comprehensive rethinking of historical sociology's basic *problématiques* has not yet fully taken place. Instead, I will proceed by making use of exemplary works and trying to show what their findings contribute to such a rethinking. Doing so, I will be working chronologically backwards, from the middle of the twentieth century to the end of the eighteenth.

Modernity and its *problématiques*: four episodes in rethinking the history of European societies

The adoption of Keynesian macro-economic policies in a number of Western societies between the 1930s and the 1960s has been explored in a comparative research project on 'the power of economic ideas', directed by Peter Hall (1989). The context in which this question could be posed had, of course, drastically changed between the early 1970s and the mid-1980s, the period of the research. By 1970, it was widely held that Keynesianism provided for the problem of the stabilization of production and exchange a solution that was functionally superior to any others that had been proposed or tried before. It was widely seen as effectively smoothing the development of the capitalist economy and at the same time providing leeway for redistribution and, thus, greater equality without, though, renouncing the benefits of capitalism, i.e., an enhancement of 'the wealth of nations', to use a time-honoured formula. The question about the reception of Keynesianism was accordingly only one about the social conditions of the acceptance of a superior idea. After the mid-1970s, in contrast, it was increasingly observed that the Keynesian treatment, if applied over long periods, produced considerable side effects. Some analysts argued that these side effects were worse than the problems caused by the disease; and the voices of those analysts were increasingly widely heard. This change, about which nothing else will be said here, had at least the advantage of opening a broader, so to say, post-Kuhnian, perspective on the social conditions of intellectual change. Peter Hall's research project was set in this intellectual context, and I will just discuss two contributions from it that pose the question of the *relation between an intellectual transformation and a politico-institutional transformation* in quite different terms.

Margaret Weir's (1989) comparison of the American and the British debates over Keynesianism is mainly interested in identifying how politico-institutional structures determine the fate of political ideas. Thus, she stays close to the structural sociology developed by Theda Skocpol, only adding the reception of ideas as an area of interest to it.[6] There is no doubt that interesting findings emerge from her analysis: the closed and hierarchical character of a centralized government structure, as in the UK, entails a longer resistance to novel ideas but

also leads to their rapid and consistent adoption once the old orthodoxy is overcome. In contrast, the comparatively open and multilay-
ered US economic policy-making apparatus provides easy access for
new ideas; it in turn also tends to slow down their adoption and to
dilute their basic messages.

However, the limits of this approach reside already in its basic
design which assumes that there just are politico-institutional structures to which ideas are brought from the outside, and the objective of
the analysis is then to find out what happens in this encounter.[7] In
contrast, Pierre Rosanvallon's (1989) analysis of Keynesianism in
France opens up broader questions. Rosanvallon's first problem in this
collaborative project was that there was hardly any reception of
Keynesianism in France until after the end of the Second World War.[8]
It is, thus, not least the absence of a phenomenon that imposes the
broadening of the research question – this is, incidentally, one of the
heuristic benefits from comparative research. In this case, Rosanvallon
opted for a broader contextualization with a view to identifying the
register of available languages for economic policy in France during
the 1930s. Importantly, he identified a tradition of government measures to alleviate unemployment that went back to at least 1848, and
that at that point became closely related to the self-understanding of
the republican political order in general. In such a politico-historical
context, there was then no apparent need for Keynesian ideas during
the 1930s; solutions to the problem had already been found much
earlier, and the only dispute was over if and how to apply them. Thus,
it becomes possible to pose the question about the specific nature of
the Keynesian innovation anew.

Rather than providing the ideal solution for stabilizing an inherently unstable market economy, Keynes's intellectual step meant a
minor transformation of the economic orthodoxy of the time, compared to the solutions offered by fascism, socialism or, as the French
and Belgians should say, *planisme* that were well under debate at the
time. All these proposals diagnosed a profound crisis of liberalism, a
view that was indeed widely shared at least since the First World War.
The specificity of Keynes's view was the limited nature of the crisis,
being namely confined to questions of economic adjustment. All
other proposals linked the problems of economic liberalism to those
of political liberalism and saw a more profound transformation of
society as necessary. Rosanvallon's analysis restores this broader
context of linguistic-discursive formations which, at that point, had
indeed been shaped over a considerable period of time.

Let me thus move a step backwards in time and look at the debates
about what is now known as early social policies or as the origins of

the welfare state. For a long time, to say this all too briefly, research on the development of the welfare state was shaped by one of two perspectives. Either social policies were seen as a functional response to problems generated by the workings of a market economy. The similarity of the problems as well as the functionality of the solutions were then derived from the apparent fact that social policies were introduced in all capitalist-industrial societies with even only relatively minor differences in timing (overlooking the minor exception of the USA). However, it is precisely the considerable differences between policies adopted that was neglected in this view, indeed was even systematically left out of focus owing to the guiding assumption of functionality. In contrast and partly in response to such functionalism, culturalist approaches emphasized the difference across states and societies. Those approaches, however, were often at a loss to explain those national political cosmologies that they needed to evoke as determining factors for policy developments.

Post-linguistic-turn historical sociology tries to deal with these issues by again linking the major political transformation that the introduction of early social policies obviously entailed to an intellectual transformation, in this case to a rethinking of the social bond, or of 'society'.[9] The background here is the observation of new forms of poverty and other social evils, such as crime, a declining medical state of parts of the population and prostitution. From the middle of the nineteenth century onwards, roughly speaking, the conviction gained ground that these phenomena were related to the processes of industrialization and urbanization, and thus that they would not disappear with the consolidation of the new industrial order but would rather get entrenched in it. Once they could no longer be seen as transitory, as side effects of the move to a new and better society, these phenomena could be addressed as a problem, in many societies indeed called 'the social question'. The formulation of this question and the attempt to find an answer to it spelt an intellectual transformation in social and political thought, most briefly to be characterized as a redefinition of responsibility in the framework of a new moral and political philosophy.

Such redefinition included two major steps. The liberal political philosophy of the nineteenth century, in as far as it prevailed,[10] had increasingly put the individual at centre-stage of political life. Individuals were responsible for their actions – in the case of work accidents, for instance, the basic assumption would be that they were caused by workers who would then also be responsible for the consequences. The decisive step towards the establishment of compulsory work accident insurance was taken when it could be argued that industrialization had transformed the standard work situation into a constitutively collective one in which it was industrial life itself, not the action of any individual, that was responsible for new risks (see, in particular, Rabinbach 1996). This was the first step, a move from the individual to the collectivity. Once this step was taken, however, for any practical or policy consequences, that collectivity needed to be defined in such a way as to be able to accept the responsibility. The second step, by and large, was the identification of the nation as the responsible collectivity (alternatives that were discussed, varying across policies, were the residence community, the employer and the company, the union or workers' corporation; see, in particular, Zimmermann 2001b). On this basis, national social policy arrangements could be introduced.

As proposed here, this intellectual transformation can be discussed in terms of moral and political philosophy. In actual practice, however, it was empirical social research, such as on accident statistics and social theory, such as Durkheim's *Division du travail social* with the idea of organic solidarity, that were in the immediate background of this change. Thus, a new form of social knowledge, in the German context sometimes indeed called an empirical philosophy of right, permitted the reconceptualization of the social bond. As a consequence of that reconceptualization, policy change became possible.

At the time of the introduction of so-called early social policies, an active and more or less self-conscious working class existed in all somewhat industrialized European societies. The political connection between the demands of this class and those social policies has been an important issue for the historical sociology of the welfare state. Not pursuing this particular question further here, I will again move a step historically backwards and look at the formation of the working class. The traditional perspective, in this case largely shared by both Marxists and modernization theorists, held that it is the commonality of their situation, *la condition ouvrière*, that created the class consciousness of the working class which, in turn, endowed this particular social group with both social visibility and potential agentiality (Katznelson 1986). If one takes a closer look at the 1830s and 1840s, when the term 'working class' became rapidly adopted in roughly its later sense, such a reasoning is, however, not very plausible in light of the relatively small number of people concerned and the wide heterogeneity of their actual social and working situations.

For France, it has been shown in some detail that a reinterpretation of a key political philosophy, namely the discourse of the French

Revolution, with a view to creating a collective actor had an important role in bringing the working class into being (Sewell 1980). To again sketch the process all too briefly: the revolutionary discourse was available as a resource for workers to place themselves and their demands in the political context of the time. It enabled them to point to the one-sidedness of the prevailing interpretation, namely with an emphasis on individual liberty at the expense of equality and fraternity. Empirically, then, they could show that such application of the discourse led to greater inequality, and that people in certain situations were particularly likely to suffer from that bias. As a consequence, they reinterpreted fraternity in terms of the right to form associations to defend themselves against the bias – contra the French republican ideology that did not want any mediators between the individual and the polity. Those who were to associate were from then on 'the workers', whose foremost commonality was to suffer from the prevailing reading of the revolutionary discourse, and fraternity became solidarity.[11]

After having said all this, the final step of this historical review certainly needs to be the French Revolution itself.[12] Similar to the historical moments of rupture and innovation already discussed, the French Revolution had hitherto been analysed in socio-economic or in politico-institutional terms. In the former view, it is seen as the seizure of power of the bourgeoisie as the rising class under increasingly capitalist conditions. In the latter, the emphasis is on the centralization and rigidity of a central state that was unable to understand, much less adapt to, societal changes. More recently, however, historical sociologists and intellectual historians – the boundaries are here entirely blurred – such as William Sewell and Keith Michael Baker have critically followed up on François Furet's (1983) attempt at 'thinking the French Revolution' that had put political ideas into the centre of attention. In his controversy with Theda Skocpol, Sewell (1994) insisted that conceptual revolutions went on in French political language during the closing decades of the eighteenth century without which numerous events in the course of the Revolution could not be understood. He summarized these changes as a transformation of metaphysical presuppositions of social and political life. While the Revolution was certainly also a peasant revolt, as Skocpol emphasized, it was at the same time a major 'conceptual transformation' (Sewell 1994, p. 181). Keith Michael Baker (1990) similarly concluded methodologically for his own work that the ideas of the Revolution cannot be regarded as a 'third level' of social life, next to socio-economic and politico-institutional factors, but that they were indeed constitutive for the social order.

Language and interpretation between historical sociology and political philosophy

What conclusions can we draw from the brief review of these studies for a historical sociology that is conscious of the use of language in history? One set of conclusions responds to the theoretical *problématique* inherent in the challenge of the linguistic turn: what does it mean to bring concern for language into historical analysis in general? But another set of conclusions should also address the substantive outcome: how will a historical sociology of modernity, of capitalism and democracy, look if it takes language seriously?

As to the first set of issues, we may note, responding to Skocpol, that, while there may be long-term 'fundamental processes of change', those are not adequately analysed as the determinate result of any constellations (or articulations) of 'large-scale structures'. This is so for two main reasons. First, rather than large-scale structures extending over grand spaces and long stretches of time (and this is what 'large scale' is supposed to mean in structural historical sociology), it is precisely the work of concepts, i.e., of phenomena of language, that stabilizes social phenomena across space and across time. This is what I take to be one of the most important insights of Koselleck's work, and in a modified way it can be found in Foucault as well.[13] Concepts homogenize situations – and social transformations are then reinterpretations of situations by means of conceptual change. Such reinterpretation, though, secondly, is the 'conceptual work' of actors that leads from one historical situation to the one that succeeds it.[14] This, contra Foucault, and at least pointing to a relative neglect in Koselleck's approach, is what we can take from Skinner's perspective.

The second set of issues needs to identify the substantive specificities of the last quarter of a millennium of the history of social configurations. Most broadly, we can possibly say that in a context of 'modernity', that is, a context in which autonomy or self-determination is a political value, institutions are in need of justification, of a justificatory discourse that underpins their rules and their ways of distributing resources. Political action, at least when it has to be public action, thus supports itself by recourse to such discourses of justification. In the examples on which I drew we have seen that, on the one hand, the broad post-Enlightenment discourse around the French Revolution provided one major such resource. On the other hand, though, as shown earlier in this volume, that discourse tended to be reduced to a mere emphasis on individual liberty as one, but only one, expression of the idea of autonomy. Later discursive struggles could then be read as situation-specific contestations of the hegemony of such discourse of individual liberty.

In those struggles, indeed in all examples selected, discursive action turned out to be transforming a political constellation. It did so by providing new justifications in – experienced, 'empirical' – contexts of situations that were analysed as problematic. Or in other words, a conceptual-linguistic transformation is created and proposed with a view to handling a new and problematic situation.

In the social and human sciences today – that means, over the past twenty years or so – a historical sociology that does not succeed in escaping from the determinist heritage of mainstream sociology (see the preceding chapter for the broader argument) exists alongside a political philosophy that does not succeed in moving away from its tradition of abstract theorizing, of theorizing at a distance from any specific situation. The linguistic turn on its own – i.e., within the tradition of philosophy, be it analytical, hermeneutic or post-structuralist – has never come close to addressing the questions raised in the older tradition of a historical sociology that wanted itself to be political theorizing at the same time. However, there is a slim chance of a post-linguistic-turn historical sociology that could alter this intellectual constellation. Such historical sociology would analyse the use of language as an interpretative intervention in the restructuring of problematic situations. As such, it would acquire the potential to link historical sociology again to political philosophy and to develop a novel sociology of modernity that is urgently needed – for general intellectual reasons, but also because we may well find ourselves currently in a problematic situation of a historical transformation that we have not yet succeeded in interpreting appropriately.

All of the above can be summarized as an attempt at providing elements of such a novel sociology of modernity. Recent work on the conceptualization of modernity has already demonstrated that modernity is not fruitfully understood as either the superior – more rational – solution to the problem of organizing social life or as an ideology in need of critique or deconstruction. Rather, it should be conceptualized as an interpretative relation to the world that lays bare, or maybe better brings about, a range of *problématiques* to which a variety of responses are possible. These responses are then always determined in a situation, defined by its space and its time, that is interpreted as problematic and in which various cultural resources are available for the solution of that which is problematic. Such a view of modernity, even though certainly not uncontested, is philosophically more or less established. However, it still needed to face its 'reality test', to use an expression employed by Luc Boltanski and Laurent Thévenot in their political and moral sociology. It needed to be shown that it could be translated into a historical-comparative sociology and anthropology, with politico-philosophical sensitivity, of Western and non-Western societies. The preceding reflections are meant to be a theoretical and historical contribution towards such contextual analysis of modernity as experience and interpretation.

Notes

Chapter 1   Ways of Understanding Modernity

1   My critiques of Beck and Giddens can be found in Wagner (1988) and Wagner (1996) respectively; see also the brief discussion in Karagiannis and Wagner (2007). I return to the analysis by Boltanski and Chiapello at various points below.

2   The works of Dipesh Chakrabarty (in particular, 2000) in post-colonial studies and William H. Sewell Jr (see now 2005) are the best antidote to these tendencies. They have been influential in the elaboration of my approach, as I will have occasion to point out again in Part IV and for Sewell in particular in chapter 13.

3   The full phrase, thus, reads: 'In Western civilization, and in Western civilization only, cultural phenomena have appeared which, as we like to think, lie in a line of development having *universal* significance and value.'

4   Mastery is a correlate because it is already entailed in the concept of autonomy. Giving *laws* means aiming at establishing control, mastery.

5   It was always a troubled relation: the long-lasting but erroneous idea that one could first solve the question of knowledge to then derive from it the solution for living together has been the major target of post-totalitarian political philosophy from Karl Popper to Hannah Arendt to Claude Lefort and Pierre Manent (see Wagner 2001a, chapter 2).

6   Probably owing to the combined effect of the impact of Marxian thought, on the one hand, and of the adversity to any 'critique of ideology' in the alternative positivism (in a broad sense) of mainstream social science, on the other, the change in the relation between the third *problématique* and the former two has been given little attention in social theory. It is touched upon, though, in critiques of determinist social theory as challenging any derivation of the solution to the 'economic *problématique*' from the solution to the epistemological one. And it is also addressed

in the few contributions that criticize the 'rise of the social' in terms of a subordination of the political *problématique* to the economic one (such as in Arendt 1958, Donzelot 1984; see also Manent 1994).

Part I   Overture: Multiple Interpretations of Political Modernity

1   Michael Walzer (1983) has used the term (conceptual) 'tyranny' in a similar way; see Karagiannis (2004) for a discussion and an application.

Chapter 2   Modernity and the Question of Freedom

1   Unless otherwise noted, further references to Berlin are to this text, and the same practice will be adopted with regard to John Stuart Mill's *On Liberty* later.
2   The passage continues with further conceptual associations to then add another note of distinction from freedom: '... fraternity, mutual understanding, need for association on equal terms, all of which are sometimes – but misleadingly – called social freedom'. He contradicts himself, though, later (p. 160 – see p. 32 below).
3   Some later critics of Berlin, such as Quentin Skinner and Philip Pettit, have tried to avoid references to the social and the economic by suggesting that different concepts of liberty exist, notably a third one beyond Berlin's distinction of two opposed concepts of liberty. Without necessarily disagreeing with those critics, this chapter suggests that a different conceptual strategy may prove more fruitful: rather than redefining liberty, conceptual efforts should concentrate on placing liberty within a comprehensive political philosophy that is articulate about the relations between the political and the social instead of separating the former from the latter. (Let me note in passing that this is said in explicit disagreement with John Rawls about the role of 'comprehensive political philosophies'. One may be somewhat able to do without those when aiming to justify a single concept, such as justice. However, the self-understanding of a polity, as laid out in a constitution, for instance, will always need to address more 'comprehensive' issues in collective terms.) For further reflections on the relation between the social and the political, see Karagiannis and Wagner (2005) as well as chapter 13 below.
4   See Freeden (1996) for a reconstruction of political ideologies around key concepts.
5   An earlier version of this chapter was published under the title 'Freedom and Solidarity: Retrieving the European Political Tradition of Non-individualist Liberalism', in Nathalie Karagiannis (ed.), *European Solidarity* (Liverpool: Liverpool University Press, 2007c).
6   The failure to state this principle becomes evident not least in Mill's use of examples, which often appear much less unequivocal, and much more open to historical change, than he thought. Among recent authors,

Berlin – in the text we use (pp. 128–30) – and more recently Gray (1989) have extensively discussed Mill's failure to accomplish his objectives. Gray's reasoning extends to a general indictment of the theoretical programme of individualist liberalism.

7   Reminiscent of Mill is also the neglect of the question how 'I', the individual thinking subject, could 'establish a society'. Despite his later critique of reason, this formulation betrays an overly rationalist approach to political theory in this essay.

8   The term 'solidarity' had become a key concept of political debate already during the first half of the nineteenth century (see, for instance, Sewell 1980), but by that time liberals could still pretend that the benefits of a free society would sooner or later accrue to all members of that society.

9   Discussing Mill's position, Berlin underlines that the individualist-liberal concept of freedom is compatible with autocracy and enlightened despotism, provided that the despot 'leaves his subjects a wide area of liberty' (p. 129). He would not have gone as far as redefining the concept of democracy with a view to justifying such kind of autocracy, as do current advocates of 'regulatory government' (Majone 1996) or government legitimated by efficiency (Scharpf 1999).

10 It is maybe not too surprising that Berlin saw communism as committed to positive freedom and to democracy; after all, many of the polities governed by communist parties were called 'democratic republics'. In contrast, one wonders whether one should find it shocking or telling that Berlin renounces the association of Western polities with the commitment to democracy at all. Would he possibly have agreed with Cornelius Castoriadis (for instance, 1997a, p. 154) in referring to those polities as 'liberal oligarchies' – and, in contrast to Castoriadis, be normatively satisfied with that diagnosis?

11 Even though his case may not be so far from the one made here, Habermas's argument (1992, 1999) about the 'co-originality' of democracy and the state of law is, at the very least, terminologically misleading since as a historical argument it clearly does not hold. See chapter 3 below for more extended discussion.

12 Long common a priori assumptions about rationality that entailed some idea about general, i.e., collective, validity and which were, thus, of concern to Berlin may have given way to the combination of individuality and rationality in economic and rational choice theory – these latter would need to be criticized by different means than those employed by Berlin (see Wagner 2001b, chapter 6, for a critique of rational choice theory).

13 For his concluding statement on the liberals' view of government and participation, see p. 165.

14 See his response to critics in the introduction to the collection of essays titled *Four Essays on Liberty* (Berlin 1971 [1958], part II).

15 Even Constant's conclusions, though, restore some lasting significance to the 'ancient' concept of liberty.

16   The suggestion that a polity should be composed of individuals with rather similar preferences only appears to offer a way out. Even if one assumed in a contractarian way that a polity is an association for mutual benefit, political communities differ from all kinds of 'clubs' in automatically accepting the children of their members as new members. This means that they have no control over the preferences of their members. My thanks to Bob Goodin for provoking this reflection.

17   Throughout this volume, unless otherwise noted, translations from non-English sources are my own.

18   For a related argument about the necessary link between democracy, trust and solidarity, unfortunately confined to the political form of the nation-state, see Offe (1998).

19   In the introduction to the collection of the four essays on liberty, Berlin acknowledges the need to analyse the 'conditions for liberty', but insists that it would be erroneous to 'identify[ing] freedom with its conditions' (p. lviii). This text also acknowledges 'the ideal of social solidarity', but again as a value distinct from freedom.

20   The insert 'in theory' is meant to suggest that 'in practice' things may be different. On the one hand, the dogmatic insistence on individual liberty as the basic principle in the West encourages the emergence of radical alternatives such as collectivist fundamentalisms of various kinds that indeed have illiberal leanings. On the other hand, the belief that Western political modernity already safely incarnates the principle of liberty opens the door to violations of liberties such as in the current 'war on terrorism' in the United States and the United Kingdom.

21   'Proper status' would be signalled not least by a telling denomination, not one confined to a negative term, such as 'non-individualism'. As a good term is not at hand, it may be worth underlining that terms such as 'social liberalism' or 'national liberalism' refer to known historical traditions that may at times overlap with the one in mind here, but not in terms of key characteristics. 'Republicanism' may be a better candidate, not least because of the recent revival in interest in it, both in intellectual history and in political philosophy. Before this term can be adopted, though, the idea, made prominent by Quentin Skinner, that republicanism subsided after the democratic revolutions and gave way to (individualist) liberalism, needs to be rethought and revised since the concern addressed by non-individualist liberalism is a key concern precisely during this period of non-existence of republicanism (for sceptical reflections on the coherence of the revived republican political theory, see Goodin 2003).

Chapter 3   The Political Forms of Modernity

1   This chapter draws on reflections that first appeared under the title 'The Political Form of Europe – Europe as a Political Form' in *Thesis Eleven* 80 (February 2005): 47–73.

2   And the recent broadening of the debate about modernity beyond its European origins and North American elaborations has allowed the insight that such recognition was not unique to Europe. See, e.g., Shin (2002).

3   Thinkers as different as Hannah Arendt (e.g., 1958) and Cornelius Castoriadis (e.g., 1986, 1990a), but also historians of ancient Greece, are sometimes prone to put their observations in similar terms (see, e.g., Meier 1990). See now Arnason, Raaflaub and Wagner, in preparation.

4   This model was one focus of Berlin's criticism of 'reason' in politics, as discussed in the preceding chapter.

5   One may add that this connection provides a context for the story of the decline of empires, which is an important part of European political modernity. The quest for individual liberty was in principle reconcilable with the political form of empire, but the idea of collective self-determination was not, at least not for actors in the nineteenth and early twentieth centuries. I will come back to this question below.

6   On the concept of political form see Manent (2001), chapter 4 and, with regard to Europe, chapter 6.

7   At the same time, politico-legal resistance to a fully liberal conception of the free movement of people across the borders of the existing polities (EU and US as the major examples) remains strong. The main topics of current debate about immigration are security concerns and (critique of) xenophobia and racism, whereas it would be important to emphasize more strongly the possibilities and limits of political participation and social inclusion under conditions of open boundaries.

8   The term 'compromise' is borrowed, even though only in a loose sense, from the work by Luc Boltanski and Laurent Thévenot (1991) on the plurality of mutually incompatible modes of justification to resolve disputes, there referring to the co-existence of such modes (see chapter 12 below).

9   For a fuller appreciation of the relevance of the Greek experience for contemporary political modernity, see Arnason et al., in preparation.

10   On the idea of 'universal empire' in the Roman Republic, see Cacciari (2002, pp. 25–7). Rémi Brague (1999) has even argued that this is the specificity of Europe: its being secondary culturally towards ancient Greece and religiously towards Judaism, its having an excentric identity. Despite all subtlety of his reasoning, Brague's 'excentric' identification makes Europe 'Western Christian' in religious terms and 'Roman' in political terms. See chapter 10 below for a fuller discussion.

11   As observed by authors as different as Gerhard Oestreich and Michel Foucault, indeed as a double process of disciplinization and individualization. Oestreich, for instance, underlines the spreading of 'contractual thinking' and the emergence of 'genuine national rights' distinct from the feudal 'regionally secured liberty' (Oestreich 1982, pp. 266, 264, 268). For a view that insists on removing all ambivalence, see Siedentop (2001, p. 19): 'The process of state formation was, especially on the continent, essentially a despotic one.'

12   As is the question of the relation between the establishment of the 'modern state' in Europe and European expansion. Despite all apparent clarity of division between 'domestic matters' and 'foreign policy matters' under this regime, such emerging globalization should to the present day blur those boundaries immediately again. The importance of this issue for political philosophy – questions of membership and responsibility, for instance – seems but little recognized; but see now Chakrabarty (2000) for a philosophico-historical account of colonial interaction, and Karagiannis (2004) for a politico-philosophical analysis of Europe's relation to her former colonies. I return to these issues in Part IV, pp. 207–8 and 213–14.

13   The term 'fraternity' furthermore suggested that it is free and equal brothers that inhabit the republic, and thus that the sisters of these men were neither free nor equal to their brothers. It is more than a sleight of hand if the term 'fraternity' is replaced by 'solidarity' towards the end of the nineteenth century, thus eliminating the gender asymmetry conceptually but most often not in practice.

14   The coincidence – in rough historical terms – of the 'democratic revolution' and the 'market revolution' and its impact on the self-understanding of European modernity will be discussed in chapter 6 below.

15   Among the exceptions, as briefly mentioned above, were authors such as Hannah Arendt, Cornelius Castoriadis and Claude Lefort who all, though, remained marginal as political philosophers during that period.

Chapter 4   Modernity as a Project of Emancipation and the Possibility of Politics

1   An earlier version of this text was published in *Thesis Eleven* 68 (May 2002), an issue devoted to '1968' and co-edited by Paul Ginsborg, Luisa Passerini, Bo Stråth and myself.

2   Offe (2002) centrally focused on this observation. For an interpretation that also emphasizes the 'intermediary' character of the events of '1968', placed between two socio-political expressions of modernity and marking that particular ambiguity, see Capdevielle and Mouriaux (1988).

3   The only sustained continuation of political practices in 'the spirit of 1968', as defined here, are the weak strands of left republicanism that can be found in many European societies, most clearly possibly in parts of the German Greens and their intellectual milieu.

Part II   Overture: Capitalism and Modernity as Social Formations and as Imaginary Significations

1   In terms of the historical approach, Wood's name stands here for a significant, even though marginalized, tradition whose most important

representative is probably Karl Polanyi. Castoriadis's interpretative reasoning is more radically innovative, in particular in its formulation as a
comprehensive perspective (for a concise discussion see Arnason 1989)
but Max Weber's work may qualify as the most important source of
inspiration.

Chapter 5   The Critique of Capitalism and its Impasse

1   This chapter goes back to work first presented at the Adorno conference
held by the Institute for Social Research and University of Frankfurt in
September 2003 and in the working group 'The Economy as a Polity' at
the Robert Schuman Centre of the European University Institute in
2004. Earlier versions have been published in German in *Dialektik der
Freiheit*, edited by Axel Honneth (Frankfurt: Suhrkamp, 2005) and in
English in *The Economy as a Polity*, edited by Christian Joerges, Bo
Stråth and myself (London: UCL Press, 2005).

2   Page numbers in what follows refer to Adorno (1974), unless otherwise
noted.

3   When pointing out the 'reduction to the human being become animal',
Adorno anticipates the idea of the reduction of human beings to their
'nuda vita', as recently discussed by Giorgio Agamben (1995). When he
qualifies: 'The historical crisis of the individual has for the time being
its limits in the biological singular being, its stage' (p. 300), the term 'for
the time being' gains an uncanny connotation in our emerging age of
human reproduction through genetic technology. See Boltanski (2002)
for a discussion of the shift of the idea of total revolution towards bio-
technological transformation of the human being.

4   There are strong reasons not only to start this history earlier, with Descartes, for instance, but also to provide a linkage to the history of the
individual in *political* philosophy, such as in Hobbes and Locke. Furthermore, Adorno also betrays here the totalizing tendency in his own
thought when he namely voices the 'suspicion that it was never much
different' (p. 310), in contrast to his attempt at historicizing.

5   'The hybris of idealism, that is, putting the human being as its creator
into the centre of Creation, has barricaded itself in the "interior without
furniture" like a tyrant whose last days have come' (p. 316; 'Intérieur
sans meubles' is the first sentence of the stage description in the original
French version of *Endgame*).

6   His few remarks about the knowledge forms of late capitalist society,
behaviourism, psychology and rational choice theory (pp. 293 and 307),
themes that are more developed in other writings, are meant to support
this observation of a loss of language and truth. In a more unusual
remark, Adorno notes that functionalist sociology sees 'the *zoon politikon* as role' (p. 312) – a remark that opens the way for linking social
theory to political philosophy, but is never followed up.

7   Mannheim (1980) – this is the revised English version that appeared
while Mannheim was in British exile.

8   Of current significance is certainly the following warning: 'One should be aware, though, not to demand of governments that they orient themselves exclusively, at all times and with regard to decisions about all issues at the vote of public opinion as it is presented in the poll results' (Adorno 1986d, p. 300).

9   *Dialektik der Aufklärung*, it may be recalled, is dated 'Los Angeles 1944'. In the absence of any specification in the text itself, this combination of date and time may be taken to suggest that emerging consumerist US and Nazi Germany are both included in the scope of the analysis. This can be seen as an intellectual misconception of highest proportions, denying a variety that was life-saving for these authors themselves, but it can also be seen as precisely reflecting the aporia of critical social theory here discussed.

10 Much of the tradition of critical theory works with a double-pronged approach, linking a philosophical argument to a socio-historical one, as, for instance, Axel Honneth (2005) demonstrates clearly with regard to the concept 'reification'. As the following discussion will show, I concur with Honneth that the philosophical part of such thinking is misconceived and in need of revision. However, this 'philosophy', I would argue, was mostly driven by a socio-historical diagnosis (see chapter 8 for my analysis of the epistemic *problématique*). Thus, an effective critique and renewal of critical theory will need to focus on the socio-historical diagnosis and recast its analysis, certainly in a philosophically more viable way, but in terms of a historical sociology that is able to say something about tendencies of societal developments in general, and about obstacles to reach normatively more desirable conditions of modernity in particular (I return to these issues in the subsequent chapter as well as in chapters 11, 12 and 13, from different angles).

11 For the sake of brevity, the discussion of epistemic modernity will be briefly suspended here, to be taken up again below in this chapter and in more detail in Part III.

12 Here, deliberation may be usefully understood as the communication about handling things in common and distinguished from regulation as the (self-) acting upon society by means of rules and policies – thus avoiding the barren opposition between a substanceless conception of the political, on the one hand, and an overly economically determined one, on the other. (As regards regulation, it is important to add that it may also occur through non-intentionally created social phenomena, such as habits, customs, trust.)

Chapter 6   Towards a Historical-Comparative Sociology of Capitalism

1   In an earlier form, some of the following reflections have appeared under the title 'Modernity, Capitalism, Critique' in *Thesis Eleven* 66 (August 2001): 1–31.

2 This is a question that would need a separate analysis in terms of economic history, not to be proposed here; see recently Wood (1991).

3 Contemporary equivalents in this respect, in our era of free trade, can be found in the principle of negative integration adopted by the European Union and in the debates within the World Trade Organisation.

4 In a certain sense, of course, European societies during the later nineteenth and the twentieth century were capitalist. 'Rise of capitalism' is here rather meant, in the terms proposed above, as an imposition of the orientation towards the 'expansion of rational mastery' without, or with only few, countervailing imaginary significations, or, in a different conceptual language, countervailing registers of justification.

5 This is not to say that individualist liberalism became the one dominant American political tradition; the debate about this question fills entire libraries. Rather, it is to suggest that it is the pivotal political theory, the thinking that is an inevitable reference point for all political debate. As Michael Walzer once noted, recent communitarianism is in this sense nothing but the contemporary expression of the critique that has always accompanied individualist liberalism in the USA, a critique that operates on the ground defined by that which it criticizes.

6 There seems to be little doubt nowadays that the alternative thesis, proposed by C. B. MacPherson (1964), that European precursors of liberalism – such as most notably John Locke – already expressed the interests of the rising industrial bourgeoisie, cannot be sustained.

7 In other words, it sees capitalism as being located on one side of modernity only, the one of mastery. An internalist critique, so to say, of the actually existing capitalism of the mid-twentieth century that emphasizes precisely this one-sidedness was provided by J. A. Schumpeter – to whose concept of 'creative destruction' unsurprisingly many observers of contemporary 'flexible' capitalism like to return (on recent debates about 'flexibility', see chapter 7 below).

8 Conventional versions of critical theorizing explain this situation as the effect of capitalism which, in its consumerist version, undermines the political, either in terms of indeed deliberately destroying alternative modernities or in terms of unintended but welcomed side effects of the workings of the profit mechanism. (This line of reasoning continues, under new conditions, the idea, of a former period, that the development of the welfare state was intended to provide mass loyalty to capitalism.) Such a view, however, appears to underestimate both the impact and the ambivalence of the experience of modernity in contemporary societies. It basically merely suggests that the workings of some force external to a normatively defined project of modernity derailed that very project, or led to its only very incomplete realization.

Chapter 7   The Exit from Organized Economic Modernity

1 A consultation of the catalogue of the British Library of Political and Economic Science (BLPES), which should give a comprehensive

overview over at least the English-language literature in the sciences of contemporary society, will easily confirm this view. Of the almost two hundred volumes that carry the term 'flexibility' in the title, a strong majority was published after 1985. The observations in the first two sections of this chapter are largely based on the literature available in BLPES.

2   The research for this chapter was pursued during 1998 and 1999. As it is meant to give an example for a type of analysis to be carried out, I considered updating not entirely necessary and have refrained from it. An earlier version of this chapter appeared in Bo Stråth (ed.), *After Full Employment: Discourses on Work and Flexibility in Europe* (Brussels: PIE, 2000, pp. 35–63).

3   On the notion of 'counter-concepts' in political language, see Koselleck 1979. Such pairs of counter-concepts regularly stand in an asymmetrical relation to each other. In this case, 'flexibility' is clearly the hegemonic concept with positive normative connotations, whereas 'rigidity' is derived from the former and has a negative ring to it. In more technical treatises, the term 'elasticity' points generically to the problem at issue, of which 'flexibility' and 'rigidity' are but two instantiations. 'Elasticity' in neo-classical economics generally refers to the inclination to react to changes in the supply–demand relation.

4   That this was a shift can be seen from the fact that the notion of 'wage flexibility' fell entirely out of such highly visible use as in book titles.

5   This broadening occurred through a digression outside of mainstream neo-classical economics, namely the theory of labour market segmentation. As recently argued by Ben Fine (1998), this theorizing, which started out from empirical observations of 'dual labour markets', opened the way to a perspective that no longer took the existence of homogeneous labour supply, defended and safeguarded by state and unions, for granted.

6   I should add that, in the social and economic sciences, the term 'flexibility' only rarely occurs with other referents than these three. Publications with the word in the title are extremely rare in BLPES before the mid-1960s, and the few that exist deal mostly with international relations and security matters. Otherwise, the term occurs in the context of urban and local planning and with reference to national developmental strategies (of countries such as Taiwan, Romania or Brazil). The socio-economic usage broadens during the 1980s and the 1990s somewhat beyond the major cases as discussed here, and some instances will be taken up below, but it is clearly influenced by the semantics of 'wage flexibility' and 'labour market flexibility'.

7   Much more common is the opposite kind of criticism: that the European Central Bank and the Euro lack a political commitment by an actual state that backs them.

8   The background to this understanding is the theory of state or popular sovereignty, defining the unit actor in global 'political' interaction.

9   All the following observations are based on the BLPES research mentioned above. For reasons of space, I will avoid giving full bibliographical details on items merely used for these observations, which can easily be accessed by checking the catalogue at <http://www.lse.ac.uk>.

10   Most of these publications point to adverse effects for certain groups of workers and employees, often for women. They, thus, raise equity concerns.

11   Published in 1973, this is by far the earliest title in BLPES that connotes flexibility to the area of work. As is now well known, this was almost exactly the last moment when such an analysis could be put forward since, as Evans makes explicit, 'underlying this report is the assumption that economic growth will continue' (p. 15). That his observations were not entirely beside the point and that they continue to have a certain attractiveness can be read from the ways temporary work agencies advertise their offers.

12   It should be remembered that the overall project of the social sciences and their problematic key term 'society' was linked to the assumption that this 'in-between' is of crucial importance for understanding human social life. This assumption seems in no way superseded (see Heilbron 1995; Wagner 2001b, chapter 8).

13   As a broad measure at least – some national economies, such as the Italian one, were obviously already highly heterogeneous.

14   'Credibility' was a key term in the debates about flexible exchange rates during the 1970s, opposed almost as a counter-concept, or at least in strong tension to, 'flexibility'. It relates to more recent debates about 'trust' as a key factor in societal situations and, more specifically, to predominantly co-operative industrial relations as a 'locational advantage' of national economies.

Chapter 8   The Critique of Science and its Prospects

1   The term 'scientific revolution' was made prominent by Alexandre Koyré in the 1930s and was widely used after the Second World War, but not much before (Shapin 1996, p. 2).

2   For the former, the Edinburgh strong programme in the sociology of scientific knowledge is the key source, though inspired by Thomas Kuhn's analysis of 'scientific revolutions' (Kuhn 1962); for the latter, Richard Rorty's review of twentieth-century philosophy seems to have provided the term (Rorty 1967), though not the research programme. For recent assessments, see Wittrock and Wagner (1987) for the former, and chapter 14 below for the latter.

3   If there is one key aversion scientists seriously need to overcome, it is their refusal to see science as a human activity alongside others. Since 'science' is what they are doing daily, this move should not be too difficult. It is their common refusal to make it, though, that turns them into dogmatics who claim to be right by virtue of their faith. And at that moment, war becomes a very likely occurrence.

4   Santos 1992 [1987]. An earlier version of the following text was first published in Portuguese in *Conhecimento prudente para uma vida decente. 'Um discurso sobre as ciências' revisitado*, edited by Boaventura de Sousa Santos (Porto: Edições Afrontamento, and São Paulo: Cortez Editora, 2003, pp. 103–21); and subsequently in English in *Cognitive Justice in a Global World*, also edited by Santos (Lanham, MD: Lexington Books, 2007), reprinted by permission of The Rowman and Littlefield Publishing Group.

5   As George Steiner (1984, p. 14) puts it: 'The epistemology of Kant is one of stoic severance. Subject is severed from object; perception from cognition. [. . .] Western metaphysics after Kant stems from the negation of this distance or from any attempt to overcome it.'

6   Scientists today often ridicule the alleged irrelevance of philosophy of science for their activity. But, to return the ball to their camp, the fact that the light goes on in my room when I turn on the switch without me knowing what happens does not mean that physics is unimportant for understanding electricity (as Friedrich Dürrenmatt has already pointed out).

7   This was not how Dewey saw it, who remained very positive about the sciences, but only because he saw them as undergoing the 'Copernican revolution' towards the understanding of knowledge he thought to be adequate. Sixty years later, Santos, while also being – overly? – optimistic, cannot reason any longer in the same terms. His 'emergent paradigm' takes distance not from philosophy, but from earlier – and still dominant – forms of scientific practice. It reflects the experience of another half century of ambivalent 'progress' in the use of instrumental reason.

8   Honneth (2005, p. 67) addresses a similar issue in related terms, comparing 'forms of knowledge that are recognition-sensitive' with those in which 'the intuition of their origins in prior recognition has got lost'. He suggests, as I would, that objectifying knowledge is justifiable under certain conditions. However, as mentioned in a different way before (see chapter 5 above), such justifiability does not solely depend on the sensitivity to recognition, but also on the situation and the problem that such knowledge is meant to address.

9   For a discussion about how such critical version of the Enlightenment optimism had an impact – a problematic one – on the emancipatory aspects of '1968', see chapter 4 above.

10 The concept of a relation between expectation and experience, borrowed from Reinhart Koselleck (1979 and elsewhere), can be translated into the metaphor of variable 'degrees of distancing' that may be required/appropriate for different kinds of questions that may be asked. My thanks to Olav Korsnaes for making me think more about the metaphor of distance with regard to knowledge-seeking practices (which is also at the centre of Carlo Ginzburg's recent collection of essays (Ginzburg 1998)).

Chapter 9   Varieties of Socio-political Interpretations of Modernity

1   An earlier version of this chapter appeared in French in Bénédicte Zimmermann (ed.), *L'Etat et les sciences sociales* (Paris: Editions de la Maison des Sciences de l'Homme, 2004).

2   I shall not take up here those parts of these debates that proceed via a critique of 'Western' social science, or even 'Western' world-views, though they could be included in a broader discussion of 'scholarly styles', beyond national ones. For an excellent example, see Chakrabarty (2000), and for some further discussion chapter 11 below.

3   In his contribution to the Münch–Alexander debate, Levine underlines that indeed he holds 'that national contexts played an important role in the development of sociology'. But he also stresses 'the international character of sociological discourse in the founding generation of 1890–1914'. For the present situation, he urges that the current network of theories be seen 'to consist not of national assertions but of theoretically and methodologically diverse orientations' (Levine 1995b).

4   The probably most articulate contemporary spokesperson for a cultural 'expressivist' theory of language, selfhood and community is Charles Taylor; see especially Taylor (1989, 1995).

5   In terms of social theory, this view emphasizes the creativity of action that goes beyond even the most sophisticated explanation by habitus and strategy; see Joas (1995). An elucidating example for the limitations of Bourdieu's approach is his discussion of 'the political ontology of Martin Heidegger' (Bourdieu 1991), which is in many respects (though possibly by now superseded) an exemplary study of the social and political, institutional and intellectual issues at stake in the 'field' of philosophy during the Weimar Republic, elaborated in co-operation with Michael Pollak, but there is very little sense of the substantive aspects of Heidegger's philosophy and its relevance or irrelevance in thought and in politics. It does not provide any means then, for instance, to understand the current sustained interest in Heidegger's work.

6   On the neglect of Max Weber's work by the Durkheimian school, see Pollak (1986); on the Durkheimian strategy, see Karady (1976).

7   Or, in other words, cross-national intellectual comparisons of 'sociologies', if they are viable at all, are quite uncertain about what it is that they compare, beyond the adoption of the common name.

8   Certainly, this observation does not hold for everything that was proposed under the name of sociology, not even during the classical era. I shall discuss other approaches in a different context of my argument, below (p. 182).

9   Crown witnesses are authors like Edmund Burke and Michael Oakeshott, but also the later, 'English', Wittgenstein. I shall avoid making this point explicitly, since its validity would have to rely not on

intellectual history but on a comprehensive cultural analysis which in itself is highly problematic.

10   No studies comparable to those pursued by the group around Michel Espagne and Michael Werner for transfers between France and Germany in philology and modern languages, or by Peter Schöttler for history, exist for the social sciences. See Pollak (1986), as one contribution to such a project in waiting.

11   Wagner (2001b, chapter 8). A more friendly international exchange took place, for instance, in the sequence of Tocqueville's reading of American democracy and James Stuart Mill's reading of Tocqueville's reading of American democracy; see Mill (1994) and for some of the substance of the concern, see chapter 2 above.

Part IV   Overture: European Integration as an Interpretation of Modernity

1   It may have been a throwaway remark by Derrida (1994, p. 89) when he recorded that it was suggested to him that the Russian term *perestrojka* should be translated as deconstruction. But the connection that is created here between a political restructuring and an intellectual proposal captures indeed the linkage between a *problématique* and an experienced situation that defines the urgency of a socio-philosophical quest.

Chapter 10   Logics of European History

1   For a discussion of the modernity of Turkey, see Kaya (2004); and for the possible significance of Orthodox thinking for understanding European political modernity, see Kristeva (2000) and now Stöckl (2007).

2   As a region rather than province, even though otherwise the approach followed here is close to Chakrabarty (2000).

3   In *A Sociology of Modernity* (Wagner 1994, chapter 4), I have discussed the tendency of modernity towards self-cancellation as inherent in certain societal implications of the liberal notion of self-regulation; thus, the focus was on self-cancellation of liberal varieties of modernity. Continuing on that train of thought, one might say that the accumulated experiences of the first half of the twentieth century bear witness to a related tendency towards self-cancellation in organized modernity (see for the above reasoning also Wagner 2001a, chapter 4).

4   Focused on experience as it is, this analysis cannot stipulate unity across such a large time-space in which similarity or even great proximity of experience is unlikely. Interpretations can tie different experiences together, but also only within limits. Let me use this conceptual remark to point to two rather obvious deviations from the analysis proposed above. First, the formerly Soviet socialist societies may have shared much of the described experience up to the Second World War but lived a very different situation between, roughly, 1948 and 1989. Secondly, the First World

War largely spared the territory of Britain and Scandinavia, and further-more many citizens of these countries also hold that their democracies have been more stable than those on the Continent and that the inclina-tion towards totalitarian ideologies was less pronounced. In both cases, the attitude within and towards Europe differs considerably from the one of 'core Europe', which was at the centre of my observations.

5 The use of the terms 'industry' and 'market' in this sense is borrowed from Boltanski and Thévenot (1991).

Chapter 11   Regionalizing European Modernity

1 Such discussion is led in Nathalie Karagiannis and Peter Wagner (eds), *Varieties of World-making: Beyond Globalization* (Liverpool: Liverpool University Press, 2007a), in which an earlier version of this chapter appeared.

2 My use of the term 'imperial' draws on Hardt and Negri (2000) and accepts the observation of a novel relatively aterritorial form of (dis-cursive) domination. Otherwise, however, as will become clear in the course of my argument, a different understanding of the novel imperial situation is proposed here, namely one that sees imperial modernism as an interpretation of modernity that is inclined towards hegemony, for reasons to be detailed below, but that is only contingently related to the rise of the USA (for a recent historico-sociological analysis of empire, see Mann 2003).

3 As will be shown in the second step of my argument below, this empty-ing out of substantive concerns by conceptual means is the core problem, rather than the main solution, in theorizing the modern polity.

4 And the elder brother, in turn, would resort to the counter-argument that these elaborations, while having sound roots, have gone too far, have misdeveloped – that was the structure of the European argument towards America during the inter-war period.

5 There is little doubt that the Anglo-American war in Iraq is also an example of robber capitalism aiming at accumulation by violent means. However, the justification it is endowed with by its commanders, with its emphasis on human rights and democracy, is an application of impe-rial modernism. As such it has created considerable havoc in political and intellectual debates in Europe and North America.

Chapter 12   The Social Theory and Political Philosophy of Modernity

1 An earlier version of this chapter appeared in Gerard Delanty (ed.), *Handbook of Contemporary European Social Theory* (London: Routledge, 2006).

2 For an interpretation of the political discourse of modernity as the attempt to decrease this necessity, by way of 'immunizing' singular human beings, see Esposito (1998).

3   For a retrieval of the emergence of a 'society'-based terminology from an earlier 'politics'-based one, see Hallberg and Wittrock (2005); for a proposal to re-weave the connections between the social and the political, see Karagiannis and Wagner (2005).

4   See very similarly Bruno Latour's observations on the separation of the natural and the social in *We Have Never Been Modern* (1993 [1991]).

5   Manent (1994, pp. 75 and 113). See Therborn (1976) for an earlier – Althusser-inspired – analysis of the emergence of sociology 'between two revolutions'.

6   See Pettit (1997) and Skinner (1998) for recent accounts; for a detailed reconstruction of republican political thought in Europe, see now Van Gelderen and Skinner (2002).

7   They are versions of 'social theory' in our current understanding of the term, even though their view of the social is extremely thin, or maybe more precisely: their substantive interest in the social is very limited; the outcome of interaction is at the centre of interest.

8   As Albert Hirschman (1977) has shown, this reasoning also suggested a transformation of social configurations towards an ever increasing importance of the 'commercial bond' at the expense of other forms of social bond.

9   Since nineteenth-century polities all worked with restrictions that are incompatible with a fully fledged individualist liberalism, one should say more precisely that such a polity was put on the horizon of political debate through the revolutions, rather than made actual in institutional form.

Chapter 13   The Conceptual History and Historical Sociology of Modernity

1   An earlier version of this chapter appeared in Gerard Delanty and Engin Isin (eds), *Handbook of Historical Sociology* (London: Sage, 2003, pp. 168–79).

2   Although her objective in this particular writing was not least a defence in terms of theory and methodology, she also added broadly and appropriately that methodology in this context cannot be understood 'as a set of techniques, but as the interrelation of substantive problems, sources of evidence, and larger assumptions about society, history and the purposes of scholarship' (Skocpol 1984b, p. x).

3   See, for instance, the evolution of the debate between Theda Skocpol and William Sewell: Skocpol (1979); Sewell (1994); Skocpol (1994); Sewell (1999); see now Sewell (2005) and the analysis of the debate by Manicas (2006).

4   This includes the insight of the need to reflect upon the very demarcation between philosophy and history. Despite all differences, it is striking to see how explorations at the margins of established intellectual modes of operation lead to neighbouring innovative insights.

5 In Foucault and Skinner, while there are also hints that this period may be approaching its end, they are not fully developed into the assertion of a new period. Similar hints are almost, though not quite, absent in Koselleck.

6 Such a step was still resolutely rejected by Theda Skocpol in the first exchange she had with William Sewell about her *States and Social Revolutions*; see Skocpol (1994, pp. 202–3).

7 Although the concept of 'policy legacies' is introduced, those are treated just as a structural element like other features of the government apparatus.

8 The *General Theory* was only published in French translation after the war and very few economists had read it in the original version.

9 My reference volumes here are Rueschemeyer and Skocpol (1996) and Zimmermann et al. (1999). But obviously works on this topic always derive some of their inspiration from the Foucauldian analyses offered by Donzelot (1984) and by Ewald (1986).

10 Important comparative and historical qualifications would need to be made here, but I will stay with this general remark for the sake of brevity.

11 Marx basically was not much more than a perceptive observer of these developments who elevated the neologism 'working class' to a key role in his social theory and philosophy of history.

12 The reference here is obviously the key works in the revisionism of the historiography of the Revolution, such as Furet (1983) as well as Baker (1990).

13 And it may be worthwhile to add that such stabilization by means of concepts is the work of both the political actors and the historian and historical sociologist.

14 'Conceptual work' is coined after 'historical work' or 'social work', as in Luc Boltanski's analyses of the formation of classes and categories; see Boltanski (1982, 1990).

References

Adorno, Theodor W., 'Versuch, das Endspiel zu verstehen', *Gesammelte Schriften 11: Noten zur Literatur*. Frankfurt/M.: Suhrkamp, 1974 [1958], 281–321.

Adorno, Theodor W., 'Neue wertfreie Soziologie. Aus Anlaß von Karl Mannheims "Mensch und Gesellschaft im Zeitalter des Umbaus"', *Gesammelte Schriften 20/1: Vermischte Schriften I*. Frankfurt/M.: Suhrkamp, 1986a [1937], 13–45.

Adorno, Theodor W., 'Democratic leadership and mass manipulation', *Gesammelte Schriften 20/1: Vermischte Schriften I*. Frankfurt/M.: Suhrkamp, 1986b [1949], 267–86.

Adorno, Theodor W., 'Individuum und Staat', *Gesammelte Schriften 20/1: Vermischte Schriften I*. Frankfurt/M.: Suhrkamp, 1986c [1951], 287–92.

Adorno, Theodor W., 'Öffentliche Meinung und Meinungsforschung', *Gesammelte Schriften 20/1: Vermischte Schriften I*. Frankfurt/M.: Suhrkamp, 1986d [1952], 293–301.

Adorno, Theodor W., 'Auf die Frage: Warum sind Sie zurückgekehrt', *Gesammelte Schriften 20/1: Vermischte Schriften I*. Frankfurt/M.: Suhrkamp, 1986e [1962], 394–5.

Adorno, Theodor W. and Max Horkheimer, *Dialectic of Enlightenment*. London: Verso, 1997.

Agamben, Giorgio, *Homo sacer. Il potere sovrano e la nuda vita*. Turin: Einaudi, 1995.

Alexander, Jeffrey C., 'Formal and substantive voluntarism in the work of Talcott Parsons: A theoretical and ideological reinterpretation', *American Sociological Review* 43 (1978): 177–98.

Alexander, Jeffrey C., 'How "national" is social theory? A note on some worrying trends in the recent theorizing of Richard Munch', *Theory* (Newsletter of the ISA Research Committee on Social Theory), Autumn 1994: 2–8.

Andrews, David M., 'The Bretton Woods agreement as an invitation to struggle', in Christian Joerges, Bo Stråth and Peter Wagner, eds, *The Economy as a Polity. The Political Constitution of Contemporary Capitalism*. London: University College London Press, 2005.

Ankersmit, Frank R., 'The reality effect in the writing of history', in *History and Tropology. The Rise and Fall of Metaphor*. Berkeley, CA: University of California Press, 1994, 125–61.

Arendt, Hannah, *The Life of the Mind*, vol. 1: *Thinking*. London: Harcourt, Brace, Jovanovich, 1978.

Arendt, Hannah, *The Human Condition*. Chicago, IL: The University of Chicago Press, 1958.

Arendt, Hannah, *The Origins of Totalitarianism*. New York: Harcourt, Brace and World, 1951.

Arnason, Johann P., 'The imaginary constitution of modernity', in Giovanni Busino et al., *Autonomie et transformation de la société. La philosophie militante de Cornelius Castoriadis*. Geneva: Droz, 1989, 323–37.

Arnason, Johann P., 'The varieties of accumulation: civilizational perspectives on capitalism', in Christian Joerges, Bo Stråth and Peter Wagner, eds, *The Economy as a Polity. The Political Constitution of Contemporary Capitalism*. London: University College London Press, 2005.

Arnason, Johann P., Shmuel N. Eisenstadt and Björn Wittrock, eds, *Axial Civilizations and World History*. Leiden: Brill, 2005.

Arnason, Johann P., Kurt Raaflaub and Peter Wagner, eds, *The Greek polis and the Invention of Democracy: A Politico-cultural Transformation and its Interpretations*, in preparation.

Asad, Talal, *Anthropology and the Colonial Encounter*. New York: Prometheus Books, 1995.

Baechler, Jean, *Les origines du capitalisme*. Paris: Gallimard, 1971.

Baker, Keith Michael, *Condorcet: From Natural Philosophy to Social Mathematics*. Chicago, IL: The University of Chicago Press, 1975.

Baker, Keith Michael, *Inventing the French Revolution*. Cambridge: Cambridge University Press, 1990.

Balibar, Etienne, *Nous, citoyens d'Europe? Les frontiers, l'État, le peuple*. Paris: La découverte, 2001.

Beckett, Samuel, *Endgame*. London: Faber and Faber, 1968 (Fr. orig. *Fin de partie*, Paris: Minuit, 1957).

Bellamy, Richard and Dario Castiglione, 'Legitimising the Euro-polity and its regime: the normative turn in EU studies', *European Journal of Political Theory* 2/1 (2003): 7–34.

Benjamin, Walter, 'Das Kunstwerk im Zeitalter seiner technischen Reproduzierbarkeit', in *Gesammelte Schriften* I/2 (eds Rolf Tiedemann and Hermann Schweppenhäuser). Frankfurt/M.: Suhrkamp, 1978 [1934], 431–69.

Berlin, Isaiah, 'Two concepts of liberty', in *Four Essays on Liberty*. Oxford: Oxford University Press, 1971 [1958].

Berman, Marshall, *All That is Solid Melts into Air. The Experience of Modernity*. New York: Simon and Schuster, 1982.

Bohrer, Karl-Heinz, '1968: Die Phantasie an die Macht? Studentenbewegung – Walter Benjamin – Surrealismus', in Ingrid Gilcher-Holtey, ed., *1968. Vom Ereignis zum Gegenstand der Geschichtswissenschaft.* Göttingen: Vandenhoeck & Ruprecht, 1997, 288–300.

Boltanski, Luc, *Les cadres. La formation d'un groupe social.* Paris: Minuit, 1982.

Boltanski, Luc, *L'amour et la justice comme compétences.* Paris: Métailié, 1990.

Boltanski, Luc, 'The left after May 1968 and the longing for total revolution', *Thesis Eleven* 69 (May 2002): 1–20.

Boltanski, Luc and Eve Chiapello, *Le nouvel esprit du capitalisme.* Paris: Gallimard, 1999.

Boltanski, Luc and Laurent Thévenot, *De la justification.* Paris: Gallimard, 1991.

Bonnell, Victoria E. and Lynn Hunt, eds, *Beyond the Cultural Turn. New Directions in the Study of Society and Culture.* Berkeley, CA: University of California Press, 1999.

Bourdieu, Pierre, 'The specificity of the scientific field and the social conditions for the progress of reason', *Information sur les sciences sociales* 14/6 (1975): 19–47.

Bourdieu, Pierre, *Homo academicus.* Paris: Editions du Minuit, 1984.

Bourdieu, Pierre, *The Political Ontology of Martin Heidegger.* Cambridge: Polity, 1991.

Bourdieu, Pierre, *Les règles de l'art.* Paris: Editions du Minuit, 1992.

Bourdieu, Pierre and Jean-Claude Passeron, 'Philosophy and sociology in France since 1945: Death and resurrection of a philosophy without subject', *Social Research* 34 (1968): 162–212.

Brague, Rémi, *Europe, la voie romaine.* Paris: Gallimard, 1999 (1st edn, 1992).

Burke, Edmund, *Reflections on the Revolution in France* (ed. L. G. Mitchell). Oxford: Oxford University Press, 1993 [1790].

Cacciari, Massimo, 'Digressioni su Impero e tre Rome', in Heidrun Friese, Antonio Negri and Peter Wagner, eds, *Europa politica. Ragioni di una necessità.* Rome: Manifestolibri, 2002, 21–42.

Cacciari, Massimo, *Geofilosofia dell'Europa.* Milan: Adelphi, 1994.

Capdevielle, Jacques and René Mouriaux, *Mai 68 – l'entre-deux de la modernité. Histoire de trente ans.* Paris: Presses de FNSP, 1988.

Castoriadis, Cornelius, 'Quelle démocratie?', *Figures du pensable. Les carrefours du labyrinthe VI.* Paris: Seuil, 1997a, 145–79.

Castoriadis, Cornelius, 'Héritage et révolution', *Figures du pensable. Les carrefours du labyrinthe VI.* Paris: Seuil, 1997b, 129–44.

Castoriadis, Cornelius, 'Pouvoir, politique, autonomie', in *Le monde morcelé. Les carrefours du labyrinthe III.* Paris: Seuil, 1990a, 113–39.

Castoriadis, Cornelius, 'Individu, société, rationalité, histoire', *Le monde morcelé. Les carrefours du labyrinthe III.* Paris: Seuil, 1990b, 39–69.

Castoriadis, Cornelius, 'Voie sans issue?', *Le monde morcelé. Les carrefours du labyrinthe III.* Paris: Seuil, 1990c, 71–100.

Castoriadis, Cornelius, 'La *polis* grecque et la création de la démocratie', *Domaines de l'homme. Les carrefours du labyrinthe II*. Paris: Seuil, 1986, 261–306.

Chakrabarty, Dipesh, *Provincializing Europe. Postcolonial Thought and Historical Difference*. Princeton: Princeton University Press, 2000.

Chakrabarty, Dipesh, '"In the name of politics": sovereignty, democracy, and the multitude in India', in Nathalie Karagiannis and Peter Wagner, eds, *Varieties of World-making: Beyond Globalisation*. Liverpool: Liverpool University Press, 2007a.

Charle, Christophe, *La crise des sociétés impériales*. Paris: Seuil, 2001.

Constant, Benjamin, *De la liberté des modernes comparée avec la liberté des anciens* ['The liberty of the ancients compared with that of the moderns'], in *Political Writings*, ed. Biancamaria Fontana. Cambridge: Cambridge University Press, 1988, 308–28.

Crouch, Colin and Wolfgang Streeck, eds, *Political Economy of Modern Capitalism. Mapping Convergence and Diversity*. London: Sage, 1997.

Dahrendorf, Ralf, 'L'Europa unita, ultima utopia', *La repubblica*, 5 September 2001.

Davis, Michael C., 'Europe, America, Asia: contemporary wars and their implications for world orders', in Nathalie Karagiannis and Peter Wagner, eds, *Varieties of World-making: Beyond Globalisation*. Liverpool: Liverpool University Press, 2007a.

Derrida, Jacques, 'Structure, sign and play in the discourse of the human sciences', in *Writing and Difference*. London: Routledge, 1978, 280–93.

Derrida, Jacques, *Of Spirit. Heidegger and the Question*. Chicago, IL: University of Chicago Press, 1989.

Derrida, Jacques, *Specters of Marx*. New York: Routledge, 1994.

Derrida, Jacques, *Politics of Friendship*. London: Verso, 1997.

Desrosières, Alain, *La politique des grands nombres. Histoire de la raison statistique*. Paris: La découverte, 1993 [Engl. tr. *The Politics of Large Numbers. A History of Statistical Reasoning*. Cambridge, MA: Harvard University Press, 1998].

Dewey, John, 'The Quest for Certainty', in *The Later Works 1925–1953*, vol. 4. Carbondale, IL: Southern Illinois University Press, 1984 [1929].

Didry, Claude and Peter Wagner, 'La nation comme cadre de l'action économique', in Bénédicte Zimmermann, Claude Didry and Peter Wagner, eds, *Le travail et la nation. Histoire comparée de la France et l'Allemagne à l'horizon européen*. Paris: Editions de la Maison des Sciences de l'Homme, 1999.

Donzelot, Jacques, *L'invention du social. Essai sur le déclin des passions politiques*. Paris: Fayard, 1984.

Dumont, Louis, 'Une variante nationale: le peuple et la nation chez Herder et Fichte', in *Essais sur l'individualisme. Une perspective anthropologique sur l'idéologie moderne*. Paris: Seuil, 1983.

Dumont, Louis, *L'idéologie allemande. France Allemagne et retour*. Paris: Gallimard, 1991.

Durkheim, Emile, *The Division of Labor in Society*. New York: Free Press, 1964.

Eisenstadt, Shmuel N., *Antinomien der Moderne*. Frankfurt/M.: Suhrkamp, 1998.

Eisenstadt, Shmuel N., *Paradoxes of Democracy*. Washington and Baltimore: Woodrow Wilson Center and Johns Hopkins University Press, 1999.

Elias, Norbert, *The Civilizing Process*. New York: Pantheon, 1982 [German orig. 1939].

Esposito, Robert, *Communitas. Origine e destino della comunità*. Turin: Einaudi, 1998.

Evans, Archibald E., *Flexibility in Working Life. Opportunities for Individual Choice*. Paris: Organization for Economic Co-operation and Development, 1973.

Evans, Peter, Dietrich Rueschemeyer and Theda Skocpol, eds, *Bringing the State Back in*. Cambridge: Cambridge University Press, 1985.

Ewald, François, *L'État-providence*. Paris: Grasset, 1986.

Fabian, Johannes, *Time and the Other*. New York: Columbia University Press, 1983.

Ferry, Jean-Marc, *La question de l'État européen*. Paris: Gallimard, 2000.

Ferry, Luc, 'Déclin de l'Occident? De l'épuisement libéral au renouveau démocratique', in Giovanni Busino et al., *Autonomie et transformation de la société. La philosophie militante de Cornelius Castoriadis*. Geneva: Droz, 1989, 339–46.

Ferry, Luc and Alain Renaut, *La pensée 68. Essai sur l'antihumanisme contemporain*. Paris: Gallimard, 1986.

Ferry, Luc and Alain Renaut, *Itinéraires de l'individu*. Paris: Gallimard, 1987, 68–86.

Fine, Ben, *Labor Market Theory. A Constructive Reassessment*. London: Routledge, 1998.

Foucault, Michel, *The Order of Things. An Archaeology of the Human Sciences*. London: Tavistock, 1974 [French orig. *Les mots et les choses*].

Foucault, Michel, *Surveiller et punir*. Paris: Gallimard, 1975.

Foucault, Michel, *L'histoire de la folie*. Paris: Gallimard, 1976.

Foucault, Michel, 'What is Enlightenment?', in *The Foucault Reader*, ed. Paul Rabinow. London: Penguin, 1984, 32–50.

Freeden, Michael, *Ideology and Political Theory: A Conceptual Approach*. Oxford: Clarendon, 1996.

Furet, François, *Penser la Révolution française*. Paris: Gallimard, 1983.

Gadamer, Hans-Georg, 'Begriffsgeschichte als Philosophie', *Archiv für Begriffsgeschichte*, 14 (1970): 137–51.

Gadamer, Hans-Georg, *Truth and Method*. London: Sheed and Ward, 1979 [German orig. 1960].

Galli, Carlo, 'L'Europa come spazio politico', in Heidrun Friese, Antonio Negri and Peter Wagner, eds, *Europa politica. Ragioni di una necessità*. Rome: Manifestolibri, 2002, 43–58.

Gander, Eric, *The Last Conceptual Revolution. A Critique of Richard Rorty's Political Philosophy*. Albany: SUNY Press, 1999.

Giddens, Anthony, *The Consequences of Modernity*. Cambridge: Polity, 1990.

Giddens, Anthony, 'Living in a post-traditional society', in Ulrich Beck, Anthony Giddens and Scott Lash (eds), *Reflexive Modernization*. Cambridge: Polity, 1994, 59–109.

Ginsborg, Paul, 'From 1968 to the Millennium – Continuities and Discontinuities: The Case of the Family', *Thesis Eleven* 68 (May 2002): 43–63.

Ginzburg, Carlo, *Occhiacci di legno. Nove riflessioni sulla distanza*. Milan: Feltrinelli, 1998 [Engl. tr. *Wooden Eyes. Nine Reflections on Distance*, London: Verso, 2002].

Glyn, Andrew and Bob Sutcliffe, *British Capitalism, Workers and the Profit Squeeze*. Harmondsworth: Penguin, 1972.

Goodin, Robert A., 'Folie républicaine', *Annual Review of Political Science* 6 (2003): 55–76.

Grantham, George, 'Economic history and the history of labour markets', in George Grantham and Mary MacKinnon, eds, *Labour Market Evolution: The Economic History of Market Integration, Wage Flexibility and Employment Regulation*. London: Routledge, 1994.

Gray, John, *Liberalism: Essays in Political Philosophy*. London: Routledge, 1989.

Habermas, Jürgen, *Theorie des kommunikativen Handelns*. Frankfurt/M.: Suhrkamp, 1981.

Habermas, Jürgen, *Der philosophische Diskurs der Moderne. Zwölf Vorlesungen*. Frankfurt/M.: Suhrkamp, 1985.

Habermas, Jürgen, *Faktizität und Geltung*. Frankfurt/M.: Suhrkamp, 1992.

Habermas, Jürgen, 'Über den internen Zusammenhang von Rechtsstaat und Demokratie', in *Die Einbeziehung des Anderen*. Frankfurt/M.: Suhrkamp, 1999, 293–305.

Habermas, Jürgen, 'The postnational constellation and the future of democracy', in *The Postnational Constellation*. Cambridge. Polity, 2001, 58–112 [German orig. 1998].

Hall, Peter, ed., *The Political Power of Economic Ideas: Keynesianism across Nations*. Princeton: Princeton University Press, 1989.

Hall, Peter, 'The political economy of Europe in an era of interdependence', in Herbert Kitschelt, Peter Lange, Gary Marks, John D. Stephens, eds, *Continuity and Change in Contemporary Capitalism*. Cambridge: Cambridge University Press, 1999, 135–63.

Hall, Peter and David Soskice, eds, *Varieties of Capitalism*. Oxford: Oxford University Press, 2001.

Hallberg, Peter and Björn Wittrock, 'From koinonía politiké to civil society', in Peter Wagner, ed., *The Languages of Civil Society*. Oxford: Berghahn, 2005.

Hardt, Michael and Antonio Negri, *Empire*. Cambridge, MA: Harvard University Press, 2000.

Hawthorn, Geoffrey, *Enlightenment and Despair*. Cambridge: Cambridge University Press, 1978.

288 References

Heelas, Paul and Paul Morris, eds, *The Values of the Enterprise Culture*. London: Routledge, 1992.

Heidegger, Martin, *Holzwege*. Frankfurt/M.: Klostermann, 1977.

Heidegger, Martin, 'Der Zeitbegriff in der Geschichtswissenschaft', in *Frühe Schriften*. Frankfurt/M.: Klostermann, 1978 [1916], 413–33.

Heilbron, Johan, *The Rise of Social Theory*. Cambridge: Polity, 1995.

Hiley, David R., James F. Bohman and Richard Shusterman, eds, *The Interpretive Turn: Philosophy, Science, Culture*. Ithaca, NY: Cornell University Press, 1991.

Hilferding, Rudolf, *Das Finanzkapital*. Frankfurt/M.: EVA, 1968.

Hirschman, Albert, *The Passions and the Interests: Political Arguments for Capitalism before its Triumph*. Princeton: Princeton University Press, 1977.

Hirschman, Albert, *The Rhetoric of Reaction: Perversity, Futility, Jeopardy*. Cambridge, MA: Belknap Press, 1991.

Hollingsworth, J. Rogers and Robert Boyer, eds, *Contemporary Capitalism: The Embeddedness of Institutions*. Cambridge: Cambridge University Press, 1997.

Honneth, Axel, *Verdinglichung. Eine anerkennungstheoretische Studie*. Frankfurt/M.: Suhrkamp, 2005.

Husserl, Edmund, *The Crisis of European Sciences and Transcendental Phenomenology*. Evanston: Northwestern University Press, 1970 [German orig. 1935].

Jessop, Bob, 'The crisis of the national spatio-temporal fix and the tendential ecological dominance of globalizing capitalism', *International Journal of Urban and Regional Research* 24/2 (June 2000): 323–60.

Joas, Hans, *The Creativity of Action*. Cambridge: Polity, 1995.

Kant, Immanuel, 'Beantwortung der Frage: Was ist Aufklärung?' ['Answer to the Question: What is the Enlightenment?'], *Politische Schriften*. Cologne and Opladen: Westdeutscher Verlag, 1965 [1784], 1–8.

Karady, Victor, 'Durkheim, les sciences sociales et l'université: bilan d'un semi-échec', *Revue française de sociologie* 17/2 (1976): 267–311.

Karagiannis, Nathalie, *Avoiding Responsibility. The Politics and Discourse of European Development Policy*. London: Pluto, 2004.

Karagiannis, Nathalie, 'Multiple solidarities: autonomy and resistance', in Nathalie Karagiannis and Peter Wagner, eds, *Varieties of World-making: Beyond Globalisation*. Liverpool: Liverpool University Press, 2007a.

Karagiannis, Nathalie, 'Democracy as a tragic regime', Lecture for presentation in the Modern Greek Program of the University of Michigan, March 2007b (forthcoming in Spanish in *Trasversales*).

Karagiannis, Nathalie, ed., *European Solidarity*. Liverpool: Liverpool University Press, 2007c.

Karagiannis, Nathalie and Peter Wagner, 'Towards a theory of synagonism', *The Journal of Political Philosophy* 13/3 (September 2005).

Karagiannis, Nathalie and Peter Wagner, 'Introduction: globalisation or world-making?', in Nathalie Karagiannis and Peter Wagner, eds, *Varieties of World-making: Beyond Globalisation*. Liverpool: Liverpool University Press, 2007a.

Katznelson, Ira, 'Working-class formation: constructing cases and comparisons', in Ira Katznelson and Aristide R. Zolberg, eds, *Working-class Formation. Nineteenth-century Patterns in Western Europe and the United States*. Princeton: Princeton University Press, 1986, 3–41.

Kawamura, Nozomu, *Sociology and Society of Japan*. London: Routledge & Kegan Paul, 1994.

Kaya, Ibrahim, *Social Theory and Later Modernities: The Turkish Experience*. Liverpool: Liverpool University Press, 2004.

Keat, Russel and Nicholas Abercrombie, eds, *Enterprise Culture*. London: Routledge, 1991.

Kitschelt, Herbert, Peter Lange, Gary Marks and John D. Stephens, eds, *Continuity and Change in Contemporary Capitalism*. Cambridge: Cambridge University Press, 1999.

Koselleck, Reinhart, *Kritik und Krise. Eine Studie zur Pathogenese der bürgerlichen Welt*. Frankfurt/M.: Suhrkamp, 1959.

Koselleck, Reinhart, *Vergangene Zukunft. Zur Semantik geschichtlicher Zeiten*. Frankfurt/M.: Suhrkamp, 1979 [Engl. tr. *Futures Past: On the Semantics of Historical Time*. Cambridge, MA: MIT Press, 1985].

Kratochwil, Friedrich, 'Global governance and the emergence of "world society": international relations analysis meets sociology', in Nathalie Karagiannis and Peter Wagner, eds, *Varieties of World-making: Beyond Globalisation*. Liverpool: Liverpool University Press, 2007a.

Kristeva, Julia, *Crisis of the European Subject*. New York: Other Press, 2000.

Kuhn, Thomas S., *The Structure of Scientific Revolutions*. Chicago, IL: The University of Chicago Press, 1962.

Lamont, Michèle and Laurent Thévenot, eds, *Rethinking Comparative Cultural Sociology. Polities and Repertoires of Evaluation in France and the United States*. New York: Cambridge University Press, 2000.

Latour, Bruno, *We Have Never Been Modern*. Hemel Hempstead: Harvester Wheatsheaf, 1993 [Fr. orig. 1991].

Latour, Bruno, 'On the partial existence of existing and non-existing objects', in Lorraine Daston, ed., *Biographies of Scientific Objects*. Chicago, IL: University of Chicago Press, 2000, 247–69.

Lefort, Claude, *La complication. Retour sur le communisme*. Paris: Fayard, 1999.

Lefort, Claude, 'Réversibilité: liberté politique et liberté de l'individu', in *Essais sur le politique xixe–xxe siècles*. Paris: Seuil, 1986a [Engl. tr. *Democracy and Political Theory*. Cambridge: Polity, 1988].

Lefort, Claude, 'Les droits de l'homme et l'État-providence', in *Essais sur le politique xixe–xxe siècles*. Paris: Seuil, 1986b.

Lefort, Claude, 'La question de la démocratie', in *Essais sur le politique xixe–xxe siècles*. Paris: Seuil, 1986c, 17–30.

Lenin, Vladimir I., *Drei Quellen und drei Bestandteile des Marxismus*. Berlin: Dietz, 1966.

Levine, Donald D., *Visions of the Sociological Tradition*. Chicago, IL: University of Chicago Press, 1995a.

Levine, Donald D., 'On the Münch–Alexander exchange', *Theory* (Autumn, 1995b): 4–5.

Löwy, Michael, 'The Revolutionary Romanticism of May '68', *Thesis Eleven* 68 (May 2002): 95–100.

Lyotard, Jean-François, *La Condition postmoderne*. Paris: Minuit, 1979 [trans. G. Bennington and B. Massumi, *The Postmodern Condition*. Manchester: Manchester University Press, 1994].

Macpherson, Crawford Brough, *The Political Theory of Possessive Individualism: Hobbes to Locke*. London: Oxford University Press, 1964.

Maier, Hans, *Die ältere deutsche Staats- und Verwaltungslehre*. Munich: Beck, 1980 (1st edn, 1966).

Majone, Giandomenico, *Regulating Europe*. London: Routledge, 1996.

Manent, Pierre, *Cours familier de philosophie politique*. Paris: Fayard, 2001.

Manent, Pierre, *An Intellectual History of Liberalism*. Princeton: Princeton University Press, 1995 (1st edn, 1987).

Manent, Pierre, *La cité de l'homme*. Paris: Fayard, 1994 [Engl. tr. *The City of Man*. Princeton: Princeton University Press, 1998].

Manicas, Peter T., *A History and Philosophy of the Social Sciences*. Oxford: Blackwell, 1987.

Manicas, Peter T., *A Realist Philosophy of Social Science*. Cambridge: Cambridge University Press, 2006.

Mann, Michael, *Incoherent Empire*. London: Verso, 2003.

Mannheim, Karl, *Man and Society in an Age of Reconstruction*. London: Routledge and Kegan Paul, 1980 [1937].

Marx, Karl, *Capital*. Chicago: Encyclopedia Britannica, 1978.

Mayer, Arno, *The Persistence of the Old Regime*. New York: Pantheon, 1981.

Meier, Christian, *The Greek Discovery of Politics*. Cambridge, MA: Harvard University Press, 1990.

Meier, Christian, *Von Athen bis Auschwitz*. Munich: Beck, 2002.

Mill, John Stuart, *On Liberty*. Indianapolis: Bobbs-Merrill, 1956 [1859].

Mill, John Stuart, *Essais sur Tocqueville et la société américaine*. Paris: Vrin, 1994.

Moore, Barrington, *Social Origins of Dictatorship and Democracy*. Harmondsworth: Penguin, 1969.

Mouffe, Chantal, *The Democratic Paradox*. London: Verso, 2000.

Mouzakitis, Angelos, 'Worlds emerging: approaches to the creation and constitution of the common', in Nathalie Karagiannis and Peter Wagner, eds, *Varieties of World-making: Beyond Globalisation*. Liverpool: Liverpool University Press, 2007a.

Münch, Richard, 'American and European social theory: cultural identities and social forms of theory production', *Sociological Perspectives* 34 (1991): 313–35.

Münch, Richard, 'The contribution of German social theory to European sociology', in Birgitta Nedelmann and Piotr Sztompka, eds, *Sociology in Europe*. Berlin: De Gruyter, 1993, 45–66.

Münch, Richard, 'Geopolitics in guise of universalist rhetoric. A response to Jeffrey C. Alexander', *Theory* (Spring 1995): 2–10.

Nancy, Jean-Luc, *The Inoperative Community*. Minneapolis: University of Minnesota Press, 1991 [Fr. orig. 1986].

Narr, Wolf-Dieter and Claus Offe, eds, *Wohlfahrtsstaat und Massenloyalität*. Cologne: Kiepenheuer und Witsch, 1975.

Nietzsche, Friedrich, *Unmodern Observations – unzeitgemäße Betrachtungen*. New Haven: Yale University Press, 1990 [1874].

Oestreich, Gerhard, 'The structure of the absolute state', in Gerhard Oestreich, *Neostoicism and the Early Modern State*. Cambridge: Cambridge University Press, 1982, 258–73.

Offe, Claus, 'Demokratie und Wohlfahrtsstaat: Eine europäische Regimeform unter dem Streß der europäischen Integration', in Wolfgang Streeck, ed., *Internationale Wirtschaft, nationale Demokratie*. Frankfurt/M.: Campus, 1998, 99–136.

Offe, Claus, '1968 – Thirty Years After: Four Hypotheses on the Historical Consequences of the Student Movement', *Thesis Eleven* 68 (May 2002): 82–8.

Palmer, Robert Rosell, *The Age of the Democratic Revolution*. Princeton: Princeton University Press, 1959.

Parsons, Talcott, 'Evolutionary universals in society', *American Sociological Review* 29 (June 1964).

Passerini, Luisa, '"Utopia" and Desire', *Thesis Eleven* 68 (May 2002): 11–30.

Patočka, Jan, *Platon et l'Europe*. Paris: Véridier, 1983.

Patočka, Jan, *Heretical Essays in the Philosophy of History*. Chicago and La Salle, IL: Open Court, 1996.

Pettit, Philip, *Republicanism. A Theory of Freedom and Government*. Oxford: Clarendon, 1997.

Piore, Michael J. and Charles F. Sabel, *The Second Industrial Divide: Possibilities for Prosperity*. New York: Basic Books, 1984.

Polanyi, Karl, *The Great Transformation*. Boston: Beacon, 1985 [1944].

Pollak, Michael, *Max Weber in France. L'itinéraire d'une oeuvre*. Paris: Cahiers de l'IHTP, 1986, no. 3.

Rabinbach, Anson, 'Social knowledge, social risk and the politics of industrial accidents in Germany and France', in Dietrich Rueschemeyer and Theda Skocpol, eds, *States, Social Knowledge and the Origins of Modern Social Policies*. Princeton: Princeton University Press, 1996, 48–79.

Rawls, John, *A Theory of Justice*. Cambridge, MA: Belknap Press of Harvard University Press, 1971.

Rorty, Richard, ed., *The Linguistic Turn: Recent Essays in Philosophical Method*. Chicago: The University of Chicago Press, 1967.

Rorty, Richard, *Philosophy and the Mirror of Nature*. Princeton: Princeton University Press, 1980.

Rorty, Richard, *Contingency, Irony, Solidarity*. Cambridge: Cambridge University Press, 1989.

Rosanvallon, Pierre, 'The development of Keynesianism in France', in Peter Hall, ed., *The Political Power of Economic Ideas: Keynesianism across Nations.* Princeton: Princeton University Press, 1989, 171–93.

Ross, Dorothy, *The Origins of American Social Science.* Cambridge: Cambridge University Press, 1990.

Rothblatt, Sheldon and Björn Wittrock, eds, *The European and American University since 1800.* Cambridge: Cambridge University Press, 1993.

Rueschemeyer, Dietrich and Theda Skocpol, eds, *Social Knowledge and the Origins of Social Policies.* Princeton: Princeton University Press, 1996.

Sabel, Charles F. and Jonathan Zeitlin, eds, *World of Possibilities. Flexibility and Mass Production in Western Industrialization.* Cambridge: Cambridge University Press, 1997.

Said, Edward, *Orientalism.* New York: Vintage, 1978.

Salais, Robert and Michael Storper, *Les mondes du production.* Paris: Editions de l'EHESS, 1993 [Engl. tr. 1998].

Santos, Boaventura de Sousa, 'A discourse on the sciences', *Review* 15/1 (1992): 9–47 [Port. orig. 1987].

Santos, Boaventura de Sousa, 'Towards an epistemology of blindness. Why the new forms of "ceremonial adequacy" neither regulate nor emancipate', *European Journal of Social Theory* 4/3 (2001): 251–79.

Scharpf, Fritz W., *Governing in Europe: Effective and Democratic?* Oxford: Oxford University Press, 1999.

Sennett, Richard, *The Corrosion of Character: The Personal Consequences of Work in the New Capitalism.* New York: Norton, 1998.

Sewell, William H., *Work and Revolution in France: The Language of Labour from the Old Regime to 1848.* Cambridge: Cambridge University Press, 1980.

Sewell, William H., 'Ideologies and social revolutions: reflections on the French case', in Theda Skocpol (ed.), *Social Revolutions in the Modern World.* Cambridge: Cambridge University Press, 1994, 169–98.

Sewell, William H., 'Three temporalities: toward an eventful sociology', in Terrence J. McDonald, ed., *The Historic Turn in the Human Sciences.* Ann Arbor: University of Michigan Press, 1999, 245–80.

Sewell, William H. Jr, *Logics of History: Social Theory and Social Transformation.* Chicago, IL: University of Chicago Press, 2005.

Shapin, Steven, *The Scientific Revolution.* Chicago, IL: University of Chicago Press, 1996.

Shapin, Steven and Simon Schaffer, *Leviathan and the Air Pump.* Princeton: Princeton University Press, 1985.

Shils, Edward, 'The calling of sociology', in Talcott Parsons, Edward Shils, Kaspar D. Naegle and Jesse R. Pitts, eds, *Theories of Society.* New York: Macmillan, 1965, 1405–48.

Shin, Jong-Hwa, *The Historical Formation of Modernity in Korea: Events, Issues and Actors.* PhD thesis, University of Warwick, 2002.

Siedentop, Larry, *Democracy in Europe.* London: Penguin, 2001.

Skinner, Quentin, *Liberty before Liberalism.* Cambridge: Cambridge University Press, 1998.

Skinner, Quentin, 'Meaning and understanding in the history of ideas' (1969), now in James Tully, ed., *Meaning and Context: Quentin Skinner and his Critics*. Cambridge: Polity, 1988, 29–67.

Skirbekk, Gunnar, *Rationality and Modernity: Essays in Philosophical Pragmatics*. Oslo: Scandinavian University Press, 1993.

Skocpol, Theda, 'Cultural idioms and political ideologies in the revolutionary reconstruction of state power: a rejoinder to Sewell', in Theda Skocpol, *Social Revolutions in the Modern World*. Cambridge: Cambridge University Press, 1994, 199–209.

Skocpol, Theda, 'Sociology's historical imagination', in Theda Skocpol, ed., *Vision and Method in Historical Sociology*. Cambridge: Cambridge University Press, 1984a, 1–21.

Skocpol, Theda, 'Preface', in Theda Skocpol, ed., *Vision and Method in Historical Sociology*. Cambridge: Cambridge University Press, 1984b, ix–xiii.

Skocpol, Theda, *States and Social Revolutions*. Cambridge: Cambridge University Press, 1979.

Smelser, Neil, *Problematics of Sociology*. Berkeley, CA: University of California Press, 1997.

Smith, Julia M. H., *Europe after Rome: A New Cultural History*. Oxford: Oxford University Press, 2005.

Soskice, David, 'Divergent production regimes: coordinated and uncoordinated market economies in the 1980s and 1990s', in Herbert Kitschelt, Peter Lange, Gary Marks, John D. Stephens, eds, *Continuity and Change in Contemporary Capitalism*. Cambridge: Cambridge University Press, 1999, 101–34.

Steiner, George, *Antigones*. Oxford: Clarendon Press, 1986.

Stengers, Isabelle, *L'invention des sciences modernes*. Paris: La découverte, 1993.

Stöckl, Kristina, *Community after Totalitarianism: The Eastern Orthodox Intellectual Tradition and the Philosophical Discourse of Political Modernity*. PhD thesis, European University Institute, 2007.

Stråth, Bo, 'Multiple Europes: Integration, identity and demarcation to the other', in Bo Stråth, ed., *Europe and the Other and Europe as the Other*. Brussels: Peter Lang, 2000, 385–420.

Stråth, Bo, '1968 – From Co-determination to Co-worker: The Power of Language', *Thesis Eleven* 68 (May 2002): 64–81.

Stråth, Bo, 'The monetary issue and European economic policy in historical perspective', in Christian Joerges, Bo Stråth and Peter Wagner, eds, *The Economy as a Polity: The Political Constitution of Contemporary Capitalism*. London: University College London Press, 2005.

Taylor, Charles, *Hegel*. Cambridge: Cambridge University Press, 1975.

Taylor, Charles, *Hegel and Modern Society*. Cambridge: Cambridge University Press, 1979.

Taylor, Charles, *Sources of the Self*. Cambridge, MA: Harvard University Press, 1989.

Taylor, Charles, *Philosophical Arguments*. Cambridge, MA: Harvard University Press, 1995.

Therborn, Göran, *Science, Class and Society: On the Formation of Sociology and Historical Materialism*. London: New Left Books, 1976.

Tocqueville, Alexis de, *De la Démocratie en Amérique*. Paris: Vrin, 1990.

Tocqueville, Alexis de, *L'Ancien régime et la Révolution*. Paris: Gallimard, 1952–3.

Toews, John E., 'Intellectual history after the linguistic turn', *American Historical Review* 92/4 (1987): 879–907.

Tönnies, Ferdinand, *Kritik der öffentlichen Meinung*. Berlin: Springer, 1922.

Toulmin, Stephen, *Cosmopolis: The Hidden Agenda of Modernity*. Chicago, IL: University of Chicago Press, 1990.

Touraine, Alain, *Critique de la modernité*. Paris: Fayard, 1992.

Tribe, Keith, 'Political economy to economics via commerce: the evolution of British academic economics 1860–1920', in Peter Wagner, Björn Wittrock and Richard Whitley, eds, *Discourses on Society: The Shaping of the Social Science Disciplines*. Dordrecht: Kluwer, 1991.

Van Gelderen, Martin and Quentin Skinner, eds, *Republicanism: A Shared European Heritage*. Cambridge: Cambridge University Press (2 vols), 2002.

Varikas, Eleni, 'The Utopian Surplus', *Thesis Eleven* 68 (May 2002): 101–5.

Wagner, Peter, 'Sind Risiko und Unsicherheit neu oder kehren sie wieder? Über zwei Versuche, größere gesellschaftliche Umstrukturierungen zu beschreiben', *Leviathan* 16/2 (1988).

Wagner, Peter, 'Social Science and the State in Continental Western Europe: The Political Structuration of Disciplinary Discourse', *International Social Science Journal* 41/122 (1989).

Wagner, Peter, *Sozialwissenschaften und Staat. Frankreich, Italien, Deutschland 1870–1980*. Frankfurt/M.: Campus, 1990.

Wagner, Peter, *A Sociology of Modernity. Liberty and Discipline*. London: Routledge, 1994.

Wagner, Peter, 'Strukturierungstheorie auf dem Juggernaut', *Soziologische Revue* 19/1 (1996): 10–15.

Wagner, Peter, 'The resistance that modernity constantly provokes. Europe, America and social theory', *Thesis Eleven* 58 (1999a): 35–58.

Wagner, Peter, 'After *Justification*. Repertoires of evaluation and the sociology of modernity', *European Journal of Social Theory* 2/3 (1999b): 341–57.

Wagner, Peter, *Theorizing Modernity: Inescapability and Attainability in Social Theory*. London: Sage, 2001a.

Wagner, Peter, *A History and Theory of the Social Sciences: Not All That is Solid Melts into Air*. London: Sage, 2001b.

Wagner, Peter, 'Soziologie der kritischen Urteilskraft und der Rechtfertigung. Die Politik- und Moralsoziologie um Luc Boltanski und Laurent Thévenot', in Stephan Moebius and Peter Lothar, eds, *Französische Soziologie heute*. Konstanz: UVK/UTB, 2004, 417–48.

Wagner, Peter, Björn Wittrock and Richard Whitley, eds, *Discourses on Society: The Shaping of the Social Science Disciplines*. Dordrecht: Kluwer, 1991.

Wagner, Peter and Bénédicte Zimmermann, 'Nation – Die Konstitution einer politischen Ordnung als Verantwortungsgemeinschaft', in Stephan Lessenich, ed., *Wohlfahrtsstaatliche Grundbegriffe*. Frankfurt/M.: Campus, 2003, 243–66.

Wallulis, Jerald, *The New Insecurity: The End of the Standard Job and Family*. Albany: SUNY Press, 1998.

Walzer, Michael, *Spheres of Justice*. Oxford: Robertson, 1983.

Walzer, Michael, 'Liberalism and the art of separation', *Political Theory*, 12/13 (August 1984).

Weber, Max, *The Protestant Ethic and the Spirit of Capitalism*. London: Allen and Unwin, 1930 (German orig. 1904–5/1920).

Weber, Max, '"Objectivity" in social science and social policy', *The Methodology of the Social Sciences* (Edward E. Shils and Henry A. Finch, tr. and eds). New York: The Free Press, 1949 [1904], 50–112.

Weir, Margaret, 'Ideas and politics: the acceptance of Keynesianism in Britain and the United States', in Peter Hall, ed., *The Political Power of Economic Ideas: Keynesianism across Nations*. Princeton: Princeton University Press, 1989, 53–86.

Werner, Michael and Bénédicte Zimmermann, 'Vergleich, Transfer, Verflechtung. Der Ansatz der Histoire croisée und die Herausforderung des Transnationalen', in *Geschichte und Gesellschaft* 28 (2002): 607–36.

Whitley, Richard, *Divergent Capitalisms*. Oxford: Oxford University Press, 1999.

Wittgenstein, Ludwig, *Philosophical Investigations*. Oxford: Blackwell, 1958.

Wittgenstein, Ludwig, *Tractatus Logicus-philosophicus*. London: Routledge and Kegan Paul, 1961.

Wittrock, Björn, 'Cultural Crystallization and Conceptual Change: Modernity, Axiality, and Meaning in History', in Kari Palonen and Jussi Kurunmäki, eds, *Zeit, Geschichte und Politik. Time, History and Politics. Dem achtzigsten Geburtstag von Reinhart Koselleck am 23. April 2003 gewidmet*. Jyväskylä: Jyväskylä Studies in Education, Psychology and Social Sciences, 2003.

Wittrock, Björn and Peter Wagner, 'Social sciences and societal developments: the missing perspective', *WZB Paper* P 87–4. Berlin: WZB, 1987.

Wood, Ellen Meiksins, *The Pristine Culture of Capitalism: A Historical Essay on Old Regimes and Modern States*. London: Verso, 1991.

Wood, Ellen Meiksins, *The Origin of Capitalism*. New York: Monthly Review Press, 1999.

Wood, Gordon S., *The Creation of the American Republic 1776–1787*. Durham: University of North Carolina Press, 1998 [1969].

Wrong, Dennis, 'The oversocialized conception of man in modern sociology', *American Sociological Review* 26 (April 1961): 181–93.

Wuthnow, Robert, *Communities of Discourse: Ideology and Social Structure in the Reformation, the Enlightenment and European Socialism*. Cambridge, MA: Harvard University Press, 1989.

Yack, Bernard, *The Fetishism of Modernities*. Notre Dame: The University of Notre Dame Press, 1997.

Zimmermann, Bénédicte, 'Work, Labour, History of the Concept', in *International Encyclopedia of the Social and Behavioural Sciences,* ed. Paul Baltes and Neil Smelser. Oxford: Pergamon, 2001a.

Zimmermann, Bénédicte, *Le chômage en Allemagne. Socio-histoire d'une catégorie nationale de l'action publique (1871–1927)*. Paris: Editions de la Maison des Sciences de l'Homme, 2001b.

Zimmermann, Bénédicte, Claude Didry and Peter Wagner, eds, *Le travail et la nation. Histoire croisée de la France et de l'Allemagne*. Paris: Editions de la Maison des Sciences de l'Homme, 1999.

Index